Nature and Art
in Renaissance Literature

Nature and Art
in Renaissance Literature

BY EDWARD WILLIAM TAYLER

COLUMBIA UNIVERSITY PRESS

New York and London 1964

Edward William Tayler is Assistant Professor of English at Columbia University.

Illustration facing page 2 courtesy Yale Medical Library

For Gup

Preface

Acknowledging indebtedness is in this case a complicated pleasure. For one thing I had been involved with the relationship of ideas to literature for a number of years without having formulated any precise aims, hence without being fully conscious of who, or what, was directing my investigations. Under this head fall the reading that has shaped my methods of analysis and the three or four teachers who taught me most of what I think I know of art and life. For another thing I differ from previous scholarship not so much in detail as in general emphasis and over-all perspective. Since my purpose is expository rather than argumentative, I record indebtedness more often than disagreement, but the necessity to work the problem through for myself has perhaps in some cases produced a combination of views beyond the grace of footnotes.

Accordingly I take pleasure in acknowledging some fundamental obligations. Of more or less direct help have been J. H. Hagstrum's brief but interesting account of the *paragone* between Nature and Art in *The Sister Arts* and Madeleine Doran's suggestive section, "Art *vs.* Nature," in her *Endeavors of Art*. Mr. Hagstrum is interested in the tradition of literary pictorialism, which lies outside my area of competence, and Miss Doran concerns herself mainly with the rhetorical tradition. Both have, however, sharpened my perception of the possibilities in the subject, and I shall be grateful for whatever direct and indirect corroboration their accounts offer my own.

The problem of "Nature vs. Art" receives more extended treatment in Hiram Haydn's brilliant and controversial *The Counter-Renaissance;* he explores more fully than other writers—there are only a few who touch on the matter at all—the broad ethical and philosophical importance of the terms. But Haydn's need to prove the existence of a "Counter-Renaissance" lends his work a quasi-polemical flavor, inviting him to emphasize the antithetic possibilities in the terms—Nature in *conflict* with Art—and to subordinate them in other ways to his thesis. My own view is, I think, more balanced, but his documentation of the ubiquitous appeal of Nature and Art corroborates the importance, if not always the interpretation, I give to the terms in Chapter I.

Equally important has been the research and criticism of Frank Kermode, who was the scholar most directly helpful in opening my mind to the more purely literary implications of the conflict between Nature and Art; he too sees the terms as primarily in conflict, rather than as a division in the order of nature that might become either antithetical or complementary. His introductions to *The Tempest* (Arden Shakespeare) and to *English Pastoral Poetry* are brilliantly suggestive of the way Renaissance poets were engaged by the conflict between Nature and Art. Kermode states unequivocally, so far as I know for the first time, the general connection between Nature and Art and the pastoral genre, a connection that has fundamental importance for my study.

My greatest debt is to a nonliterary source, the monumental, documentary *History of Primitivism and Related Ideas in Antiquity* by Arthur O. Lovejoy and George Boas. This volume is in effect a source book for the study of primitivism, collecting in one place most of the significant documents relating to that subject; since the history of Nature and Art is inextricably a part of the history of primitivism, the seminal labors of Lovejoy and Boas offer a convenient point of departure for work in the Renaissance.

For grants allowing me to complete my research I am indebted to the Huntington Library and to the Council for Research in the Humanities of Columbia University; my debt to the Huntington is much more than financial, for the friendly efficiency of the staff has made the Library a place of pleasure as well as profit. The help and guidance of Columbia University Press have been represented most immediately for me in the person of Mr. William F. Bernhardt. In preparing the manuscript for publication I have been grateful for the curious care and intelligent industry of Miss Dora Odarenko.

Some personal acknowledgments remain. To my colleagues, Professors Marjorie H. Nicolson and William Nelson, I am deeply grateful for wise encouragement and helpful suggestions. To my teachers at Amherst and Stanford I owe much that is not appropriately summarized in words. The present work, in particular, would have been impossible without the patient understanding of Professors L. V. Ryan and Yvor Winters. To my wife, critic and comforter, I owe the most personal debt of all.

E. W. T.

Columbia University
February, 1964

Contents

Nature and Art
in Renaissance Literature

Introduction

It may be that Aristotle was right in supposing that human nature is always and in every place the same, just as fire burns both here and in Persia. But if man's nature persists unchanged, the words by which he expresses his awareness of himself and his world do not; and sometimes words may come to have the importance of human nature itself, for they have the power to shape as well as to express thought. The shift from such words as form, substance, quality, and essence to mass, acceleration, inertia, and energy has accompanied, at times even determined, changes in our notions of reality, causality, and the human mind. For the scientist these verbal revolutions seem to lead to progress, but for the student of literature they generally diminish the means by which he may re-create within himself the experience of great and vanishing art. Such at least has been the case with our loss of the Renaissance use of the words Nature and Art.

Not that we no longer use the terms. The association of Nature and Art has always been important in human history because it involves many of man's most cherished assumptions about himself and his proper place in the universe. As late as the nineteenth century Coleridge and Wordsworth could find in the shifting meanings of Nature and Art a measure of their theoretical disagreement,[1] and even today some of the most venerable notions rise, unclear but recognizable, behind the "natural rights" granted by the United Nations or lurk obscurely in justifications for nudism. But by and large we have today no exact counterpart of the Renaissance uses of Nature and Art. Art for us usually means fine art, and Nature has been stripped of the veils that made her a figure of mystery and power for Spenser. Coupling the terms is no longer for us (as it was for the Renaissance) a marriage of convenience, even of necessity. Our meanings for Nature and Art are at once more limited and more vague than they were in Shakespeare's day. A glance at the accompanying illustration, taken from a learned treatise by Robert Fludd, will suggest relationships—significant and familiar to Spenser, Shakespeare, Marvell—that must seem meaningless or merely quaint to most of us today.

What Fludd gives us is the universe, together with the powers that shape and maintain it: the mirror of Nature and the image of Art. From the shining cloud appears the hand of God, grasping the chain that symbolizes His mastery over *Natura,* who is His agent in the earthly realm. *Natura,* whose "sun" breast fecundates the earth, stands on sea and land; her head reaches the sphere of the stars, beyond which lies the ethereal region where play the angelic hosts. She, too, grasps a chain, this one attached to the simian *Ars,* who squats below her on the round earth, holding in his paws the globe and compasses that symbolize his attempts—that is, the attempts of Art—to ape the handiwork of God and Nature. In the natural world there are two efficient causes—*Natura scilicet, & ejus Simia, quam Artem appellamus* [2]—and both owe their power to God, who is the final cause of nature. The chain of command, as we say, is perfectly clear. Art imitates Nature, and Nature is the Art of God.

Fludd's universal diagram helps visualize what was in fact the case, that in the Renaissance the concepts of Nature and Art enjoyed a dignity and popularity never equaled before or since. The terms are as ubiquitous and pivotal in Renaissance thought as the pairing of "heredity" and "environment" in a modern textbook of social psychology; they dominate the thinking of the age. One reason for their extraordinary popularity lies of course in their general, abstract character and their multiplicity of meanings, which made of them, particularly when used together, a unique conceptual instrument that was felt to be almost uni-

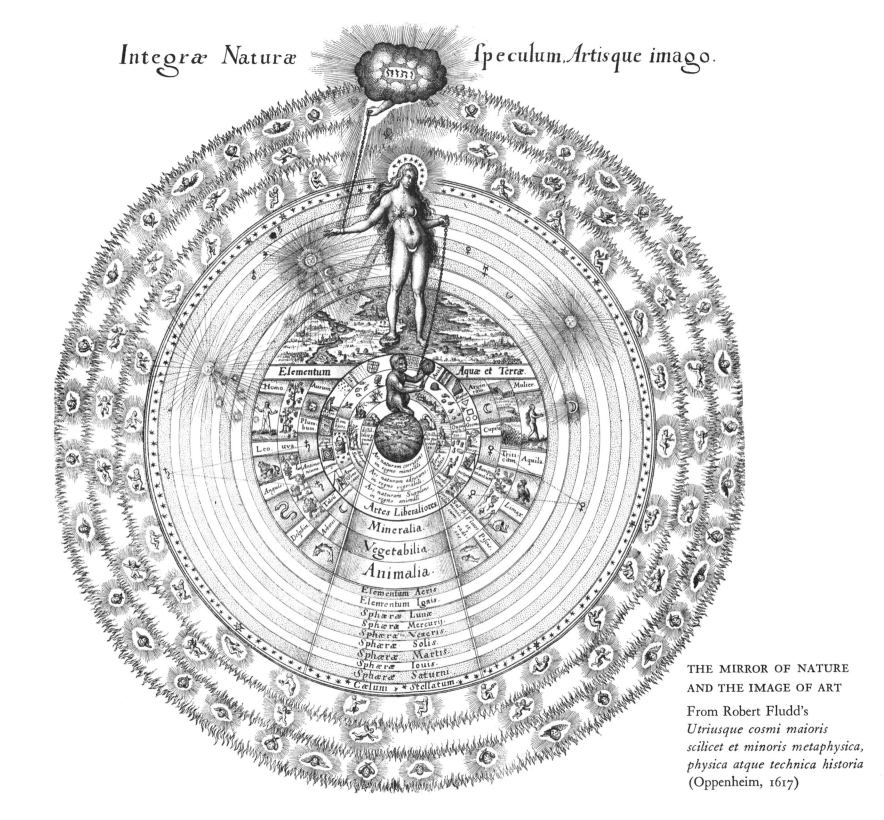

THE MIRROR OF NATURE
AND THE IMAGE OF ART

From Robert Fludd's
*Utriusque cosmi maioris
scilicet et minoris metaphysica,
physica atque technica historia*
(Oppenheim, 1617)

versally applicable. As Simon Goulart understates it in annotating Du Bartas' use of the word Nature, "Ce mot se prend en diuerses significations entre les Theologiens, Medecins, & Philosophes"; [3] and while Art does not possess the sixty-odd significations attributable to Nature, [4] it is in itself a considerable semantic phenomenon, being applicable during the Renaissance to any specifically human activity or production. It was the universal pertinence of the terms on which William Rand relied when in 1657 he referred to those "vast and all-comprehending Dominions of Nature and Art." [5]

Of course, the equivocal quality of the terms does not explain, it merely helps to explain, why the words were so prevalent and important in the Renaissance. Nor is it possible to account for the pairing of Nature and Art by labeling it a theme, a commonplace, or, as the fashion now has it, a *topos*. Flaubert rightly warns us of the difficulty of assessing the amount of genuine feeling and thought that may animate a cliché. It is therefore not enough to point to rhetoric books and Erasmian *copia*, to Plato, Aristotle, Cicero, and Seneca, for the terms are in this respect like the hackneyed language of Madame Bovary: their life, their connection with the nerve-endings of humanity, lies far below the surface. The fact is that during the Renaissance the terms were more than a commonplace, more even than an extraordinarily flexible analytic convenience. As Fludd's picture of the world implies, their variety of significations received ultimate meaning and precision in relation to the Elizabethan idea of an ordered universe: Nature and Art pointed to what appeared to be a "real" division in man's experience of himself and the cosmos.

The marriage, not always happy, of Nature to Art therefore requires considerable investigation before we can hope to place the terms in historical perspective and relate them to other intellectual movements of the Renaissance. But the business of defining these kinds of historical relationship must be approached with circumspection: understanding how general attitudes toward the pairing of Nature and Art may be identified with "Christian humanism" and *"libertin* naturalism" has its value only so long as it does not invite the historian to regard the past as dead, possessing nothing more than a kind of pseudo-life that resides in the intellectual categories used to talk about it. Ideas do not grow, like potted plants, in restricted areas, which is to say that Nature and Art have roots in other than philosophic soil; among other possibilities, a philosophic idea may become a literary one, and vice versa.[6]

Furthermore, the floating commonplaces or "ideas" of the Nature-Art division are not discrete entities that may be regarded as the "same" in a variety of authors. Although it has probably occurred many times to all of us that we have encountered the "same" idea elsewhere, it will not do to confuse, say, the "soft" primitivism of Longus even with the "soft" primitivism of Hesiod or Ovid. Because of differences in dramatic context these "same" ideas will inevitably manifest and demand different degrees of emotional assent. The origin of an author's ideas may therefore be less important than their intellectual and emotional status in a particular work, for regarded simply as "ideas" they are only materials or commonplaces, potentially scientific, philosophical, literary, theological, or other. For example, Longus' pastoral romance, *Daphnis and Chloe,* is a literary analogue of the antithesis of Nature and Art in philosophy; that is, the literary form, in so far as it exploits the contrast between court and country, reflects the division between Nature and Art, but whether the genre is cause, the division effect, seems impossible to determine. The impulse behind different manifestations of interest in Nature and Art appears to be a fundamental gesture of the human spirit that has, at various times and places, found diverse channels for its expression.

In the Renaissance the habitual pairing of Nature and Art is the philosophical equivalent of an extraordinary efflorescence of pastoral literature.[7] Of course, the very existence of pastoral as a distinct genre has always been, in effect, an acknowledgment of the distinction between Nature and Art. Pastoral is by definition implicitly concerned with the discrepancies that may be observed between rural and urban, country and courtly, simple and complex, natural and artificial. Such literature, no matter what its pretensions to simplicity of form or matter, proves on inspection to be highly stylized and carefully calculated. The reason is simple. Bucolic fiction requires before all else a poet and audience sufficiently civilized to appreciate primitive simplicity, to recognize that the gain of Art means the loss of Nature. To regard pastoral literature as simple stuff because it sings of simple things is to confuse the symbol with the thing symbolized.[8] After all, nostalgia for natural simplicity is a sentiment denied those who have experienced only natural simplicity. Although the popularity of the pastoral genre may in any age be used as a convenient measure of the intensity of man's concern with the relation of the natural to the artificial, it was only during the Renaissance that writers began to use the eclogue to deal overtly with the philosophical problem of Nature and Art.

Because of what we may be sure is a variety of complicated reasons, the thinkers of the Renaissance had reached a stage of sophistication that brought them to investigate with unparalleled energy the differences between the natural and the artificial. The investigation proved to be both philosophical and literary, often a little of both, leading in great writers like Spenser, Shakespeare, and Marvell to the distinctive variety of philosophic pastoral that forms the subject of this book. During the later sixteenth and earlier seventeenth centuries, the terms Nature and Art actually appear, as terms, in pastoral verse—for the first time making explicit the tension between Nature and Art that is implicitly the basis for all pastoral literature. In *England's Helicon,* for example, an eclogue by "J.M." devotes several stanzas to the usual business of "shadie Bowers," "harmlesse sheepe," and "pensive Swaines," but then begins to explain and evaluate in a way inconsistent with more modern notions of the pastoral form:

> Thus did heaven grace the soyle:
> Not deform'd with work-mens toile.

Behind this simple couplet lie some complex notions: not only that of the Golden Age when Nature dispensed food and shelter to man without "toile," but also that of the Garden of Eden when "heaven" did indeed "grace the soyle." And both are involved in the moral judgment implied by the word "deform'd." The judgment is made explicit in the next stanza where the speaker's preference for untouched land, for this fusion of Arcadia, the Golden Age, and Eden, receives conceptual formulation in terms of Nature and Art:

> Purest plot of earthly mold,
> Might that land be justly named:
> Art by Nature was controld,
> Art which no such pleasures framed.[9]

A literary convention has thus become the vehicle for philosophic controversy. Or is it the other way around?

The poem by "J.M." is conventional, as poetry undistinguished; and yet its moral frame of reference, conceptual vocabulary, and rich allusiveness point both to a kind of pastoral that had disappeared before the age of Dr. Johnson and to a way of categorizing experience that vanished with the universe anatomized by Robert Fludd.

The fact is that broadly speaking there are two sorts of pastoral verse, two main traditions within the same genre: one is the allegorical or symbolic pastoral, which is no longer generally recognized for what it is; and the other is the "decorative" or "sugared" pastoral, which is no longer fashionable. Dr. Johnson appears to have had little or no imaginative understanding of the former—the successful religious use of the form died with the seventeenth century—but he was familiar enough with the decorative tradition to want to judge all pastoral in terms of it.[10] He was quite certain that Milton *really* had no flocks to batten . . . and hence those vigorously commonsensical criticisms of "Lycidas" that have reappeared in our own day in the naïve notion that the pastoral is a cotton-candy genre—sugary, pinkly-pretty, and not very substantial. C. S. Lewis, on the lookout for philistinism, tries to circumvent such criticism by arguing that the genre affords us an opportunity to escape to a "region in the mind which does exist and which should be visited often," [11] saying in effect that Johnson rightly understands the pastoral but is mistaken in his notion of triviality. My own concern is not with the decorative tradition—the butt of criticism since the close of the seventeenth century—but with the other tradition of pastoral, to which the remarks of Dr. Johnson and C. S. Lewis are not so much wrong or right as simply irrelevant.

My concern is with the *use* of the pastoral *kind* (the old word for genre means "nature" and in itself suggests half-forgotten relationships) as a vehicle for conveying and exploring ideas, particularly the ideas of Nature and Art. For the greater writers of the Renaissance, as well as for minor poets like "J.M.," this kind of pastoral was what Moses Hadas calls a "laboratory" world in which might be clearly demonstrated relationships that appeared only fragmentarily and obscurely in the everyday world. It was, specifically, a showcase that exhibited the ideal or holiday relationship of Nature to Art, as in the summary evaluation by "J.M." of the significance of his pastoral landscape: "Art by Nature was controld," an explicit formulation of the ideal that Fludd symbolizes in the chain that is held by *Natura* and holds the simian *Ars*. The ideal superiority of Nature to Art, glimpsed only imperfectly and intermittently in the world of post-lapsarian man, may be made to operate consistently and without qualification in the paradise of the pastoral form.

It will perhaps be obvious that I have undertaken to record the *interaction* of a philosophical idea with a literary genre. Since the one is in effect the counterpart of the other, there is nothing arbitrary about such an undertaking; indeed, from the point of view of the Renaissance poet this particular association of genre with idea seemed right and inevitable, so that Shakespeare and his readers must have felt perfectly comfortable in the presence of a long philosophical debate over Nature and Art in the middle of the pastoral episode of *The Winter's Tale*. Concentration on crucial instances of interaction means that this book is nothing like a complete history of pastoral, nor is it even intended as an exhaustive account of Renaissance pastoral; adequate studies of these matters already exist. Neither is the book a history of the idea of "Nature" or even of "Art." Despite the work of Lovejoy and others it might be argued that such histories need writing, but here it has seemed discreet to limit myself to the way Nature and Art interact with pastoral, a limitation that permits a relatively unencumbered view of a specific connection between "philosophy" and "literature" and that also helps circumscribe a subject that might otherwise balloon almost infinitely.

Although the interaction of genre with idea begins in classical antiquity and has its effects on later practice, the unique cross-fertilization that occurred during the Renaissance issued in a unique kind of great poetry, poetry that I believe has rarely been properly understood since the time of Pope and Ambrose Philips. In the minor verse of "J.M.," as philosophical concepts interrelate with literary genre, there may be glimpsed techniques and conventions that are realized more amply in Book VI of Spenser's *The Faerie Queene,* in Shakespeare's *The Winter's Tale,* and in Marvell's pastoral verse. These writers could assume in their audience a common nucleus of thoughts and feelings about Nature, Art, and pastoral, a nucleus that invites renewed understanding and, in so far as it remains possible, imaginative recovery. The history of genre and the history of ideas combine happily enough in achieving such aims. Results may be complementary since both kinds of history allow the critic to come at the personal preoccupations of an author from a well-defined point of departure, from the point at which he begins to assimilate and then modify the materials of tradition. In this way we may begin to appreciate with some exactness how a writer manipulates the expectations of his readers, turns their presuppositions about poetry and life to his own artistic ends.

Admittedly, the study of intellectual history, even of genre history, is a risky business, largely because it involves the disquieting assumption that the materials dealt with may be isolated from context without undergoing essential change. The risk is unavoidable; it is an occupational hazard, akin to the critic's assumption that dissection does no permanent harm to the poem on the operating table. Ideas are heady items, especially ideas that like Nature and Art are so broad as to induce the intoxicating belief that they are present everywhere; hence I consider the terms not separately but only as a pair and confine myself to documents in which appear the words themselves as well as the ideas they represent. Success seems to depend first on the skill employed in excising the idea from the organism and in comparing it elsewhere with the results of a similar amputation, then on one's ability to resuscitate the patient by revealing the vital interdependence of the idea and its literary context. Final success doubtless depends on literary tact; and though I cannot claim immunity from risks that are more easily described than avoided, I have at least tried hard to remember that it is the better part of literary tact to allow a poet to own his own ideas.

The order of the following chapters represents an attempt to respond to occupational hazards: Chapters I–III treat mainly the history of idea and of genre; Chapters IV–VI deal rather with literary consequences. The division, though purely arbitrary, does help in considering history as history, literature as literature. My ultimate aim, of course, is the recovery of the kinds of imaginative experience that lent vital meaning both to Fludd's picture of the universe and to the pastoral literature of writers like Spenser, Shakespeare, and Marvell. Since "history" and "literature" are in this case probably not separable, results again depend in the last analysis on literary tact, the success of which must be left, tactfully, to the judgment of my reader.

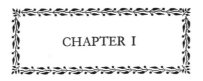

CHAPTER I

Renaissance Uses of Nature and Art

The pairing of Nature and Art occurs with such numbing frequency in Renaissance literature that there is a tendency to label the terms a "commonplace" or *"topos"*—and then to forget them. Similarly, we may look at Fludd's "mirror of Nature and image of Art" and respond with the feeling that it is quaint or curious, which is yet another way of acknowledging the existence of the terms without allowing them to confront the mind directly. Both reactions are ways of anesthetizing the brain, of seeing a division between Nature and Art without scrutinizing it with Plato's eye of the mind. It is therefore worth while to emphasize that during the Renaissance the coupling of Nature and Art was neither quaint nor commonplace. These terms, these categories, were the intellectual tools man used in understanding himself and his world, in organizing his views of himself and experience. It was primarily for this reason that the pairing of Nature and Art became an habitual instrument of analysis appearing in a variety of different contexts.

Suppose the subject to be ale and tobacco, the form a madrigal:

> One clears the brain,
>   The other glads the heart,
> Which they retain
>   By nature and by art.
> The first by nature clears;
>   By art makes giddy will.

> The last by nature cheers,
> By art makes heady still.[1]

Or the subject smut, the intent the Earl of Rochester's explanation of his sexual "Disappointment" (the speaker has the Desire but not the Power):

> Natures support, without whose Aid,
> She can no humane being give;
> It self now wants the Art to live;
> Faintness, its slacken'd Nerves invade.[2]

Or the subject parasitic rascality. In *Volpone* Jonson has Mosca discourse on what it takes to be a fine parasite, and the audience must have perceived in the use of Nature and Art an adjunct to the mock seriousness of the speech. Although in "nature" there is nothing but "Parasites or Sub-parasites," nevertheless a "fine, elegant rascall" like our Mosca is not to be classed with those that have only "your bare towne-arte," for he is

> the creature, had the art borne with him;
> Toiles not to learn it, but doth practise it
> Out of most excellent nature.[3]

Passages such as these, illustrating the habitual association of Nature and Art, presuppose a whole body of rather more seriously philosophical literature devoted to use and analysis of the terms. Jonson's contemporary readers were accustomed to see Nature paired with Art in such apparently unrelated areas as moral education, cosmetics, gardening, and literary criticism.

Plutarch, in writing of the education of the young, had advanced the thesis that "Nature without doctrine is blynde, and doctrine without Nature is a thinge mutilate,"[4] and this fine balance between conflicting claims lives again in much of Renaissance moral philosophy, as writer after writer seeks to reconcile the roles of Nature and Art in attaining perfection in one or another sphere of human activity. It is as if the use of one term automatically called forth the other, as if a subject could only be analyzed completely through recourse to both the terms. Thomas Wilson's *Arte of Rhetorique* (1553) typifies the effort to develop the (usually) balanced view of antiquity in order to make sense of man and his mysterious talents. Wilson admits that

> though many by nature without art, haue proued worthy men, yet is arte a surer guide then nature, considering we see as liuely by arte what we do, as though we read a thing in writing, where as Natures doings are not so open to all men. Againe, those that haue good wittes by Nature, shall better encrease them by arte, and the blunt also shall bee whetted through arte, that want Nature to helpe them forward.[5]

With Wilson the final balance swings slightly but surely to the side of Art, which is in general the emphasis of orthodox opinion —and, one must add, befits a book advocating the art of rhetoric.

Lyly's *Euphues: The Anatomy of Wit* (1578) echoes Aristotle and Plutarch: "For Nature without Discipline is of small force, and Discipline without Nature more feeble." But the voice of the young Euphues juggles the traditional terms in such a way as to undermine the balance sought by Plutarch and other writers on education:

> Now whereas you seeme to loue my nature, and loath my nurture, you bewraye your owne weakenesse, in thinking that nature may any wayes be altered by education. . . . It is natural for the vine to spread, the more you seeke by Art to alter it, the more in the ende you shal augment it. . . . education can haue no shewe, where the excellencye of Nature doth beare sway. . . . plante and translate the crabbe tree, where, and whensoeuer it please you, and it wyll neuer beare sweete Apple, vnlesse you graft it by Arte, which nothing toucheth nature.[6]

As everyone knows, however, the young Euphues is what the Renaissance called a dandy-prat. Most writers remained more sanguine about the potentialities of their erected wit and the educability of the human animal. They had need of such optimism if they were to deal morally with the scriptural fact of the Fall. It was only the primitivists, the fideists, or the naturalists like Montaigne who depreciated at all consistently the products of human reason, undercutting at times the *raison d'être* of education and, indeed, of all intellectual endeavor.

For the moment, however, opinions on the relative values of Nature and Art are less important than seeing clearly the Renaissance habit of approaching a problem such as education with these two alternatives almost inevitably in mind. When used to explain another and unrelated aspect of human experience, Renaissance cosmetics, Nature and Art again serve the same analytic function of discriminating alternatives. Hamlet's eschatological warning—"Now get you to my lady's chamber, and tell her, let her paint an inch thick, to this favour she must come"—is but one of a long series of moral commonplaces provoked by a feminine habit that has from antiquity with some show of reason been thought to smack of darkest deceit. If carried to the point of philosophical generalization, such animadversions usually turned on the concepts of Nature and Art. Any number of positions were possible, even in the same writer. Robert Herrick, better known for his praise of Julia's artlessness, seems to restore the balance in an epigram amiably entitled "Painting Sometimes Permitted":

> If Nature do deny
> Colours, let Art supply.[7]

Few Renaissance authors displayed such tolerance.

Thomas Kyd's translation (1588) of Tasso's essay on domestic management is quite specific: "And truely as a woman of discretion will in no wise marre her naturall co[m]plexion, to recouer it with slime or artificiall coullered trash, so ought the husband in no sort to be consenting to such follies."[8] Sound advice . . .

that falls far short of the fine Juvenalian violence of which the Middle Ages was capable in this connection. George Pettie's translation (1581) of Stefano Guazzo's *Civile Conversation* reveals a similar lack of genuine involvement as he retails the familiar phrases: "They thinke themselves made bewtiful by the force of those artificiall colours: not knowing, as a Poet sayth, That painting could not Hecube Helene make." [9] Robert Burton's tone in *The Anatomy of Melancholy* (1621) characteristically differs from Kyd's and Guazzo's, but Nature and Art reappear easily enough in the more learned context he provides:

But why is all this labour, all this cost, preparation, riding, running . . . dear bought stuff? Because forsooth they would be fair and fine, and where nature is defective, supply it by art.

Who blushes not by nature, doth by art, (Ovid)
and to that purpose they anoint and paint their faces, to make Helen of Hecuba—a distorted dwarf an Europa.[10]

One of the most interesting variations on the theme occurs in that extraordinary book of seventeenth-century anthropology, *Anthropometamorphosis* (1653), which in its extended attack on "Nature-scoffing art" includes a "VINDICATION of the Regular Beauty and Honesty of NATURE":

. . . Faces of effeminate Gallants, a bare-headed Sect of amorous Idolaters, who of late have begun to vye patches and beauty-spots, nay, painting, with the most tender and phantasticall Ladies, and to returne by Art their queasie paine upon women, to the great reproach of Nature. . . . Painting is bad both in a foule and faire woman, but worst of all in a man [for] such counterfeit stuffe . . . be made of ointments, greasie ingredients, and slabber-sawces, or done by certaine powders, Oxe-galls, Lees, Latherings, and other such sluttish and beastly confections.[11]

Again, the variations in tone and meaning, ranging all the way from Burton's wry pedantry to the Nashe-like vigor of *Anthro-*

pometamorphosis, do not obscure the simple fact that "painting" as well as moral philosophy is treated habitually, at least on the level of abstract generalization, in terms of Nature and Art.

The treatises on gardening, such fine barometers of taste during the sixteenth and seventeenth centuries, reveal a similar use of Nature and Art; there appears again the shared assumption that really important distinctions may most conveniently be made by manipulating the ideas of naturalness and artificiality. The "natural garden" is for most historians of taste identified with the eighteenth century, and yet one suspects that the ideal order of the axial pattern decried by the eighteenth century must have seemed nothing so much as "natural" to the Elizabethan who could see formal order everywhere in Nature. In this sense many painters, gardeners, and writers may be said to anticipate the "natural" *furor hortensis* that agitated later generations. Even Milton, given propitious prelapsarian circumstances, was ready to describe the truly "natural" garden. In Eden there are

> Flours worthy of Paradise, which not nice Art
> In Beds and curious Knots, but Nature boon
> Powrd forth profuse on Hill and Dale and Plaine.
> (IV.241–43)

The Garden itself, because it is the product of unfallen Nature, seems to be

> A Wilderness of sweets; for Nature here
> Wantond as in her prime, and plaid at will
> Her Virgin Fancies, pouring forth more sweet,
> Wild above Rule or Art; enormous bliss.
> (V.294–97)

Writers like John Rea, John Worlidge, and Sir Hugh Plat also relied on the pairing of Nature and Art to express their reaction to new tastes in gardening, often directing polemics against what seemed to them to be an excessive emphasis on the artificial as against the natural.

In *Flora* (1665) John Rea decries the "Gardens of the new model," to which a "green Medow is a more delightful object":

> There Nature alone, without the aid of Art, spreads her verdant Carpets, spontaneously imbroydered with many pretty Plants and pleasing Flowers, far more inviting than such an immured Nothing.[12]

Such a text might serve as gloss for Andrew Marvell's "The Mower against Gardens," and other poets, such as James Shirley and Abraham Cowley, similarly asserted their preference for Nature over Art where gardening is concerned. In "Of My Self" Cowley remarks his Horatian retreat, a modest garden

> painted o're
> With Natures hand, not Arts.

And in "Of Solitude" he speaks with complacent satisfaction of sylvan delights:

> Here Nature does a House for me erect,
> Nature the wisest Architect,
> Who those fond Artists does despise
> That can the fair and living Trees neglect;
> Yet the Dead Timber prize.[13]

There are various and complex reasons—more various and complex than perhaps would appear at first glance—why men like Rea, Milton, and Cowley might in garden literature depreciate Art and praise Nature and yet in other areas of discourse, for example in speaking of education, endorse a balance between the two terms. At present, however, it will be enough to recognize that here again Nature and Art appear in their usual analytic form.

The use of Nature and Art as pivotal terms in treatises and poetry on gardens closely parallels their use in the criticism of poetry. By a familiar migration of metaphor, what one does in the garden becomes analogous to what one does in writing poetry —and vice versa. In *Poetica* (1536), Bernardino Daniello, in the course of an argument designed to show that a writer's Nature needs also Art, introduces the traditional analogy from gardening:

For nature produces what is useful to human life mixed indiscriminately with thorns and brambles . . . trees are apt to degenerate and bring forth sour or insipid fruit if left to their own development. But if these are diligently and artfully grafted with the proper scions of other fruit trees, the fruits become sweet and savory.[14]

This is the position transformed through a kind of dramatic casuistry by Polixenes in *The Winter's Tale* (IV.iv):

> Yet nature is made better by no mean
> But nature makes that mean. So, over that art
> Which you say adds to nature is an art
> That nature makes. You see, sweet maid, we marry
> A gentler scion to the wildest stock
> And make conceive a bark of baser kind
> By bud of nobler race. This is an art
> Which does mend nature—change it rather; but
> The art itself is nature.

Puttenham, in *The Arte of English Poesie* (1589), surpasses Daniello in his respect for the gardener's ingenuity, producing a commensurate and added respect for poetic craft. Art, it seems, may not only aid but "surmount" Nature:

And the Gardiner by his arte will not onely make an herbe, or flowr, or fruite, come forth in his season without impediment, but also will embellish the same in vertue, shape, odour and taste, that nature of her selfe woulde neuer haue done: as to make the single gillifloure . . . double . . . a plumme or cherrie without a stone . . . a goord or coucumber like to a horne, or any other figure he will: any of which things nature could not doe without mans help and arte.[15]

William Lawson's *New Orchard and Garden* (1618) exhibits the same terms and much the same attitude, this time from the point of view of the gardener rather than the critic. The rhetorical question of his Preface—"For what is Art more than a provident and skilful Correctrix of the faults of Nature in particular works, apprehended by the Senses?"—receives answer directly or by implication on every page of his treatise. His opinion is, for example, that trees, after all else has been attended to, must be pruned and "dressed." Although the "unskilful Arborist" may object that "Trees have their several forms, even by nature," there is nevertheless "a profitable end and use of every Tree, from which if it decline, (though by nature) yet man by art may (nay, must) correct it." Lawson's uncompromising view of Art as perfecter and improver of Nature extends to every living thing, including man himself. Indeed he goes so far as to use a human analogy to support his position on horticulture:

Such is the condition of all earthly things, whereby a man receiveth profit, or pleasure, that they degenerate presently without good ordering. Man himself left to himself, grows from his heavenly and spiritual generation, and becometh beastly, yea, devilish to his own kind, unless he be regenerate. No marvel then, if Trees make their shoots, and put their sprays disorderly. . . . It is a common, and unskilful opinion, and saying, Let all grow, and they will bear more fruit.[16]

The process of cross-fertilization is complete, the two areas of discourse having thoroughly interpenetrated each other.

The alliance of horticulture and poetic—often involving through grafting the practice of the physician—will be familiar almost *ad nauseam* to readers of antique and Renaissance criticism; such analogies, together with their conceptual equivalents Nature and Art, appear to dominate thought and expression.

The question of the part played by Nature and Art in the creative process had been the subject of discussion well before Horace embalmed it for posterity in the *Ars poetica:*

'Tis now inquir'd which makes the nobler Verse,
Nature, or Art. My Judgement will not pierce
Into the Profits, what a meere rude braine

Can; or all toile, without a wealthie veine:
So doth the one, the others helpe require,
And friendly should unto one end conspire.[17]

Plato had used Nature and Art in depreciating painting and
poetry as inferior sorts of imitation, and the terms had gained
currency in a less pejorative context from Aristotle's famous
dictum that Art imitates Nature, but it is Horace's passage that
seems to be the *locus classicus* for Renaissance attempts to explain poetic talent on the level of abstraction. Drayton's advice
in "The Sacrifice to Apollo" begins with Horatian balance and
then varies the formula slightly. If "yee list to exercise your
Vayne,"

> Let Art and Nature goe
> One with the other;
> Yet so, that Art may show
> Nature her Mother.[18]

Such use of the terms occurs with particular frequency in what
may be referred to as elegiac criticism.

Poets as well as gardeners could allow the terms to do their
thinking for them; in poems like Denham's on the death of
Cowley, Nature and Art seem to appear almost involuntarily to
inflate a few lines of elegiac criticism:

> Old Mother Wit, and Nature gave
> Shakespear and Fletcher all they have;
> In Spenser, and in Johnson, Art,
> Of slower Nature got the start;
> But both in him [Cowley] so equal are
> None knows which bears the happy'st share.[19]

Nature and Art receive an emphasis probably more palatable to
modern taste in Jonson's elegiac criticism of Shakespeare contributed to the First Folio (1623), where the terms nevertheless
again serve to deal abstractly with the problem of poetic talent:

> Yet must I not give Nature all: Thy Art,
> My gentle Shakespeare, must enjoy a part.
> For though the poet's matter Nature be,
> His art doth give the fashion.

Jonson's eulogy exemplifies a position approximating that of both Horace and Thomas Wilson, Nature and Art in fine balance, complementing each other and contributing together to the making of poets and poetry, of men and fine art. It is the position of the orthodox moral philosophers of the Renaissance who, respecting the Senecan *sequere naturam,* appreciated as well the Senecan qualification: "For Nature giueth not vertue; it is an art to be made good." [20]

Serious occasions invite the dignity of theory, the enunciation of first principles, the invocation of Nature and Art. Activities like criticism or even gardening require thorough analysis, and Renaissance writers remained consciously and unconsciously ready to conduct such examinations in terms of Nature and Art.

So far this survey has recorded the habitual pairing of Nature and Art in a variety of "logically" unrelated areas of human endeavor—education and rhetoric, cosmetics, gardening, literary criticism. Still other aspects of human experience might have been drawn within this purview,[21] but enough has been said to indicate the way the traditional coupling of Nature and Art became indispensable to the thinkers of the Renaissance. When in tandem, so to speak, the words possessed the glamour of completeness: they summed up a situation, almost any situation, so that no more need be said. They were there to be used, customarily, habitually, often without conscious effort, in any act of defining or exhibiting relationships. The use of one term seems automatically to suggest the other, as if the absence of one of the words must betray the fact that the subject had been examined incompletely. Together these two terms encompassed the totality of specifically human experience as it was understood by Renaissance thinkers.

It will perhaps be obvious from the examples offered so far
that to Renaissance writers Nature and Art were often more
than dead words interred in commonplace contexts, that they
were often used and felt with the solidity of fact, not merely as
analytic symbols but as signs possessing direct connection with
the world. For a variety of historical reasons the terms are no
longer used in the old ways, but in any case we no longer share
the optimism of earlier ages in the efficacy of labels like Nature
and Art. For us Darwin's "survival of the fittest," Hegel's "thesis-
antithesis-synthesis," and Freud's "superego" are symbols for experience, certainly not experience itself, nor even, usually, are
they presumed to correspond directly to "reality" in the way
words do so obligingly for Plato in the *Cratylus*. But doubts
about language and reality, while certainly not unknown to
many early theoreticians, only very rarely troubled the Renaissance users of Nature and Art.

Nature and Art signified a real division in the structure of
the universe, a division that in accord with accepted Elizabethan
thinking appeared also in the state and in man himself. The
Renaissance had inherited from the Middle Ages the Stoic-
Christian emphasis on order in the universe.[22] Allegiance to the
concept of order was remarkably widespread, so that controversies—the Renaissance had no dearth of controversies—flared
up within relatively limited areas and rarely threatened to ignite
the whole. Men might debate even the inerrancy of Scripture,
but doubts about its being in some sense the Revealed Word
were extremely rare; one might question *how* the hand of God
was made manifest in the cosmos, but it was apparent to virtually
all that it *was* in some way made manifest. The unanimity of
opinion, the homogeneity of assumption, that existed at this time
included the widest ranges of experience, comprehending everything from God to a stone, from the most complex to the most
simple—all conceived within an incredibly detailed and yet in-

clusive system of hierarchies, correspondences, analogies, and parallels.

The fundamental principle of this variegated but clearly patterned fabric, the idea of order, was realized most grandly in the empyrean heavens and the astronomical system derived from Plato, Aristotle, and Ptolemy. Ideally it appeared as well in the sublunary world that was composed like man of the corruptible and changeable four elements. Even man himself, viewed as he ought to be, was thought to reveal law, order, symmetry, and proportion. Man is the state in little, the state is the cosmos in little; and the three main areas of human experience, interlocking and interdependent, form a single unity under the Providence of God.[23]

Renaissance writers customarily divided their ordered world into two main areas, variously labeled matter and spirit, human and divine, corporeal and noncorporeal, Nature and Grace, and so on. The two areas or categories may perhaps most conveniently be called the order of nature and the order of grace.[24] Whether we encounter the two orders in connection with Bacon's explicit attempt to segregate one from the other or with Hooker's effort to reconcile them, we may still see them as together constituting the frame of reference within which the Renaissance mind easily and habitually moved; and though both are of course comprehended by God's Providence, it nevertheless remains possible to recognize in each order certain differentiating and characteristic features.

To the order of grace belong man as the possessor of an immortal soul and all things that under the new and old dispensation pertain directly to his salvation. The law of this order derives from God's revelation as received and interpreted through the faith of His creatures, and the kind of experience appropriate to it is religious. To the order of nature, on the other hand, belong man in his role as reasoning animal and the whole physical world of animate and inanimate creation. The law of this order

appears in the regularities of physical existence, in natural morality and ethics, and in natural as distinguished from revealed
theology. Man therefore lived simultaneously in two orders of
existence, in what Sir Thomas Browne calls "divided and distinguished worlds"; and his separate functions and responsibilities were customarily discriminated with the utmost nicety, for
man's moral life depended upon his ability to understand in the
cosmos, in the state, and in himself the functional relationship
of the two orders.

Man's was the "middle and participating nature" that uniquely
occupied the position halfway between the order of grace and
the order of nature. As Raleigh says:

God created three sorts of living natures, to wit, angelical, rational,
and brutal [and] he vouchsafed unto man both the intellectual of
angels, the sensitive of beasts, and the proper rational belonging unto
man; and therefore . . . "Man is the bond and chain which tieth
together both natures." [25]

Traditional morality taught that it was a matter of rational
choice, a matter of man's free will, which order should claim man
most completely, which of his two "natures" should dominate
the other:

Now MAN being placed (as it were) in the Bounds betweene the
Reasonable-nature, and that which is Irrationall; if he incline to the
Bodie . . . he chuseth and embraceth the life of unreasonable-
creatures; and, for that cause, shall be numbred among them, and
be called (as Saint Paul terms him) An earthly MAN. . . . But, if he
incline rather to the Reasonable part, and . . . shall make choice to
follow that blessed and divine life which is most agreeable unto MAN,
he shall, then, be accounted a Heavenly MAN.[26]

But for us at this moment it is Nature and Art, rather than Nature
and Grace, that is important, as indeed it often was for Renaissance writers like George Wither:

For in what age, will the knowledge of the humane nature bee impertinent, or to what person of that kinde? nay, what knowledge, save the knowledge of GOD is more pertinent? Or, how can GOD be well knowne, by him, that knoweth not himselfe? It is that knowledge which this Booke teacheth. . . . Let no man, therefore . . . prejudicately conceive . . . that NATURE is here magnified above GRACE.[27]

Of man's two natures and the possibilities of both glory and degradation they hold for him, only one—his "humane nature," man considered as part of the order of nature—relates directly to an understanding of what Nature and Art meant to the Renaissance.

Not recognized by scholarship, but equally important to an appreciation of Renaissance moral experience and literature, is the further division that marks the order of nature itself. Within the order of nature, and clearly distinguished from the order of grace, lie two distinct and often conflicting areas of experience. The Renaissance referred to them as "the vast and all-comprehending Dominions of Nature and Art." [28] Although the fundamental division crops up in many other and related terms— usually in controversies opposing the universal and natural to the customary and conventional, primitivism to progress, the contemplative to the active, the pastoral to the courtly, genius to education, even good to evil—the two categories are most often subsumed by the terms Nature and Art.

Generally taken for granted, assumed rather than expounded, Nature and Art point to the two main kinds of specifically human experience. As we have seen, the terms appear habitually in a variety of contexts, floating like most commonplaces somewhere below the level of conscious intellection: ages, like men, rarely demand that the language they allow to think for them be brought to the surface of consciousness. Occasionally, of course, a didactic purpose requires the explicit reassertion of commonplace material, as, for example, in Robert Herrick's epigram "Upon Man," which has considerable historical interest:

> Man is compos'd here of a two-fold part;
> The first of Nature, and the next of Art:
> Art presupposes Nature; Nature shee
> Prepares the way to mans docility.[29]

These four rather prosaic lines distill some fifteen hundred years of controversy over the conflicting claims of Nature and Art.

The "here" of the first lines demonstrates by its sheer unobtrusiveness what Herrick could afford to take for granted in his time. Serving to do more than pad out the metrical line, it is in fact crucial to a proper appreciation of the epigram, for it refers to this dull, sublunary world, to the order of nature rather than that of grace. The lines are not part of the "Noble Numbers" —that is, not part of the collection of sacred poems published in the same book with *Hesperides* but having a separate title page —and therefore Herrick quite appropriately confines his attention to Wither's "humane nature," to man in his role as reasoning animal, not man as the possessor of an immortal soul but man as part of the order of nature. Herrick is expounding for his readers the fundamental division in the order of nature, the division between Nature and Art, so that he may go on to explain its application to the moral life of man. The epigram does not presume to define man's role in the order of grace; in this second area he has other functions and other attributes.

A controversy over the relative values of Nature and Art is thus in effect a controversy over man's role in the order of nature, and the terms themselves are therefore when paired, when used in tandem, a "complete" and "real" principle of classification by which man may organize his perceptions of what is right and legitimate in this corporeal and terrestrial world, of what is good and valid for him in his role as reasoning animal alive in the physical world of animate and inanimate nature.

The possible combinations of Nature and Art, together with the relative values assigned to each term, were of course virtually infinite. Since the division between the two terms offered a convenient way—apparently *the* most convenient way—for man to organize his view of natural experience, Nature and Art were combined, according to a writer's temperament, training, and purpose, in innumerable and sometimes contradictory ways.

The terms might of course in rare instances merely indicate a neutral division in the order of nature, with little or no observable preference for either Nature or Art, and in one passage from Bacon there appears the explicit assertion that the terms refer to a division and nothing more: "It matters not whether it be done by art and human means, or by nature unaided by man; nor is the one more powerful than the other." But generally, as Bacon admits contemptuously, "it is the fashion to talk as if art were something different from nature." [30] In which case, as Burton says: "It is a question much controverted by some wise men, whether natural or artificial objects be more powerful? But not decided." [31] Bacon aside, it was "the fashion to talk" as if "the vast and all-comprehending Dominions of Nature and Art" were capable of interaction, so that the way a given writer pairs the terms indicates (or betrays) his preference for one or the other.

The key to the "question much controverted" lies in Renaissance assumptions about human reason. The use of the division almost invariably reveals some sort of moral position in regard to the order of nature because the relative values assigned to Nature and Art are tightly linked to what was perhaps the main moral problem of the Renaissance—the use (or misuse) of human reason. Reason was Renaissance man's most cherished possession, the faculty that separated him from the bestial hordes, allied him with the angelic hosts, and permitted him to understand an essentially rational universe. For Cicero (and most Renaissance moralists) to follow Nature meant to conduct oneself according to law and reason:

For those creatures who have received the gift of reason from Nature have also received right reason, and therefore they have also received the gift of Law, which is right reason applied to command and prohibition. And if they have received Law, they have received Justice also.[32]

Where Nature is virtually equivalent to (right) reason, the relationship between Nature and the product of human reason, Art, will be complementary, as in Herrick's epigram and in most of the writings of the Christian humanists of the Renaissance.

Puttenham sums up the orthodox position thus:

Arte is an ayde and coadiutor to nature, and a furtherer of her actions to good effect, or peraduenture a meane to supply her wants, by renforcing the causes wherein shee is impotent and defectiue, as doth the arte of phisicke, by helping the naturall concoction, retention, distribution, expulsion, and other vertues, in a weake and vnhealthie bodie. Or as the good gardiner seasons his soyle by sundrie sorts of compost . . . and prunes his branches, and vnleaues his boughes to let in the sunne. . . . And in both these cases it is no smal praise for the Phisition & Gardiner to be called good and cunning artificers.[33]

Art perfects and complements Nature. At the same time Puttenham's phrasing betrays the stigma that could be attached to Art because of its connotations of the counterfeit or even the dishonest.[34] And Nature and Art might come into conflict for still more fundamental reasons. An obvious example would be Calvin, whose doubts about fallen nature and corrupted reason extend to art. Similar results appear in a man like Swift, growing out of his ironic vision of man's perversity to man through "art and reason":

I expected every moment that my master would accuse the yahoos of those unnatural appetites in both sexes, so common among us. But Nature, it seems, hath not been so expert a schoolmistress; and these politer pleasures are entirely the productions of art and reason, on our side of the globe.[35]

Less obvious but equally important is a writer who sees the law of nature as *opposed* to human reason, an opposition that in turn leads automatically to the opposition of Nature and Art.

Montaigne finds in the opposition of Nature to Art and Reason a standard and a constant theme. Following Nature makes the unexamined life worth living:

> I have (as elsewhere I noted) taken for my regard this ancient precept, very rawly and simply: That "We cannot erre in following Nature": and that the soveraigne document is, for a man to comforme himself to her. I have not (as Socrates) by the power and vertue of reason, corrected my natural complexions, nor by Art hindered mine inclination. Looke how I came into the World, so I goe-on: I strive with nothing.[36]

Charron is more orthodox, especially in his refusal to see Reason in conflict with Nature, but even orthodox Christian Stoicism often ignored Seneca's qualification—"For Nature giueth not vertue; it is an art to be made good"—in favor of a position approximating Montaigne's idiosyncratic stand:

> Doubtlesse, Nature in euery one of vs is sufficient, and a sweet mistris and rule to all things, if we will hearken vnto her, employ and awaken her; and we need not seeke elsewhere, nor begge of Art . . . the meanes, the remedies, and the rules which we haue need of. . . . [Unfortunately] we prefer Art before nature, we shut the windowes at high noone, and light candles.[37]

It is in such ways that the division between Nature and Art becomes an opposition, so that the pairing of the terms becomes antithetical: "Art is Nature's rival." [38] Usually, however, when human reason functions properly, it is possible to "aid nature with a little art," [39] to acknowledge "that Art might helpe where Nature made a faile." [40]

These conflicting interpretations of the division—Nature and Art as complementary, Nature and Art as opposed—represent the two main alternatives for Renaissance thinkers. Yet it remains

dangerous to try to identify these fundamental attitudes with
particular figures or even with general intellectual trends.[41] On
one occasion a writer may maintain that Art perfects Nature,
on another that Art perverts Nature. An opinion about the relationship of the terms in one area of discourse, say the grafting
of fruit trees, may be completely reversed in another area, say
intermarriage between different social classes. (It is just this
ambiguity between different areas of discourse that lends ironic
and dramatic point to the speeches of Perdita and Polixenes on
Nature and Art in *The Winter's Tale,* where Shakespeare clearly
intends such lines as "we marry/ A gentler scion to the wildest
stock" to carry social overtones.) As a way of organizing and
labeling aspects of moral experience, the division remained so
infinitely flexible that it could be used entirely differently in
different contexts.

The responsibility for the "right" alignment of Nature and
Art finally devolves upon man, as George Turbervile points out
in "That All Things Are as They Are Used," a poem that investigates in some detail the way the Art of man may alter
Nature for the better and the worse. The first stanza states un-
compromisingly the possibility of misusing human reason:

> Was neuer ought by Natures Art
>   Or cunning skill so wisely wrought,
> But Man by practise might conuart
>   Too worser vse than Nature thought.

The middle stanzas catalogue the predictable examples—law,
medicine, the use of fire, learning—of activities that reveal both
the use and the abuse of Art. The last stanza then states, as
unequivocally as the first, the opposite side of the coin, exhibiting
confidence at last in what Sidney would call man's "erected wit":

> Againe there is not that so ill
>   Bylowe the Lampe of Phoebus light,

> But man may better if he will
> Applie his wit to make it right.[42]

Art, the product of human "wit," may either perfect or pervert Nature. The relationships between the two terms, the values assigned to each, depend finally on a writer's view of human reason in general and his application of this view to a particular case.[43]

One answer to the "question much controverted" was that "artificial objects be more powerful": "Art can breake Nature." [44] It might even be argued "by some wise men" that Art *ought* to be "more powerful," a stand taken infrequently during the Renaissance because the word Nature possessed so much sanctity. Baltasar Gracián, however, in Maxim XII of *The Courtiers Manual Oracle* (printed 1647, Englished 1685) adopts this extreme position as unequivocally as Oscar Wilde:

Art corrects what is bad, and perfects what is good. Nature commonly denies us the best, to the end we may have recourse to Art. The best Nature without Art is but a Wilderness: and how great soever a Man's Talents may be, unless they be cultivated, they are but half-talents. Without Art a man knows nothing as he ought to do, and is Clownish in every thing he sets about.[45]

Such extreme statements are rare. It is Puttenham's exposition of this view that is sufficiently well qualified to be representative:

Arte is [an alterer of] nature in all her actions . . . and in some sort a surmounter of her skill. . . . The Phisition by [his] cordials . . . shall be able not onely to restore the decayed spirites of man . . . but also to prolong the terme of his life many yeares ouer and aboue the stint of his . . . naturall constitution . . . any of which things nature could not doe without mans help and arte.[46]

Even when admitting that Art may be "in some sort a surmounter" of Nature, Puttenham clings to the orthodox notion that ideally the two terms should work together.

The other extreme response to this "question much contro-verted" lies in the preference for Nature to the exclusion of Art: "Certainly nothing artificial is pleasing." [47] Propertius was con-vinced that "birds sing sweetlier from their lack of art," and Montaigne quotes the line in support of a similar argument.[48] John Wilson's translation (1668) of Erasmus' *Praise of Folly* reads decisively: "Much better in every respect are the works of Nature than the adulteries of Art." [49] This extreme view, gen-erally advanced for aesthetic reasons, may also appear in writers like Fulke Greville who derive it from religious principles of a Calvinistical turn:

> Hence weake, and few those dazled notions be,
> Which our fraile Vnderstanding doth retaine;
> So as mans bankrupt Nature is not free,
> By any Arts to raise it selfe againe:
>   Or to those notions which doe in vs liue
>   Confus'd, a well-fram'd Art-like state to giue.

Art corrupts rather than perfects man's fallen Nature:

> Nature we draw to Art, which then forsakes
> To be herselfe, when she with Art combines.[50]

But the more orthodox position—"without Art, Nature can ne're bee perfect; &, without Nature, Art can clayme no being" [51]— can also find a religious justification in men like Sir Thomas Browne: "Now Nature is not at variance with Art, nor Art with Nature, they being both servants of his Providence. . . . In brief, all things are artificial; for Nature is the Art of God." [52] The direct opposition of Nature and Art, so neatly reconciled in Browne, indicates only the extreme possibility. The spectrum reveals infinite gradations of more or less direct conflict.

One kind of conflict that falls short of complete opposition appears in the idea that Art produces effects altogether different from Nature, that arte is as it were an encountrer and contrary to nature, producing effects neither like to hers, nor by participation with her operations, nor by imitation of her paternes, but makes things and produceth effects altogether strange and diuerse, & of such forme & qualitie (nature alwaies supplying stuffe) as she neuer would nor could haue done of her selfe.[53]

The more important and widespread kind of "neutral" opposition, familiar to readers of Renaissance criticism, grows out of the concept of imitation.[54] There is no need to emphasize the importance of this concept for an understanding of Renaissance poetic; all we need note is its tendency—*Illud tamen in primis testandum est, nihil praecepta atque artes valere nisi adiuvante natura* [55]—to subordinate, if not actually oppose, Art to Nature. Most of the rhetoric books held that *Naturam incipere, artem dirigere,*[56] but in many writers, as in La Primaudaye, there is little feeling that Art has value independently of Nature:

This word Artificer is deriued of the worde Arte. Nowe bicause that nature is most perfect next to God, the neerer that arte approcheth to nature, the better and perfecter it is, as appeereth in images and pictures: so that arte is nothing else but an imitation of nature.[57]

Such is the result of placing the dicta of Aristotle's *Physics* and *Poetics* in the context of Christian aesthetic; Nature and Art are working together, but there is no doubt as to which is the leader.

Although imitation was generally an activity of great dignity during the Renaissance, vestiges of Plato's pejorative use of the term linger on, perhaps even in Puttenham's choice of simile to describe the process of imitation:

In another respect, we say arte is . . . onely a bare immitatour of natures works, following and counterfeyting her actions and effects, as the Marmesot doth many countenances and gestures of man, of which sorte are the artes of painting and keruing. . . . So also the Alchimist counterfeits gold, siluer, and all other mettals, the Lapidarie pearles and pretious stones by . . . substances falsified and sophisticate by arte. These men also be praised for their craft, and their credit is nothing empayred, to say that their conclusions and effects are very artificiall.[58]

If the negligible role of "bare immitatour" suggests the less than flattering simile of the "Marmesot," [59] at least this kind of Art is not explicitly condemned as it was by many a Platonist. Clearly, however, Puttenham is attempting to anticipate Platonic criticism, so that he is careful to distinguish, here and elsewhere, the proper from improper uses of Art, concluding in most instances (sheer dandyism in dress or speech being an important exception, for him if not for Baudelaire) that "their credit is nothing empayred, to say that their conclusions and effects are very artificiall." It is nevertheless easy to see how attitudes toward an imitation "falsified and sophisticate by arte" could shade imperceptibly into rather less neutral contexts.

Hence the tirelessly repeated maxim that the real aim of Art is to conceal Art, to efface itself by so closely imitating Nature that it is impossible to distinguish the "Marmesot" from the man: "Art is only perfect when it looks like nature." [60] Quintilian asserts that the "height of art is to conceal art," [61] and Nicholas Breton's gentlewoman in the seventeenth century is but one of a long line of "rhetoricians" to second him dutifully: "I haue heard scholars say, that it is art to conceal art." [62] Thus the classical canon that Art imitates Nature could lead finally, if not to outright conflict between the two terms, at least to implicit opposition or a kind of wary neutrality.

The preceding pages outline possible relationships between Nature and Art without much regard for either context or historical development. The purpose has simply been to suggest the large number of ways the terms might be combined, even after showing that they were generally viewed either as opposed or as complementary. But an attempt has been made to establish a thesis as well as to offer a survey. I have been arguing throughout that the words were felt to be universally applicable to any activity within the order of nature, whether gardening, cosmetics, the moral life, or rhetoric: thus Puttenham could presume to show "where arte ought to appeare, and where not, and when the naturall is more commendable than the artificiall" not only in poetry but also in "any humane action or workmanship." [63] Organized thinking in the Renaissance relied so heavily on the pairing of Nature and Art not only because of the equivocal and flexible character of the words but also because the "vast and all-comprehending Dominions of Nature and Art" marked a "real" division in man and his universe. For this reason Nature and Art, though sometimes paired out of copybook habit as the result of hackneyed thinking, were generally apprehended as more than a verbal formula, as more than a rhetorical flourish to trick out a line, just as in *Religio Medici* the idea of man as microcosm is understood to be more than a "pleasant trope of Rhetorick."

Both Nature and Art were necessary to any accurate, complete view of the world: "If Nature could produce all her works in perfection, there would be no need of Art, and if Art could make them by herself, there would be no need of Nature." [64] As simple as that. The relationship between Nature and Art was thus fixed in so far as it was felt to correspond to reality—

> Man is compos'd here of a two-fold part;
> The first of Nature, and the next of Art—

but we have seen that the balance of the correspondence, hence the values assigned to each term, lay open to varying interpretation and vigorous controversy. The relationship posited between Nature and Art could vary according to a writer's assessment of a particular situation in the light of his assumptions about the efficacy of human reason, so that it is therefore risky to attribute a "consistent" or "invariable" attitude toward Nature and Art to an individual writer or even to a group of writers. Some observations of a general character are nevertheless possible.

When Art is viewed eulogistically—as the product of man's "erected wit," of a faculty not entirely impaired by the Fall, of a faculty capable of rational creativity—then Nature usually signifies the unformed, the inchoate, the imperfect, or even the corrupt:

> But all these naturall Defects perchance
> May be supplyed by Sciences, and Arts;
> Which wee thirst after, study, admire, aduance,
> As if restore our fall, recure our smarts.[65]

In this view Nature is that which has been more or less impaired by original sin and Art represents the means by which man, to borrow Milton's phrasing on education, may repair the ruin of his first parents' Fall. Such an attitude toward Nature and Art characterizes the morality, if not the gardening, of the Christian humanists, and in literature it may be associated with courtly rather than pastoral society. Shepherds, from Longus on, were presumed to do quite well without Art in the green world of pastoral, but neither Sidney nor Spenser allows his knights to dwell too long in their natural Arcadias. Beyond the green world of the shepherds the Blatant Beast runs mad, the unspoiled Nature of golden lads and lasses is not enough, and a knight must assume his true responsibilities where fallen Nature is insufficient, where "it is an art to be made good."

When, on the other hand, Art is viewed pejoratively—as mere imitation, falsification, reprehensible counterfeit, or even perversion—then Nature signifies the original, the unspoiled, the transcendent, or even the perfect. So with Montaigne's cannibals:

There is ever perfect religion, perfect policie, perfect and compleat use of all things. They are even savage, as we call those fruits wilde, which nature of her selfe, and of her ordinarie progresse hath produced: whereas indeed, they are those which our selves have altered by our artificiall devices, and diverted from their common order, we should rather terme savage. . . . there is no reason, art should gaine the point of honour of our great and puissant mother Nature.[66]

Nature in this view is associated with Eden and the Golden Age and is represented as having preserved some of the communication between heaven and earth relinquished through the Fall. Art thus becomes the product of defective human reason, the instrument of man's further alienation from Nature, the reenactment of his Fall from the harmony of Eden:

> Nature we draw to Art, which then forsakes
> To be herselfe, when she with Art combines.[67]

Art corrupts the pristine integrity of Nature. This attitude toward Nature and Art was exploited primarily by the Renaissance naturalists, especially those of a *libertin* cast, and was felt to be appropriate to pastoral rather than courtly society.

So much for survey and large generalization. It seems clear that there can be little doubt of the importance of the terms in understanding Renaissance thought. Indeed, the pairing of Nature and Art is so frequently a mental habit of Shakespeare's England that at times it must appear to dictate rather than express thought; the habitual pairing many times betrays perfunctory thought or, worse yet, no thought at all. And yet when used by men like Spenser, Shakespeare, and Marvell, the terms suddenly become a "commonplace" of rare vigor and precision. The reason is that these writers not only thought *with* but also *about* the "vast and all-comprehending Dominions of Nature and Art." Standing at the end of a tradition that took shape before the time of Plato, these writers used individual talent to produce the art that Robert Frost calls a momentary stay against confusion.

CHAPTER II

Classical Backgrounds

It is good occasionally to look to the rock whence we were hewn and unto the hole of the pit whence we were digged. And the attempt to search out beginnings may be particularly useful in dealing with the literature of the Renaissance, for this was a time before the activity of imitation became confused with the business of plagiarism. The Renaissance division between Nature and Art has its ultimate source in antiquity, where may be found also, only to a lesser extent, the origins of Renaissance pastoral poetry. Classical philosophy had explored the main possibilities in the relationship of Nature to Art fairly thoroughly, bequeathing the Renaissance an authority for all the alternative combinations outlined in the last chapter. Writers as important for the Renaissance as Plato, Aristotle, Cicero, and Seneca were all preoccupied at one time or another with Nature and Art: they thought with and about the terms, using them both as a means of organizing thought and as objects worthy of scrutiny in themselves. The pastoral genre, on the other hand, did not develop until the Renaissance its full potentiality as a vehicle for exploring the division between Nature and Art. Although the pastoral did develop in antiquity its concern with idealized Nature and the Golden Age, it did not exploit fully the moral aspects of the antithesis between Nature and Art. It was concerned only implicitly and in a relatively neutral fashion with the possibilities for conflict between the terms. But these are difficult distinctions, and it will be best to consider them in greater

detail, one at a time, beginning with some etymological observations that reveal the source of the power and appeal of Nature
and Art in classical philosophy.

Nature and Art, considered merely as words, represent an
extraordinarily complicated semasiological process beginning with
the pre-Socratics and not yet concluded in modern times. The
word Art alone comprehends a variety of meanings—Webster's
New International Dictionary subsumes at least fifteen under
the two main headings—but it is the word Nature, of course,
that has encouraged the almost infinite proliferation of ways to
combine the terms. Lovejoy and Boas enumerate fully sixty-five
normative meanings of the term,[1] and there is no doubt that
the list might be extended to include senses which, though minor
and derivative, nevertheless play a discernible part in the "etymol-
ogy" of the Renaissance division in the order of nature. Fortunately we need not be concerned with the entire history of
primitivistic thought.

During the Renaissance the distinction between Nature and
Art depends on whether man himself or man's view of the
universe is being observed: in respect to man himself the distinction may be formulated in terms of the dichotomy between
the instinctive or spontaneous (Nature) and the voluntary or
conscious (Art); with respect to the universe the terms segregate
the work of God (Nature) from the work of man (Art). With
meanings as inclusive as these, the terms appear very early in
Western philosophy and are applied to a wide range of activities.

In the *Laws* (x.889) Plato summarizes the views of certain
philosophers who believe (erroneously) that the best things occur
by "chance" and by "nature," not by "art." According to their
misapprehension,

art sprang up afterwards and . . . produced in play certain images
and very partial imitations of the truth, having an affinity to one
another, such as music and painting create and their companion arts.
And there are other arts which have a serious purpose, and these

co-operate with nature, such, for example, as medicine, and husbandry, and gymnastic. And they say that politics co-operate with nature, but in a less degree, and have more of art; also that legislation is entirely a work of art, and is based on assumptions which are not true.[2]

These assertions—that in the fine arts Art imitates Nature, that in medicine and husbandry Art cooperates with Nature, and that in society Art may either complement or oppose Nature—are commonplace in the Renaissance. Apparently they were equally well known in Plato's day, and apparently even then Nature and Art were thought to be applicable to a wide variety of human activities. Karl Popper argues that the distinction represented by Nature and Art goes back at least to the generation of Protagoras, who in Popper's estimation was one of the first to make a conscious program out of the process of differentiating the natural from the social environment of man. Popper maintains that primitive man, part of a tribal society, does not clearly recognize the difference between "natural laws," such as those that govern the succession of the seasons or the science of thermodynamics, and "normative laws," such as the Ten Commandments or those that regulate the activities of automobile drivers.[3] However plausible these speculations may be, unfortunately they do not explain the division between Nature and Art, which by the time of Plato had reached a point of sophistication where study of its origins throws only incidental light on its later manifestations.

The process by which the division between Nature and Art became such an important opposition that it penetrated large areas of analytical thought is initially linguistic, depending finally on the genesis of the normative function of the word Nature. Lovejoy and Boas have investigated the development thoroughly,[4] and it will consequently be sufficient to review only those aspects of the process pertinent to an understanding of how Nature and Art became a "problem" for ancient philosophy.

The word Nature (*physis*) in its earliest literary use (*Odyssey* x.303) appears already to have undergone a semasiological change from "birth" to "innate characteristic," and then to "characteristic" in general. It was also used to distinguish between reality and appearance, between the inherent, permanent characteristics of a thing as opposed to its superficial, transitory qualities.[5] Meanwhile the Greek for "by law" or "in accordance with accepted mores" was submitting to another long semasiological development, ending finally in its use as an antonym for Nature. By the fifth century B.C. philosophers were employing *nomos*—the word for law or custom—to express the doctrine of the subjectivity of the secondary qualities of matter. Since it had acquired by this time the connotations of "subjective" or even "erroneous," it was conveniently paired antithetically with Nature in distinguishing secondary from primary characteristics.

The appearance of the linguistic antithesis coincided with a related development in Greek ethics. In Athens by the second half of the fifth century, faith in traditional moral precepts and existing laws had been threatened, notably by the relativistic implications of Herodotus' catalogue of cultural oddities and differing customs, so that it became fashionable to advocate a kind of ethical skepticism. The skepticism was then balanced by a search with renewed urgency for some sort of objective, universally valid, moral criteria.[6] It was at this point that the linguistic antithesis between "physis" (Nature) and the word for "by law" came to have crucial significance. The search for objective criteria indeed produced a new standard or norm—"by nature" or "according to nature" rather than "by law."[7] When transferred to the vocabulary of ethics, "physis" comes to be synonymous with that which is attested by the *consensus gentium*, that which is normal and healthy, that which has the indication or even the certainty of objective reality. Here lies the basis for opposition between Nature and Art.

The honorific connotations that clustered ever more persistently around the word Nature have obvious primitivistic implications, and less directly they have far-reaching consequences for the division between Nature and Art as well. The meaning of Nature as a generic label for that which is not made by man and is free of his contriving, together with the collateral assumption that Nature is a divine or semidivine power that invariably "does things" better than man, had inevitably a prejudicial effect on words like "custom," "use," "convention"—all of which everyday usage opposed to Nature. The honorific meanings of Nature automatically lent pejorative connotations to those words that referred to human alteration or addition to the "natural" order of things. This result was paralleled by the tendency of popular usage to oppose Nature, in its senses of "original endowment" and "spontaneous movement," not only to "accepted mores" but also to culture, instruction, and *techne* or Art.[8] And because Nature had acquired meanings such as "objectively valid" and "normal," the word that stood in linguistic opposition to it automatically became suspect.[9] It was through such a process that Art became a pejorative term and that the products of Art, the results of deliberate education and conscious volition, became by definition inferior to "spontaneous" intuitions and "natural" feelings.

The division between Nature and Art is therefore in Greek primitivistic thought a radical opposition, and even in Plato and Aristotle, whose philosophies are fundamentally anti-primitivist, the words are often used antithetically. Represented in sufficiently broad terms the contrast between Nature and Art becomes the conflict between reality and appearance, which was the concern not only of primitivistic thought in particular but also of other areas of Greek ethics and philosophy. In the Platonic dialogues there is the treatment of the Sophists, who are represented as taking care to distinguish between nature and convention in order to depreciate the validity of "objective" morality. The crucial distinctions—between Nature and Art, reality and appearance, the universal and the local, and so on—are brought to bear on the whole range of human endeavor: in the *Gorgias* on ethics, in the *Republic* and *Laws* on politics, in the *Cratylus* on language. The division between Nature and Art is as clearly present in Plato as it is throughout Greek thought, and yet his final position in regard to the words remains hard to define precisely.

The division between Nature and Art often proves intractable because of the multiple significations of the word Nature; in Plato this resistance to easy definition is aggravated by the dramatic ambiguities involved in using the dialogue form. Montaigne, for example, managed to find in Plato an authority for one of his attempts to depreciate the value of Art and (hence) the power of human reason: "'All things' (saith Plato) 'are produced, either by nature, by fortune, or by art. The greatest and fairest by one or the other of the two first, the least and imperfect by the last.'"[10] This misrepresentation of Plato will be considered shortly, but it may be admitted that there is much in the philosopher that might be brought into at least superficial alignment with such an assertion. Lovejoy and Boas argue that Plato was in revolt against his period, and that his social ideal, emphasizing austerity, simplicity, and communism, has many elements in common with "hard" primitivism. Moreover, the theory of forms and his political prose seem to imply an endorsement of the idea that the "original" and "natural" state of a thing is best, for again and again a reader is invited to see that human history has been marked by progressive deterioration from the ideal.[11] And yet to leave Plato here, rubbing shoulders companionably with Montaigne, is to mistake the part for the whole. It ignores Plato's consistent advocacy of the examined life and hence distorts the relative proportions within his philosophy considered in its entirety.

Although Plato nowhere devotes an entire dialogue either to Art or to Nature and Art, much of his dialectic depends on distinguishing the natural and true from the artificial and merely apparent. In the *Sophist,* for example, the Eleatic Stranger constructs an elaborate dialectic of division and subdivision in order to discover, with a trace of malicious humor, that the Sophist fits the last and most odious category. It is the process, however, and not the result, that is important here. First we are asked to agree that the Sophist is an artist and that all art is either creative or acquisitive. The dialectic then proceeds by analogy and analysis through a variety of classes, through kinds of imitation and kinds of being, until we have been prepared to look in more detail at the branches of the creative arts. There are in Plato, as in most Renaissance theorists, two kinds of creative art—one divine and one human. The Eleatic Stranger points out that "the world and all the animals and plants" are the work of "divine art" and not, as the vulgar suppose, the product of "nature" which "brings them into being from some spontaneous and unintelligent cause," for

things which are said to be made by nature are the work of divine art, and . . . things which are made by man out of these are work of human art. And so there are two kinds of making and production, the one human and the other divine.[12]

Then productive art is again divided into real and apparent creation, later subdivided into ignorant and intelligent imitation, the Sophist finally and at long last being revealed as an acquisitive imitator of mere appearance and not at all—had we suspected it?—the true philosopher.

In its emphasis on Nature and Art, the real and apparent, and the theme of imitation, the dialogue anticipates many commonplace Renaissance notions. Moreover, Plato thinks *with* Nature and Art—they are organizing terms in the dialectic—and also *about* them—they are discussed as objects in themselves. The *Sophist* may therefore be considered a convenient *locus classicus* for many of the uses of Nature and Art in the Renaissance.

Although the terms Nature and Art possess exact meanings only within the dramatic context of the dialogues themselves, Plato's philosophy in general (and the *Sophist* in particular) rejects the "vulgar" notion that Nature is equivalent to truth and reality while Art always means the false and apparent. Unlike Montaigne, Plato is committed to a belief in the dignity and efficacy of human reason; he inveighs constantly against reliance on the instinctive and spontaneous. Indeed, the passage—about Nature, fortune, and Art—that Montaigne seems to have had in mind when quoting Plato is not what "saith Plato" at all; the Athenian in the *Laws* is merely repeating views about Nature and Art that he wishes finally to refute: *"They* say that the greatest and fairest things are the work of nature and of chance, the lesser of art." For Plato the consequence of such (mistaken) attempts to praise Nature at the expense of Art is ethical relativism:

These people would say that the Gods exist not by nature, but by art, and by the laws of states, which are different in different places . . . and that the principles of justice have no existence at all in nature . . . and that the alterations made by art and by law have no basis in nature.[13]

It is clear that Plato's own position directly opposes the relativistic views of "these people"; Art, saith Plato, when it involves conscious reflection and the use of "right reason," is itself a product of Nature, of universal Nature, and must be respected; men should "support the law and also art, and acknowledge that both alike exist by nature, and no less than nature [whenever] they are creations of mind in accordance with right reason."[14] Nature and Art for Plato are not necessarily in conflict, although he sometimes uses the linguistic opposition to make a point in one or another of his dialogues. In the particular cases where he permits himself to pair the terms antithetically, he usually means, as in the *Sophist,* a kind of Art that is unreal, acquisitive, and inimical to true philosophy. The general tendency of his thought as a whole is to find that Art, as the product of "right reason," is superior to uninstructed and instinctive Nature.[15]

Aristotle also uses Nature and Art in a variety of senses, and his final view of the division is much the same in its emphasis upon the value of Art, properly used, as Plato's. And although in Aristotle there is no need to reckon with the equivocality of the dialogue form, the two words reveal a variety of significations even in his expository prose. Art for Aristotle, as for most writers of antiquity and the Renaissance, pointed to a much wider range of experiences than it does today. It meant for him a disposition ("habit" or "virtue") of the intellect and referred to any act of making that involves intellectual judgment:

It is by art that the architect makes the plan of a house; it is by art that the shipbuilder makes a ship; it is by art that the doctor makes health to exist in the patient's body; it is by art that the rhetorician makes up a plausible argument; it is also by art that Homer makes up the story of Odysseus.[16]

This comprehensive use of the word Art was matched in breadth if not in precision by Aristotle's use of the word Nature. Two main meanings of Nature, one psychological and one meta-physical-biological, underlie most of Aristotle's normative uses of the term. The psychological sense implies that the Nature of a man predestines him to a certain kind of life; the psychological may become confused with the moral at this point, so that it may appear that a man has an ethical obligation to pursue a certain mode of existence. This sense, transferred to an external, half-personified power—"Nature makes nothing without an end in view, or in vain"[17]—might be taken to assume that anything that Nature provides for the use of man *ought* to be used. The second, and more important, normative use of Nature derives from Aristotle's metaphysical biology in which Nature becomes the logical "what" of something, the defining attribute of class.

This use is restricted to organisms, to things that change or develop internally, as the oak tree develops from the acorn. And since, according to Aristotle, the formal cause of an organism, that which makes it what it is, exists at first potentially and only after a series of transitional phases in actuality, an organism does not possess its own Nature until the last stage. This metaphysical-biological meaning of the word, when combined with its psychological sense, leads to the conclusion that the end of something in a temporal sense may be identified with its end in a normative sense.[18]

Aristotle has retained the normative function that Nature possessed in popular usage, but has converted its meaning so that the word now expresses a new standard of value. Not the original but the final, not the simple but the complex, is the best condition of a thing subject to change. This broad, complimentary use of Nature apparently leaves little room for the honorific use of Art, and yet in Aristotle, as in Plato, the terms are not necessarily antithetical. Although Art, in so far as it may be held to hinder the spontaneous realization of the potentiality of an organism, is obviously opposed to Nature, Aristotle did not pursue the implications of this possibility because his philosophy, like Plato's, is fundamentally anti-primitivist. Indeed, so far as the organism man is concerned, his potentiality is most fully realized through Art. Nature provides a beginning, but this must be supplemented through education and discipline: "He who is to become good must be properly brought up and habituated." [19] Since man is capable of Art, Nature must have intended him to realize the capacity; and until he does, man's own Nature remains potential rather than actual. There is little appreciation in Aristotle for the spontaneous and instinctive when it lacks shape and direction, when it is not governed by the rational principle, "for in the world both of nature and of art the inferior always exists for the sake of the better or superior, and the better or superior is that which has a rational principle." [20] In the final

analysis, Art, considered as the product of human reason, is itself
the end of Nature in what Aristotle seems to regard as the basic
sense of the word,[21] and in this view the disadvantage, if any,
lies with Nature: "All art and education aim at filling up Nature's deficiencies," [22] for "in general art partly completes what
Nature cannot bring to completion, and partly imitates her." [23]
But even when Art is spoken of as having "completed" Nature,
in reality it is Nature who has completed herself, as "may be best
illustrated by the case of a physician curing himself; for nature
is like that." [24] Aristotle refuses to permit the antithesis of Nature
and Art to become a philosophical problem; no sooner does the
opposition appear than it is resolved.

Roman thinkers inherited the normative uses of the Greek
physis, so that the Latin *natura,* in combination with *ars,* came
to express many of the relationships already observed in Plato
and Aristotle. Cicero, the eclectic synthesizer whose work satu-
rates so much of Renaissance thought, made current most of the
honorific uses of *natura,* sometimes equating it with *ratio* but
more often using it simply as a kind of pious label for what he
approved. Despite his immense importance as a channel of transmission, however, the real significance of Cicero's writings in
regard to Nature and Art seems to lie in his constantly reiterated
notion of man as an animal whose gifts are at first poorly developed. From the Greeks Cicero had learned to discriminate
the *prima naturae,* the basic impulses in man, from that which
becomes part of man through education and the exercise of reason. Virtue is not acquired fortuitously or by Nature. Art must
shape and develop the basic impulses, must complement and
guide the work of Nature. The primary gifts of Nature are in
many cases underdeveloped, for example man's latent faculty of
reason and the "germs of virtue." Of

virtue itself she merely furnished the rudiments; nothing more.
Therefore it is our task (and when I say "our" I mean that it is the

task of art) to supplement those mere beginnings by searching out the further developments which were implicit in them, until what we seek is fully attained.[25]

For Cicero Art supplements Nature and both are requisite to the moral life.

And yet, despite his enthusiastic appreciation of human Art, Cicero's writings, like those of Plato and Aristotle, could often be turned to the service of a variety of (sometimes conflicting) theses. As Lovejoy and Boas point out, Cicero probably did more than any other Latin author to give currency and sanctity to Nature as a standard of conduct; and this standard, though it did not carry primitivistic connotations for Cicero, could still be easily used in arguments for primitivism and ethical "naturalism."[26] Hiram Haydn maintains further that the well-known passage on the "bent and tendency of a man's genius" might similarly be turned to the cause of ethical individualism, and this despite Cicero's careful qualifications to the effect that one's "peculiar character" is to be allowed full play *only* when it is not "contrary to that universal character which Nature has imprinted on every one of us."[27] These are minor caveats: the influence of Cicero overwhelmingly supported the "orthodox" view that Nature and Art are complementary rather than antithetical.

Seneca's influence, despite the overriding emphasis that Stoicism gives to Nature as norm, is similar to Cicero's, in its balance between Nature and Art in the field of ethics. Although *sequere naturam* is the unconditional standard of Senecan Stoicism and of Stoicism in general, this did not mean for Seneca an endorsement of the ethical state of Nature or a rejection of the benefits of Art. The Stoic tendency to identify God and everything valuable with Nature leads him to describe the Golden Age with a certain respectful nostalgia, but he is nevertheless quick to point out that life then was unexamined and consequently less virtuous.

For Nature giueth not vertue; it is an art to be made good. They [the race of the Golden Age] sought not for Gold, nor Siluer, nor glistering stones shining amongst the lowest dregges of the earth. . . . What therefore? did the ignorance of things make them innocent? but there is much difference, whether one will not, or else know not how to sinne. They wanted iustice, prudence, temperance, and fortitude. This rude life had certaine things which had some resemblance of all these vertues. Vertue entereth, and is entertained in no mind, except it be instructed and taught, and brought to the highest by continuall exercise. We are borne to this, but without this, and in the best men also before thou instructest them, the matter of vertue remaineth, not vertue it selfe.[28]

Stoic criticism of civilization, grounded in the ideals of self-sufficiency and conformity to Nature, could often make the life of Art, of court and city, seem ill-considered, but Senecan Stoicism does not extend the criticism to moral sophistication. Civilization may have multiplied man's desires and corrupted his simple piety, but nevertheless the "stuff of virtue" is not enough; "it is an art to be made good." It is, by extension, an Art to follow Nature properly, and once again the linguistic opposition dissolves under the pressure of the moralist to provide for the discipline of the purely spontaneous and instinctive in recommending virtue.

This glance at Senecan Stoicism, so influential in the sixteenth and seventeenth centuries, concludes the examination of Nature and Art in antiquity. The outline has been brief, but sufficient to attest to the vitality of the tradition. Even such sketchy testimony to the complexity and range of its origins helps to place in perspective the Renaissance involvement in the traditional division between Nature and Art. Initially linguistic, the opposition between Nature and Art reflected in popular usage the Greek feeling that reality (Nature) might be discerned beneath appearance (Art). The terms were thus a linguistic convenience that later came to be an analytical convenience. Finally they became a philosophical "problem," a matter for speculative concern. A primitivistic position required the exploitation of the division; Nature and Art are paired antithetically, with Art as the pejorative term. More orthodox opinion, however, resisted the "vulgar" opposition between the terms, even while it adopted as a matter of course the normative function of Nature. The terms were therefore used habitually as foci for arguments about man and his place in the universe, just as today our controversies about juvenile delinquency and capital punishment may suddenly become clarified and intensified through recourse to such words as "heredity" and "environment."

The ancient division between Nature and Art appears at well-defined points in intellectual history, forming a line, not always straight but never broken, from the greatest and most representative thinkers of antiquity to the writers of the Renaissance. In Plato, Aristotle, Seneca, even in Cicero, there are passages open to primitivistic or "naturalistic" interpretation, but the balance in all of these minds falls finally against Nature in the sense of the spontaneous and unreflective. Whatever their opinions in regard to Nature and Art on some specific point, their general position on questions of ethics is almost invariable: "For Nature giueth not vertue; it is an art to be made good." Consequently each of them, in his own way and with his own concerns primarily in mind, resists the notion of a radical opposition between Nature and Art. For each of them the reflective and reasoning faculty is as much a part of man's Nature as his instinctive and nonrational characteristics, and the rational takes precedence over the instinctual; "for in the world both of nature and of art," as Aristotle says, "the inferior always exists for the sake of the better or superior, and the better or superior is that which has a rational principle." Consequently the analytical distinction between Nature and Art which these representative thinkers use and explore, which they think with and about, proves at last to be a division rather than an opposition. And it is thus, as a division, capable nevertheless of becoming, in a particular writer at a particular time, a radical opposition, that Nature and Art reappear as paired terms in the Renaissance.

The Greek and Roman pastoral genre or *kind* developed, independently of philosophical controversy, several of its own ways of dealing with the division between Nature and Art. It was probably inevitable that it should. The philosophical division and the literary form are, essentially, two aspects of the same thing. Both require the same kind of self-consciousness in man and about the same degree of sophistication in regard to the external world; both depend finally upon the ability to distinguish the natural from the artificial. Before one can argue the respective merits of Nature and Art or write pastoral verse it is necessary to become civilized. Development of Art entails a loss of simplicity, and the growth of civilization leads to alienation from Nature. The response may be literary as well as philosophical. Of course, when man becomes sufficiently civilized to appreciate that the gain of a value may only be achieved at the loss of another, he may find still other channels to express his awareness of (in this case) the gain of Art and the loss of Nature.

Nostalgia for a time of lost harmony and simplicity remains one of the perennial yearnings of mankind, appearing as myth long before its embodiment in pastoral literature and philosophical debate. In a period before philosophy, when speculative thought is mythical,[29] nostalgia for artless nature found a vehicle in the myths of the Golden Age and Prometheus. Primitivist nostalgia took shape from the concept of the four ages (Golden, Silver, Bronze, and Iron), a concept that is at once organizational and evaluative. The four ages form a descending series of value, the Golden Age being the first in time and in excellence. According to Hesiod and other writers, it was (with variations) a period of happy innocence, when men lived without strife or injustice and when the earth, unwounded by the plough and without any human labor, brought forth food abundantly, entirely of its own accord. Byron (*Beppo* LXXX, 7-9) knew but could not feel its charms:

> Oh, for old Saturn's reign of sugar-candy!—
> Meantime I drink to your return in brandy.

Montaigne implies that our lapse from the Nature of the Golden Age coincided with the introduction of Art, for the savages of the New World who "have lately bin discovered, so plenteously stored with all manner of naturall meat and drinke, without care or labor, teach us" that

> without toyling, our common mother nature, hath with great plentie stored us with whatsoever should be needfull for us, yea, as it is most likely, more richly and amply, than now adaies she doth, that we have added so much art unto it.[30]

In brief, it was a time when man lived naturally and artlessly, when he lived in harmony with Nature and had no need of Art.

The matter was of course open to debate. Seneca's approval of the Golden Age, for example, was sharply qualified by his conviction that "Nature giueth not vertue; it is an art to be made good." In a writer like Ovid, however, the delineation of the Golden Age emphasizes the languorous delights of pastoral life and evades questions of moral responsibility. The alternative ways of regarding the Golden Age are neatly formularized by two famous Renaissance choruses on the legendary time of peace and plenty. The earlier is from Tasso's *Aminta* (1573):

> . . . legge aurea e felice
> Che Natura scolpi: S'ei piace, ei lice.

The second is from Guarini's later and more "moral" pastoral, *Il Pastor Fido* (1580–89):

> Cura d'onor felice,
> Cui dettava Onesta: Piaccia se lice.

For Tasso "what pleased was proper," while for Guarini "what was proper pleased."[31] In these Golden Age choruses lie the possibilities for controversy over the ethical state of Nature and for opposition between Nature and Art. In Tasso, where Nature takes precedence over Art, the terms conflict; in Seneca, on the other hand, Nature is insufficient and Art is necessary, so that balance is preserved between the two terms.[32]

The myth of Prometheus similarly expresses man's concern with the division between Nature and Art, but it does so, in general, from the point of view of an entirely different philosophy of history. The myth of the Golden Age implies that history reveals progressive decline, often because of the corrupting influence of Art, and asserts in one way or another that original Nature is best. The story of Prometheus, on the other hand, has usually been taken to depend upon the opposite view of history, for the tale of a hero who first introduces the practical arts to mankind seems to assume that man in a state of nature is weak, ignorant, and brutish. And yet even a myth such as this lends itself to various interpretations: Prometheus is only a hero so long as one approves of the results of civilization, so long as one does not believe that Art corrupts Nature. For the primitivist who is attracted emotionally to the idea of a Golden Age Prometheus may seem, as he did to Zeus, to be the arch-villain of history. Since the artifices of civilization are only rarely unmixed blessings, the Promethean gift, especially in a time before the modern adherence to the idea of progress, may be seen according to temperament and experience as either good or evil.

Although Plato's attitude toward the Promethean myth is complicated by his wavering attitude toward certain kinds of Art, the *Protagoras* nonetheless provides a clear statement of the more orthodox interpretation of the myth. Epimetheus and Prometheus have agreed that during creation the first will distribute the proper qualities to each of the creatures while the second will inspect them before they are brought into the light of day. Unfortunately Epimetheus,

not being very wise, forgot that he had distributed among the brute animals all the qualities which he had to give,—and when he came to man, who was still unprovided, he was terribly perplexed. Now while he was in this perplexity, Prometheus came to inspect the distribution, and he found that the other animals were suitably furnished, but that man alone was naked and shoeless, and had neither bed nor arms of defence. The appointed hour was approaching when man in his turn was to go forth into the light of day; and Prometheus, not knowing how he could devise his salvation, stole the mechanical arts of Hephaestus and Athene, and fire with them (they could neither have been acquired nor used without fire), and gave them to man.[33]

Protagoras is represented as having a point to make with his (slightly amused) rehearsal of the myth, and had his point been different, Plato might have allowed him to interpret the myth rather differently. As an excerpt from the sixth oration of Dio Chrysostom (A.D. 40–120) will show, there was a tradition that Diogenes had in fact done just that:

And the reason, as it seemed to him [Diogenes], why the myth says that Zeus punished Prometheus for the discovery and bestowal of fire was that that was the origin and starting-point of softness and luxury amongst men. . . . For men do not use their intelligence to promote manly virtue and justice, but in the pursuit of pleasure. . . . their life becomes constantly less pleasurable and more wearisome; and while they imagine that they are exercising forethought about their own interests, they perish miserably through just this excess of care and forethought. Thus Forethought [Prometheus] is altogether justly said to have been bound to the rock and to have had his liver torn out by the eagle.[34]

Prometheus as hero, Prometheus as villain: the two attitudes neatly illustrate the way in which the simple division between

Nature and Art might become, especially in connection with the moral and ethical implications of the terms, an extreme opposition. The nostalgia for a time of lost simplicity and harmony, then, appears most obviously in the myth of a Golden Age, but the primitivist praise of Nature at the expense of Art could be conveyed even by the myth of Prometheus.

Pastoral literature expresses a more highly developed but kindred concern with Nature and Art. Unlike the Prometheus myth, pastoral usually idealizes the original gifts of Nature and either ignores or depreciates the contribution of Art; its preoccupation with Nature and Art opposes that of the more orthodox treatment in the myth of Prometheus. Pastoral idealizes the original condition of man, or at least what it represents to be man's original condition; like the myth of the Golden Age, which it embodied almost from the first and later assimilated to its own purposes, the pastoral generally conveys formal nostalgia for a lost time of happiness and natural simplicity. Thus its potentiality for moral assertion is, in a sense, built in; the form of the pastoral is itself an expression of the division between Nature and Art. Although the expression of the division was at first, as in Theocritus, little more than a literary acknowledgment of the fact of social division, residing almost exclusively in a poet's simple recognition of a difference between country and court, this kind of recognition can seldom remain neutral: there is usually a preference either for Nature or for Art, with the result that the terms come into conflict. Pastoral is a form of meditation, over the difference between the condition of the poet and the condition of those about whom he writes, which explains why his descriptions of Nature, of the simple shepherd and clean sheep, constitute at least an oblique comment on Art, on the complex virtues and vices of the audience. Pastoral has, therefore, a satirical reflex,[35] and possesses, despite its reputation to the contrary, a definable moral dimension. As God preferred the shepherd Abel before Cain, symbolizing the superiority of the contemplative to the active life, so pastoral prefers Nature before Art. But the morality of the literary form rarely derives from anything more complicated than a simple aesthetic preference for Nature.

The recognition of a difference between country and court remains fairly neutral in Theocritus. His Idyls celebrate country life with tolerant affection but without nostalgia. It is believed that Theocritus introduced himself and his fellow poets into the Seventh Idyl as shepherds, but he does not do so in order to state or even to imply that Sicilian Nature is somehow superior to Alexandrine Art. In general, the pastoral pieces (Idyls I, III–VI, X) do not attempt to idealize Nature: they reveal an affection for shepherd life tempered by amusement and by ironic acknowledgment of its shortcomings. The "dissonance between the bucolic simplicity of the pasture and the literary refinement of the city is never completely resolved, nor was it ever intended to be, for the whole point of Theocritus' humour lies in this dissonance." [36] The source of the dissonance is the division between Nature and Art, but the "bucolic simplicity of the pasture" is not preferred before the "literary refinement of the city." Theocritus sees pastoral steadily and sees it whole; Nature remains in balance with Art. In short, the Idyls of Theocritus resemble later examples of the genre in relying on the division between Nature and Art, but the division is exploited for a humorous rather than a didactic end. Consequently the division remains a division, rather than becoming a moral opposition in which Nature is preferred before Art.

In Vergil, however, the pastoral begins to display moral direction. The *Eclogues* represent an aesthetic ordering of primitivist sentiments, and in such sentiments, as usual, lies the possibility of opposition between Nature and Art. There is no direct evidence of Vergil's having intended to take a stand in the controversy over Nature and Art, and it seems doubtful that even so well-read a young man as he was consciously preoccupied with the philosophical division. Nevertheless, the effect of the *Eclogues* is to idealize the bucolic existence and hence implicitly to prefer Nature before Art. It is Vergil who asks us to believe, if not in Nature, at least in what Nature ought to be. Vergil, according to Bruno Snell, was in 42 or 41 B.C. the discoverer of Arcadia: not the Arcadia of geographies and encyclopedias—that Arcadia had always been known—but the Arcadia of literature, the world of shepherds and Pan, of love and natural simplicity, of delicate feeling and artless tranquillity.[37] In Arcadia Nature has no deficiencies and hence no need of Art to supply them; perfection may not be improved. Not all antiquity shared Vergil's literary enthusiasm.

Polybius, for example, was Arcadian in a geographical rather than a Vergilian sense; he describes his country as rocky and bare. Juvenal, even less Vergilian in his attitude toward this pastoral people, refers to a dull orator as an "Arcadian youth." And as for Philostratus, without a trace of hesitation he dismisses the Arcadians as "acorn-eating swine." [38] Vergil obviously drew on different sources in constructing the ideal world of the *Eclogues*. He elaborated and refined the myths of Arcadia as the dwelling place of Pan, as a land of isolated innocence and purity, as a place where much music was heard—and out of such materials he fashioned the literary Arcadia that has survived into modern times. But whether Vergil created Arcadia in this way, or even whether he created Arcadia at all, makes little difference in this outline of the history of pastoral in relation to Nature and Art.[39] The point is that at least as early as Vergil "Arcadia" had come to be used figuratively as a synonym for an unattainable ideal and that it signified in this figurative sense the ideal landscape of Vergil's pastoral poetry.

Unlike Theocritus, Vergil seems relatively uninterested in realistic descriptions of shepherd life; unlike Sicily, Arcadia is governed by delicate thoughts and ruled by tender feelings. Vergil's herdsmen are never crude, though they lack the overnice Art of the city. They toil not and neither do they draw milk and make cheese; they play the oaten reed and sing mildly of un-requited love. This is all perhaps incipient in Theocritus, but in the *Eclogues* "Virgil has ceased to see anything but what is im-portant to him: tenderness and warmth and delicacy of feeling. Arcadia knows no reckoning in numbers, no precise reckoning of any kind. There is only feeling which suffuses everything with its glow." [40] For our purposes the main points are clear: pastoral is from this time on not necessarily concerned with the realistic depiction of rustic life; it has taken one step toward the symbolic use of the form examined in the next chapter in connection with medieval examples of the genre; and, most important of all, it has come to express not merely Nature but Nature suffused and finally transformed by fragile feelings and sentimental nostal-gia.[41]

The last point, that Vergil's bucolic verse exhibits the workings of ideal Nature in the never-never land of Arcadia, is particularly important for the symbolic use of pastoral, for in such a world it is impossible that Art should take precedence over Nature. The ideal landscape of Vergil's bucolics, that paradisiacal scene that we associate with Arcadia, has no need for Art, no need of improvement of any kind: Nature in this variety of pastoral is already perfect, either entirely beyond the reach of Art or, in some instances, susceptible to it as a corrupting influence. This is indeed the Nature of the Golden Age, that legendary time when Nature dropped food of her own accord into the lap of man. In Ovid, for example:

> And Earth, unplowed, brought forth rich grain; the field,
> Unfallowed, whitened with wheat, and there were rivers
> Of milk, and rivers of honey, and golden nectar
> Dripped from the dark-green oak-trees.[42]

Or later in Marvell:

> Ripe Apples drop about my head;
> The Luscious Clusters of the Vine
> Upon my Mouth do crush their Wine;

The Nectaren, and curious Peach,
Into my hands themselves do reach.[43]

Marvell's understanding of Nature, so superficially similar to
Vergil's, is modified by his knowledge that man lost this relationship with Nature through the Fall from the Garden of
Eden, but Marvell does not change the ideal landscape of Vergil
so much as assume that it will mean something different to his
readers. I am, however, anticipating material that must be approached more slowly. At this time it will be enough to note
that the aesthetic organization of primitivist sentiments in Vergil's *Eclogues* may also become under certain circumstances—
particularly, of course, in treating the Golden Age or the Garden
of Eden—a moral organization of experience. All that is necessary is that the opposition of Nature to Art, latent in Theocritus
and primarily aesthetic in Vergil, should be accepted as a scheme
of values and as the more or less explicit principle of moral organization in a work of art. This is in fact the case with Longus'
Daphnis and Chloe, a prose romance perhaps of the third century
A.D. that anticipates Renaissance uses of Nature and Art in pastoral.

The Greek romances are a relatively late product of the Hellenistic imagination—fairly long, highly melodramatic, rhetorical,
erotic, sensational. The glory and grandeur of antiquity has thus
furnished us with a genre that includes as one of its more recent examples *The Perils of Pauline.* These "disreputable" fragments of ancient civilization represent a problem for the classical
scholar. It has apparently been possible to treat seriously the
question of sources, later influences, and philological cruxes, but
what is one to do with their embarrassing lack of serious purpose? Usually the problem is solved by avoiding it—although
a passing reference to plot or style is almost invariably the occasion for a little quiet irony. There is no need to quarrel with this
general attitude, for a reading of the extant romances brings with
it the evident conviction that when a later teller of tales, Nicetas

Eugenianus, wrote an induction to his twelfth-century verse romance, he might with an appropriate change of names have been speaking with equal exactitude of his predecessors.

> Here read Drusilla's fate and Charicles'—
> Flight, wandering, captures, rescues, roaring seas,
> Robbers and prisons, pirates, hunger's grip;
> Dungeons so deep that never sun could dip
> His rays at noon-day to their dark recess,
> Chained hands and feet; and, greater heaviness,
> Pitiful partings. Last the story tells
> Marriage, though late, and ends with wedding bells.[44]

Only a few specimens of what was apparently an extremely popular genre have survived, and they are with two exceptions notably alike and notably undistinguished, their principal charm being the direct and unabashed way in which they make the most outrageous demands on the sensibility of the reader. Their influence has nevertheless been considerable, not only among the medieval monks who were perhaps inordinately fond of them and upon Byzantine and Roman imitators, but also during the Renaissance, when their plots were reworked by such writers as Greene and Shakespeare and their formal devices may have exerted a diffuse effect on the origins of the modern novel.[45]

That *Daphnis and Chloe* is an atypical romance will quickly be granted, but the primary reason for its unique quality—the philosophic and ethical conflict between Nature and Art—needs explanation and documentation, especially in this instance, where the conflict is dramatized and does not receive expression in direct, abstract language. In this case the ideas of Nature and Art, the main terms of what might have been a purely philosophical opposition, have been assimilated to the dramatic structure of the pastoral romance, thus giving it shape and purpose, the strength and direction that result from a definable moral position. But since, in the case of Longus, the assimilation has been so successful as to leave few traces of the process of absorption, it will be helpful to approach *Daphnis and Chloe* by way of Dio Chrysostom's *Hunters of Euboea*,[46] which represents a more simple and crude attempt to adapt the philosophical opposition between Nature and Art to a fictional form.

Dio Chrysostom is the only author in Moses Hadas' collection of Greek romances about whom anything in particular is known. He lived A.D. 40–120, was a teacher in the Cynic-Stoic tradition, wrote at least eighty orations and an essay in "Praise of Hair." The *Hunters of Euboea* is actually a part of his seventh oration, but it stands by itself as an intelligible, unified whole. The story purports to be told by a garrulous old man who assures the listener that he is about to report a kind of life he has observed with his own eyes, lived by "some men I met practically in the heart of Greece" (p. 173). Having lost his ship on the rugged coast of Euboea, the old man is cared for by a hardy, generous, self-sufficient, happy hunter of the region, who judges the old man to be from "the city" because he looks so "thin and poorly" (p. 175). The hunter tells the old man of his strong, happy, self-sufficient life, taking care to contrast it with the luxurious, weak, decadent life of the city, which he has twice visited.

That is what I saw [the hunter is speaking of courts of law]. It is a great crowd of people shut into the same place and a frightening roar and shouting: I thought they were all fighting with one another. . . . Their angry fits were awful. The people they shouted at were terrified; some of them ran around begging for mercy and others flung their cloaks off for fear. . . . Some men would step forward and some rise in their places and address the crowd. . . . To some the crowd would listen for quite a long while; with others they grew angry as soon as they opened their mouths, and would not let them so much as cheep. (p. 178)

The calculated naïveté of the hunter repeats an old and obvious satirical device. Enough has been quoted to indicate the general tenor of all the incidents recounted by the hunter, in whom Dio has united the Socratic ideal of self-sufficiency and the Cynic-Stoic precept of following Nature. The hunter is less a man than a moral principle, used to exalt Nature above the Art of the corrupt and decadent city. The division between Nature and Art, observed in philosophy, myth, and pastoral, appears again—this time in the form of a short novel or romance—and the division has become more than the aesthetic opposition noted in Vergil: here it has become a moral opposition. Here it is a matter of moral principle to acknowledge that Nature ought to take precedence over Art and that the terms are rightly considered antithetical.

Dio's denigration of urban life is so obvious and exaggerated, his abilities as a romancer so minimal, that the story is little more than a document in the history of primitivism. Such literary pretensions as the tale possesses are carefully subordinated to Cynic propaganda, and the laboratory aspects of the piece float unmistakably uppermost in the author's mind. Dio is writing about what Lovejoy and Boas would call "hard" primitivism to distinguish it from the descriptions of "soft" nature associated with pastoral and most versions of the Golden Age. Although the Cynic "return to Nature" did not include mortification of the flesh, the philosophers of this school were unusually ready to emphasize the "hard" aspects of man in a state of nature, especially in connection with a rigorous discipline of the desires. Dio's tale expresses, more or less directly, the chief ideals of Cynic life in accordance with Nature: things are best as made by Nature uncontaminated by the Art of man; cultural "improvement" is therefore to be resisted and where possible reversed; those human desires are "natural" (and therefore good) that are spontaneous and universal rather than conscious and local; moral codes and customs are usually "artificial" and therefore to be resisted unless they happen to be attested by the *consensus gentium*.[47] These tenets of the Cynic program are advanced with such directness in *The Hunters* that the ideas, together with the

author's preference for Nature over Art, are easily isolated from
the flimsy fiction with which Dio has sought to disguise them.
The ideas of Nature and Art have been imperfectly assimilated
to the form of the romance, and consequently *The Hunters* remains propaganda rather than a work of literary art.

The pastoral romance of *Daphnis and Chloe* is rather different
and far more successful as fiction. The moral burden is equally
present in Longus, as a result of his having adopted the division
between Nature and Art along with the pastoral form. But apparently because the moral opposition between the terms does
not appear crudely and overtly, as it does in Dio's *The Hunters,*
the ethical purport of *Daphnis and Chloe,* the basic seriousness
with which the plot is shaped, has been overlooked by commentators on the work. Thornley's translation of 1657 seems to have
set the critical tone in this respect when he advertised his work
as a "most sweet and pleasant pastoral romance for young
ladies." [48] The attitude has persisted, and thus Longus' kindly
humor, technical brilliance, and psychological insight are much
praised. But this is partially to miss the point, for it distinguishes
Daphnis and Chloe only in degree from the other romances and
says nothing about moral differences. It ignores Longus' incor-
poration of the bucolic concern with Nature and Art into the
form of the romance and fails to note that the amalgam represents a new product. There seem to be two main reasons for such
critical neglect: pastoral, with its implied contrast between Nature and Art, is unfashionable and perhaps therefore little understood; further, Longus' treatment of the division between Nature
and Art is not explicit, as in philosophy, the conflict between the
two being dramatized through plot and character rather than
expressed directly in expository prose. Yet, behind these "dramatized ideas" a particular moral stance exists, and it is one that
will yield at least its general outlines to analysis.

A brief summary of *Daphnis and Chloe* will indicate the moral
tendency or direction of the plot itself. Daphnis and Chloe are

found where they had been abandoned by their parents and are brought up respectively by goatherds and shepherds; the simple country people are taught to cherish the children by the "humane" (p. 18) "compassion" (p. 20) of the she-goat and the sheep that suckle the foundling infants in the absence of their mothers. As the children grow up in the green world [49] of pastoral, they are shown to be under the protection of Eros and are therefore soon to experience the awakening of love. Yet their love, in the tradition of the romance, is to be delayed in its consummation, although the complications that develop in Longus are different from those of his fellow novelists. First, there is the much-emphasized psychological barrier of the lovers' naïveté, a matter that is not so much neglected as totally ignored by other romancers. Second, the external obstacles—represented by Dorcon, the gallants of Methymna, Lycainion, Lampis, the pirates, and Gnathon—differ in important respects from their stereotyped counterparts in the other romances. Finally, however, all such obstacles are overcome, and the action proceeds in the invariable pattern of the romance toward prosperity, the requital of true love, and social acclaim. There is, however, this difference: because the chaste lovers find they can "not endure their sojourn in the city" (p. 97), they reject their new social position and their joyous, legitimate parents in favor of the green world: "And not only then, but as long as they lived, for the greater part of the time Daphnis and Chloe led a pastoral life. . . . Their male child they put to a goat to suckle, and their little daughter, who was younger, they made to nurse from a ewe" (p. 98).

A reader, coming to *Daphnis and Chloe* after having read other romances, brings with him a certain pattern of expectation. Some of his expectations are fulfilled: chaste and beautiful lovers separated by a series of hazardous adventures, pirates, false lovers, and unscrupulous rascals, and in the end virtue triumphant as wedding bells chime. But here the resemblance ends. Longus is interested in psychological motivation, and the plot of *Daphnis and Chloe* shows that the virtues of his heroine do not simply proceed from the Horatio Alger-like morality of the other romances. Longus should be read not so much in terms of the romance as in terms of the pastoral, a form that is the direct articulation of the sensed contrast between Art and Nature, between urban and rural values. For in Longus it is the simple values of the Theocritean green world that triumph, not only over pirates, but also over the bourgeois ideals of such typical romances as the *Ephesiaca* of Xenophon and the *Aethiopica* of Heliodorus.

The pastoral innocence of Daphnis and Chloe, their closeness to Nature and the rural deities, protects them from harm much in the same way that the simple virtue of Dio's hunter is more than a match for the unscrupulousness of the city-lawyer. The shepherds learn their humanity from goats, whereas Lycainion, the city wench, has acquired her "wolfish" arts in a sophisticated society. The gallants of Methymna have departed so far from natural virtue that they are unable to use simple honesty in dealing with the direct, innocent inhabitants of the green world. Even the cowherd, Dorcon, betrays habits associated with the urban rather than the rural: he boasts to Chloe, for example, that he is "white as milk," to which the sun-blackened Daphnis replies that the cowherd is "white," yes, "like a city wench" (p. 26).

All this "evil," which for Longus is somehow the result of Art, of urban sophistication, is neutralized and made ineffective in the green world. Lycainion teaches Daphnis the cure for love, and thereby involuntarily furthers the affair with Chloe; the gallants of Methymna are no match for the simple honesty of the shepherds; the Methymnaean army is roundly defeated without bloodshed by the pastoral deities; and Dorcon considerately dies after providing the means for Daphnis' rescue from the pirates. Even the most genuinely corrupt figure in the story, Gnathon the parasitic pederast—"a fellow all jaws, belly, and the parts beneath" (p. 83)—eventually rescues Chloe and returns her to the arms of Daphnis. Virtue in Longus, then, consists in conformity to Nature, and corruption is the result of Art, of the complexity and sophistication of civilization.

Daphnis and Chloe is thus informed by a particular moral point of view, and the source of its morality lies in the pastoral contrast between Nature and Art. Longus' evident moral preference for Nature makes him a primitivist, but it will not do to think of him as the same kind of primitivist as Dio in *The Hunters of Euboea*. The noble savages of the classical period— the Getae, the Scythians, the Germans—were rude, powerful, and simple; Nature to them was not indulgent, nor were animals friendly. Like Dio's hunters they were admired for the fewness of their desires and their indifference to civilization, for their self-sufficiency. These "children of Nature" were extolled for their "hard" primitivism, mainly by the Stoics and Cynics, whose view of man in a state of nature is clearly more rigorous than that of Longus. There is obviously a profound opposition between the Cynic view and the "soft" primitivism of Longus' idyl of a Golden Age. Although *Daphnis and Chloe* may from this point of view be regarded simply as another scrap of evidence in the persistent historical controversy between Nature and Art, it is neither Stoic nor Cynic in total attitude or intention.

Ideas may enter into a work of literature in a variety of ways and with more or less successful results. In Dio's *Hunters* the ideas seem to have been intruded directly, the motive of Cynic propaganda remaining obtrusively evident despite the plot and the literary fiction of the old man. In *Daphnis and Chloe,* however, the ideas have been assimilated to such a degree that they are conveyed indirectly, not in abstract language or through explicit illustration but by means of the tendency of the plot, the direction of the dramatic action, and through the motives of the characters. The antithesis of Nature and Art has been absorbed along with the pastoral form, so that the philosophic controversy has become inextricably a part of the structure of the romance of Daphnis and Chloe. Philosophic ideas have become literary ideas.

Much of pastoral poetry, of course, simply does not possess the moral energy that informs Dio's *The Hunters* or even *Daphnis and Chloe*. In Theocritus the dissonance between Nature and Art is exploited for a humorous rather than a didactic end. There is no question of Theocritus' wanting to use the Idyls as Cynic propaganda. Nature and Art are held in balance, each helping to qualify Theocritus' appreciation of the other, so that the division remains a division. In Vergil the division is at least latently an opposition, for the idealization of Nature has a corollary in the depreciation of Art. But the primitivist sentiments are so thoroughly subordinated to the aesthetic end that a reader will not ordinarily be aware of the implied opposition of Nature and Art. The creator of Arcadia is primarily interested in the way an ideal landscape may be suffused with literary feeling and not at all concerned with philosophic argument. It seems clear that Longus is also primarily committed to aesthetic ends, but *Daphnis and Chloe* reveals that in his hands the pastoral form has developed the possibilities latent in Vergil's treatment of the division between Nature and Art.

In Longus, moreover, there is no doubt that the division has become an opposition. Whether the opposition was for Longus a matter of settled philosophical conviction, psychological inclination, or even *ad hoc* convenience makes little difference here. Whatever its origins and relation to Longus' intention, this "scheme of general propositions that are implied by, rather than directly asserted," [50] in *Daphnis and Chloe* is extremely important—from the point of view of both the individual work and literary history. So far as the individual work is concerned, Longus' stand on the controversy between Nature and Art is the distinguishing mark of *Daphnis and Chloe,* for it represents his most radical departure from the stereotype of romance. Doubtless his preference for Nature over Art impresses us as naïve and ill considered, especially since the idea of progress dominates so much of our intellectual life, and yet Longus' attitude has been endorsed or seriously considered by a fairly large number of responsible thinkers. We can understand his position in regard to Art if we cannot assent to it. Moreover, the opposition of Nature to Art has led in the case of Longus to a moral outlook that possesses considerably more dignity than the crass ethics of the other romancers. It is the ultimate source of the feeling of depth, of fundamental clarity, that the work imparts to critics who nevertheless try to explain their response simply in terms of Longus' technical brilliance and literary *taxis*. But in the last analysis it is Longus' moral consistency, his unequivocal attitude toward the opposition between Nature and Art, that lends direction and a degree of serious purpose to a plot that would otherwise be nothing more than a "most sweet and pleasant pastoral romance for young ladies."

From the standpoint of literary history and my argument, *Daphnis and Chloe* represents the final phase in the development of classical pastoral. It represents, for one branch of the tradition, the triumph of Nature over Art. Vergil's literary fabrication of the green world of Arcadia, in which ideal Nature has no need of Art, disturbs the equipoise between the terms achieved by Theocritus, but it was some time before writers like Dio Chrysostom and Longus actually perceived in the terms a profound moral opposition. The tension between town and country values has always been the source of whatever interest pastoral may possess, but not until Longus did the form become, in effect, an active element in the philosophical controversy over the relationship of the terms. In Longus the literary dream of Arcadia and the poignant myth of a Golden Age have coalesced to produce the pastoral world of Nature, fundamentally opposed to the corrupt and decadent world of Art.

Such distinctions as these about Theocritus, Vergil, and Longus are worth particular emphasis because of the later history of the pastoral *kind,* for the association of pastoral with the philosophic controversy, specifically with the moral position that prefers Nature to Art, has great importance for Renaissance writers like Spenser, Shakespeare, and Marvell. In them the relationship between the literary genre and the philosophical controversy appears as something fixed and given; for them the pastoral traditionally represents the green world in which Nature takes precedence of Art. Indeed the writers of the Renaissance often reveal a conscious awareness of the relationships between literary conventions and the philosophical concepts; then poets may make explicit use of the ideas that Longus never formulates conceptually. The result may be the poem by "J.M." already examined or the famous debate between Perdita and Polixenes over Nature and Art in Shakespeare's *The Winter's Tale.*

That pastoral should become in the hands of some writers a vehicle for the injunction to follow Nature rather than Art is quite within the limits of probability. What is perhaps surprising is that the Renaissance poet, acutely aware of his responsibility to moralize, should accept a convention that appears to carry so much ethical dynamite. There was no problem for a "naturalist" like Tasso,[51] to whom "what pleased was proper," or for the French *libertins,* but Milton assumed that his readers would see through the attempts of Comus to justify the life of the senses through an appeal to Nature, and Sidney obviously expects his readers to see that Cecropia argues perversely in appealing to Nature as a sanction for sensual pleasure.[52] Pamela is not taken in for a moment, no more than would be any Elizabethan trained in orthodox moral philosophy. Further, Nature in the Renaissance is often opposed to Grace, and if we take Seneca's formulation—"For Nature giueth not vertue; it is an art to be made good"—as typical of orthodox opinion, then it is difficult to see how Spenser and Shakespeare can unquestioningly accept, and apparently expect their readers to accept, the pastoral convention that equates Nature with the perfect and regards Art either as superfluous or as downright corrupting. The answer is that during the Middle Ages the tradition of pastoral was "Christianized," so that the pastoral ascendency of Nature over Art became properly purged of its "naturalistic" and primitivist implications.

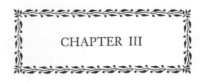

CHAPTER III

The Medieval Contribution

The medieval period contributed much to the development of pastoral, very little to the division between Nature and Art. And yet there is sufficient evidence even about Nature and Art to provide a sense of historical continuity. At the very least it is possible to take note of the ways that Nature and Art, both as a conceptual pair and as an element of pastoral, became part of the intellectual equipment of Renaissance thinkers. Differentiating sources and assessing influences is of less importance, and in regard to the transmission of Nature and Art it is perhaps impossible. Seneca, for example, was supposed by the Middle Ages to have corresponded with St. Paul; even St. Jerome, ordinarily wary of pagan authors, lists him in *catalogo sanctorum.* Also, Senecan Stoicism occupies common ground with Christianity.[1] How, then, do we assess the influence on the Renaissance of Seneca's attitude toward Nature and Art? and do we label it "classical" or "medieval"? The situation is less complicated in dealing with pastoral because the medieval elements are so distinctively Christian that they are relatively easy to isolate.

The division between the natural and artificial retains little interest for the philosophers of the Middle Ages. As a philosophical issue it lacks immediacy. Aquinas follows Aristotle in defining Art as right reason (*ratio recta*) applied to making, but it is no longer urgent, as it was for Aristotle and Plato, to determine what is *really* the work of Nature and what of Art. Stated most simply, a shift of emphasis has occurred—from the classical concern with the order of nature to the medieval preoccupation with the order of grace. The Christian God lies outside the older universe of discourse: "Nature contains him not, Art cannot shew him."[2] Now the primary questions will be raised in connection with Nature and Grace rather than Nature and Art. Enough of the medieval attitude remains even in the seventeenth century to form the ultimate ground of Donne's witty interpretation of a marriage benediction: "Nature and grace doe all, and nothing Art."[3]

Where Nature and Grace "doe all," there is little reason to debate the place and value of Art. Instead, the tenacious issues grow out of a consideration of the relation of Nature to Grace. One view, deriving ultimately from Paul, is that Nature, "being fallen through the offence of the first man," sank into corruption so that "the motion left vnto it tendeth alwaies vnto euil, and inferior things." In many medieval minds, from St. Paul to Thomas à Kempis, Nature appeared to be separate from and opposed to Grace:

Nature is bent vnto the world, vnto the flesh, vnto vanitie, and to vagaries: but Grace allureth vnto God, and vnto wel dooing; biddeth al creatures fare-wel, flieth the world, abhorreth the desires of the flesh, abstaineth from idle gaddings, & blusheth to be seene abroad.[4]

Nature in this view is no longer the province of man's study of man; it is the kingdom of the devil, the world of the flesh. And man's business is to discriminate accurately between the two realms. After all, his salvation depends upon it. The necessity for discriminating between the possibly conflicting claims of Nature and Art was consequently less urgent, and this once vital issue submitted to a process of intellectual petrifaction.

The process went on, though for different reasons, even in areas where Nature was treated with reverence. The Middle Ages managed to assimilate two (contradictory) views of Nature, the one Pauline, the other pagan, and entertain both simultaneously.

When Nature is not the playground of the devil, it is personified as the handmaiden or vicegerent of God, as in Bernardus Silvestris and Alanus ab Insulis.[5] In this sense Nature remains, even in the medieval period, worthy of investigation and imitation, especially when Nature, as in Stoic Christianity, signifies in one of her aspects the order of the universe revealing the form and pressure of God the Artist. Granted that Nature in this sense should be imitated, still Art cannot hope to touch (*attingere*) a natural perfection that comes from God.[6] Human Art must be assumed in this view to be more feeble (*debilior*) than divine Nature.[7] The chain of command, the order of the terms, is as irrevocably fixed in Dante as we saw it to be in Robert Fludd:

Philosophy . . . notes, not in one place only, how nature takes her course from the divine mind and its art; and if thou note well thy *Physics* thou wilt find, not many pages on, that your art, as far as it can, follows nature as the pupil the master, so that your art is to God, as it were, a grandchild.[8]

Aristotle's dictum that Art imitates Nature has been assimilated to a Christian view of experience; for Dante, as later for Sir Thomas Browne, Nature is the Art of God, and human Art does what it can to counterfeit the operations of divine Art. The relationship between the terms remains inflexibly determined within the medieval hierarchy.

Evidence of petrifaction, of hardening of the intellectual arteries, appears conveniently and clearly in Jean de Meun's portion of *The Romance of the Rose*. It is the medieval hierarchy, rather than the author, that determines the scope and value of Nature and Art. Which is not to say that Jean de Meun is a poor poet. There is a tendency to dismiss his achievement because he is less "original" than "encyclopedic," and, as we think we know from reading John Keats, a true poet is not "encyclopedic." But if vigor, humor, and wisdom have anything to do with poetry, Jean de Meun is worthy of respect. Read, for example, the wise

and witty account of the Lover's sexual "pilgrimage," stripped
of all resources save Nature's gift of a "scrip" of "supple leather"
and "staff so stiff and stout," to the Tower of his virgin Rose.[9]
Of course, when Jean comes to consider Nature and Art his purpose is frankly encyclopedic—he is communicating information
—and consequently his statements fall into predictable patterns.
In explaining how Nature forges species in despite of Death and
Corruption the poet slides down a short simile into a long digression on Nature and Art:

> No better plan
> Can she conceive than to imprint the stamp
> Of such a letter as shall guarantee
> That they are genuine; as men are wont
> To stamp the various values on their coins,
> Of which by Art we some examples have,
> Though Art can never fashion forms so true.

The result is one kind of medieval poetry, that is, the spontaneous overflow of powerful learning, collected without too much
thought in tranquillity.

The familiar propositions follow, seeming to arise almost unconsciously out of the simile. Art imitates Nature, Art is inferior
to Nature, Art is Nature's ape, Art must copy but cannot create:

> With most attentive care, upon his knees,
> Of Nature Art implores, demands, and prays,
>
> · · · ·
>
> That she will teach him how she manages
> To reproduce all creatures properly.
>
> · · · ·
>
> He watches how she works, and, most intent
> To do as well, like ape he copies her.
> But Art's so naked and devoid of skill
> That he can never bring a thing to life
> Or make it seem that it is natural.

The delightful and unabashed pedestrianism of these ideas continues through a section on the fine arts and into a discussion of alchemy, that science in which, according to many Renaissance theorists, Art actually had the ability to correct and perfect Nature. But Jean de Meun, in spite of his being vastly intrigued by the subject, manages to preserve the orthodox medieval view of Nature's superiority to Art. Although

>   'tis well known that alchemy
> Is veritably an art,

and although the alchemist can reduce metals to their common substance no matter how "Nature may have sundered them," in the last analysis he "ne'er one species could transmute to other kind." Since the alchemist can work only with "individuals,"

> He'll ne'er attain to Nature's subtlety
> Though he should strive to do so all his life.

The "scholastic" distinction between species and individuals allows the use and dignity of Art to be fixed precisely within the medieval hierarchy.

The distinction perhaps appears factitious to us, but to Jean de Meun it offers a way of integrating kinds of knowledge and opinion that come to him from a variety of different, often conflicting, sources; his eclectic vigor attracts intellectual filings from all quarters. Here he is not really thinking either with or about Nature and Art: he is reiterating in orderly fashion some traditional opinions. The conventional praise of Nature produces the inevitable citations of Zeuxis and Pygmalion and all the usual commonplaces about "imitation," even so far as the simian metaphor that has swung indefatigably through the standard treatises of criticism from Aristotle to John Dennis. The terms Nature and Art have become fossils, deeply embedded in certain literary contexts, so that like the bones confronting the early opponents of evolution they are present to the eye but not the mind. Such calcified fragments typify what remains from the urgent philosophical issues of antiquity, lumps of poetic allusion that mean everything or nothing, proverbial responses that, like He Who Hesitates Is Lost and Look Before You Leap, might sometimes even be contradictory and nevertheless represent "truth." [10]

The most persistent use of Nature and Art appears in the treatises on rhetoric, and even here the old controversies have somehow been neutralized and transformed into maxims and precepts. J. W. H. Atkins points out that from Plato to Quintilian two of the three fundamental requirements for good speaking and writing were natural endowment (*natura*) and knowledge of the craft (*ars*).[11] The *locus classicus* for this use of Nature and Art is of course Horace's conservative passage in the *Ars poetica* on the old question—pursued in Cicero and the Hellenistic rhetoricians, perhaps derived ultimately from Plato—of whether Nature or Art is the more powerful force in the writing of poetry.[12] Horace resolves the difficulty, or rather disposes of it, by asserting that both are necessary. The Horatian resolution was itself a commonplace and was treated as such throughout the Middle Ages. Its authority was reinforced by such minor writers as Simylus, a didactic poet of the Hellenistic period, fragments of whose work were later (*ca.* A.D. 500) collected by Stobaeus. The relevant lines—

> Nature of Art bereft will not suffice
> For any work whate'er in all the world;
> Nor Art again, devoid of Nature's aid—

closely parallel Horace's position on Nature and Art; the lines were known to the Middle Ages, and they are cited with a passage of similar tenor from Cicero as late as Ben Jonson.[13]

The part of Nature and Art in the creative process is held in suspension during the Middle Ages in such passages as those of Horace and Simylus, cited often but seldom thought about.

Similar notions about the complementary relationship between the terms are accepted for the most part unquestioningly, so that from Horace, through John of Salisbury in the twelfth century, to Robortellus and Madius in the sixteenth century there occurs no essential change in the traditional attitude toward the role of Nature and Art in the creative process.[14]

Although the relevance of the terms was not entirely circumscribed by Horace's discussion, controversies seldom or never excited ripples on the theoretical level. Disagreements about practical criticism, about what should be considered Nature and what Art in a particular instance,[15] apparently never reached the rarefied atmosphere in which nearly everyone professed allegiance to the same general principles. This remarkable uniformity of theoretical opinion doubtless implies a certain reluctance to generalize independently about the function of Nature and Art. But for our purposes it will be enough to see that classical views of the division have persisted into the Middle Ages, that in treatises considering the creative process, as in poems like *The Romance of the Rose,* the terms are present even if they are no longer centers of argument.

One problem, the real problem, remains. This main difficulty lies in understanding how chips of fossilized learning, relayed by a Jean de Meun or collected by a Stobaeus, could regain during the Renaissance the immediacy they had for classical antiquity. But since it is a fact that the old issues became in the Renaissance the subjects of new debates, it is possible, with the knowledge of hindsight to steady speculation, to find symptoms of renewed concern with the relationship of Nature to Art as early as the twelfth century.

For example, the *Metalogicon* (*ca.* 1159) of John of Salisbury uses the old terms in a contemporary debate, defending the Trivium against the attacks of one "Cornificius." (Since Donatus had mentioned one "Cornificius" as the detractor of Vergil and the liberal arts, he serves John as the representative of philistinism in general.) The Cornificians, apparently primitivists, maintain that

there is no point in studying the rules of eloquence, which is a gift that is either conceded or denied to each individual by nature. Work and diligence are superfluous where nature has spontaneously and gratuitously bestowed eloquence, whereas they are futile and silly where she has refused to grant it.

This position, that Nature is sufficient and Art either superfluous or detrimental, strikes at the foundation of all learning. John's reaction comes instantaneously. "Art is a system that reason has devised in order to expedite, by its own short cut, our ability to do things within our natural capabilities." Art therefore "avoids nature's wastefulness, and straightens out her circuitous wanderings." The Cornificians believe out of stupidity and confusion that the division between Nature and Art is an opposition. But in reality, says John, the filiation is that of mother to child, so that there is finally no conflict between the terms:

However vigorous it may be, nature cannot attain the facility of an art unless it be trained. At the same time, nature is the mother of all the arts, to which she has given reason as their nurse for their improvement and perfection.[16]

John's position here represents considerably more than a simple elaboration of Horace (*Ars poetica,* ll. 408–11), whom John quotes in support of his own conviction that natural endowment should be supplemented with training. John has thought the problem through on his own, in direct response to the meretricious simplicity of Cornificius.

For John and his classical guides the close connection they believed to exist between *ratio* and *oratio,* between mind and communication, provides the basis for manners and morals in human society.[17] From this conviction of the dignity of rhetoric and reason flows the corollary proposition that Nature and Art must complement each other in the life of the whole man as well as in society and the creative process. The balance that produces fine rhetoric likewise makes for the noble life. These fundamental convictions and John's polemical purpose animate the entire discussion of Nature and Art. In the last analysis there is for John, as for the Athenian in the *Laws* and Polixenes in *The Winter's Tale,* such close kinship between Nature and Art that to hurt one is to injure the other: "The mother of the arts is nature, to despise whose progeny amounts to insulting their parent."[18] The *Metalogicon,* then, reproduces a view possibly less Christian than classical, but such distinctions cannot take us very far. What is important is that John of Salisbury, unlike Jean de Meun, adopts the role of polemicist rather than popularizer. Consequently he accepts the traditional views only after investigating the problem for himself, only after thoroughly assimilating orthodox attitudes to his own convictions about the relationship of rhetoric to life. He carefully thinks *about* the terms, and then, much like Plato in the *Sophist,* he thinks *with* them, going on to use Nature and Art as primary categories in his attack on Cornificius.

The thorough examination of the terms in the *Metalogicon* illustrates the possibility of renewed interest in the old division between Nature and Art. And it is with how the Renaissance adopted and revivified the old issues that we are ultimately concerned. Even John of Salisbury cannot illustrate the process of revival, but examples lie ready to hand in the literature of travel. In voyage literature it is possible to see how the commonplaces about Nature and Art could suddenly regain the meaningfulness and intensity they had for the thinkers of antiquity.

Contrary to the opinion of some literary historians, the literature of travel was extremely important not only because of the allusions it contributed to poetry and drama but also because of its influence on intellectual history.[19] Specifically, the descriptions of savage men provided a nexus in reality for common-places about the Golden Age and Nature versus Art. During the Renaissance, the literature of travel forced the civilized European to acknowledge the existence of men who looked, acted, and apparently thought rather differently than he. Theories about man in a state of nature suddenly had concrete application to the Indians of the New World, and some of the most venerable principles of moral philosophy abruptly received the pragmatic test in the wilds of New Guinea.

One might imagine that actual encounters with savage men would instantly settle all the perennial debates about the relative merits of Nature and Art. At the very least, one would expect the philosophers and moralists (not, of course, the pastoral poets) to admit that Nature, unaided by either Grace or Art, is nasty, brutish, and atrabilious. In fact, however, the voyagers found what they wanted to find, and some of them may perhaps be excused for not wanting to find the Hobbesian man. It may even be that they found what their literary heritage and intellectual background required them to find. From antiquity and the Middle Ages the Elizabethan had learned two main ways of seeing man in a state of nature, and when he actually encountered the savages of the New World, he did not hesitate to explain shiny experiences in tarnished terms.

Although the weight of classical opinion fell against the merely instinctive and spontaneous in man, the literature of antiquity often turned to the savage Scythian or Ethiopian as a standard of moral virtue.[20] The Stoic and Cynic traditions offer many examples of the Noble Savage who was recommended because of his robust self-sufficiency, honest simplicity, and rugged comradeship with Nature; or at certain other times because of his unspoiled tenderness, delicacy of feeling, and idyllic harmony with Nature. In short, the shepherds of Arcadia might be, according to one's literary and other experience of Nature and

Art, "acorn-eating swine," admirable diamonds in the rough (their roughness, their lack of Art, being of course a virtue), or sensitive, unspoiled figures of Vergilian pastoral.

The medieval period reveals a slackening of interest in primitive man, partially because the men of the Middle Ages were in many cases descended from the savages eulogized from afar by writers of antiquity, and mainly because primitive man was usually ignorant of Christianity. Of course, it would at times be possible to extol savage Nature uncorrupted by Art, so long as one conveyed regret at the absence of Christian truth.[21] The satirical use of primitive virtue would be particularly hard to relinquish: in confronting Golden Age virtue a reader must ask himself, as he does in thinking about More's *Utopia,* Is it not a shame that civilized man, sustained by Revelation, is in many respects inferior to the savage who is ignorant of Christianity? Finally, the faraway lands of primitive men, idealized in the numerous medieval accounts of the earthly paradise, helped preserve the classical tradition of Arcadia,[22] that land that reflects in the present the paradisiacal characteristics of the Golden Age: "When Nature raign'd instead of . . . Arts." [23] Somehow better and more perfect than anything available to civilized man, the earthly paradise represented, as does Samoa to many moderns, the oasis of simplicity in a land scorched by the multiplication of demands, the source of untouched, untroubled Nature in a world complicated beyond all endurance by the intricacies of Art. In both antiquity and the Middle Ages, then, it was possible to see the savage, according to one's inclination and moral philosophy, as either noble or ignoble; and the voyagers of the Renaissance had this double literary experience to condition their response to the savages of the New World.

The Savage Man was the product of Nature without Art, and there were, as we have seen, many writers of the Renaissance who might be presumed to approve of him for that reason. These writers were generally primitivists of some sort, standing in the

Cynic-Stoic tradition of "hard" primitivism or in that of the "soft" primitivism of Vergil and Ovid. Amadas and Barlowe were voyagers of this second type, for in 1584 they described the Indians of the New World as "most gentle, loving, and faithfull, voide of all guile and treason, . . . such as live after the maner of the golden age."[24] Peter Martyr (Pietro Martire d'Anghiera), some seventy years earlier (1511), was equally impressed, and even more literary in his description:

A fewe thinges contente them, hauinge no delite in suche superfluites, for the which in other places men take infinite paynes and commit manie unlawfull actes, and yet are neuer satisfied, wheras many haue to muche, and none inowgh. But emonge these simple sowles, a fewe clothes serue the naked: weightes and measures are not needefull to such as can not skyll of crafte and deceyte and haue not the use of pestiferous monye, the seede of innumerable myscheues. So that if we shall not be ashamed to confesse the truthe, they seeme to lyue in that goulden worlde of the whiche owlde wryters speake so much: wherin men lyued simplye and innocentlye without inforcement of lawes, without quarellinge Judges and libelles, contente onely to satisfie nature.[25]

The passage is a largely literary response to new experience. Nathanael Culverwel, as late as 1652, follows Salmasius, who sought the Law of Nature in the "naked Indian" and "rude American" rather "then in a spruce Athenian," because

Those Nations that have more of Art and emprovement amongst them, have so painted Natures face, have hung so many Jewels in her eare; have put so many Bracelets upon her hand; they have cloth'd her in such soft and silken rayment, as that you cannot guesse at her so well, as you might have done, if she had nothing but her own simple and neglected beauty: you cannot taste the Wine so well, because they have put Sugar into it, and have brib'd your palate.[26]

Here again a mosaic of commonplaces, evoked by and focused upon the Savage Man, that creature of Nature who has escaped the corrupting influence of Art.

And yet the Elizabethan had been taught to be suspicious of the desires of the natural man—whether those desires proceeded from within the Elizabethan himself or whether they were displayed in the New World. R. H. Pearce's extensive study of travel literature clearly documents the conclusion that the greater number of Elizabethans viewed the Savage Man with contempt and distaste. Far from placing him in the golden world, most Elizabethan accounts of the Savage Man emphasized his brutishness, irrationality, excess, and lack of true religion. The Indians encountered by Frobisher, for example, on his second voyage to America are implicitly censured for their failure to eat in a civilized manner and are compared to animals:

If they for necessities sake stand in need of the premisses, such grasse as the countrey yeeldeth they plucke up and eate, not deintily, or salletwise to allure their stomacks to appetite: but for necessities sake without either salt, oyles or washing, like brute beasts devouring the same.[27]

Henry Hawks is equally unimpressed by man in a state of nature, equally without illusions in regard to the Savage Man: "They are soone drunke, and given to much beastliness, and void of all goodnesse. In their drunkennesse they use and commit Sodomy; and with their mothers and daughters they have their pleasures and pastimes." [28]

Primitivism or no primitivism, Hawks knows savagery when he sees it, and this is an ability he shared with a large majority of his contemporaries. Most Elizabethans would have had little sympathy with Ruth Benedict's program of cultural tolerance. There was no place for moral relativism in sixteenth-century England: the Elizabethan never doubted for a moment that man, even a great man like Macbeth, might lapse into bestiality. This was the lesson enforced by the Fall. Unremitting vigilance was required, at least in the eyes of most Elizabethan moralists, to preserve man from his own naked naturality. The Elizabethan dedication to reason as a primary good made for distrust of the purely natural man, so that most accounts of the voyagers emphasize the theme of brutishness, telling of men who are not quite men because they lack discourse of reason and are ignorant of civilized behavior, especially Christian behavior.

Two themes emerge from this look at travel literature, themes that appear first in antiquity, persist throughout the medieval period, and then reappear with renewed emphasis in the Renaissance. The first is the theme of the Noble Savage. It communicates a vision of natural man living in a present-day Golden Age; if Arcadian simplicity does not appeal to the writer, he may seek the nobility of the savage in the ideals of self-sufficiency and physical hardiness. In either case the Savage Man becomes a model of virtue, providing the standard of conduct against which the writer measures the iniquity of civilized man. It will be obvious that this theme is, with a change of terminology, the primitivist thesis that Nature is superior to Art. Satire and pastoral both exploit this theme, the one negatively through castigation and the other positively through the depiction of exemplary shepherds.

The second theme is less well known, probably because of its very pervasiveness, its very obviousness. Nevertheless it possesses independent existence and deserves a name. It may be called the theme of the Ignoble Savage, and it represents the usual Elizabethan attitude toward the natives of the New World. In this instance there is no talk of the virtues of the simple life, of the harmony of Eden, or even of self-sufficiency as an ideal. Instead the Savage Man is reproached for his treachery, uncivilized conduct, immorality, and inhumanity; he is a literal illustration of what is expressed allegorically for the Renaissance in the Circe myth—man may, after the Fall from Eden, tralineate further, into complete bestiality. In so far as the Savage Man fell short of the rational and religious ideals embodied in conservative Elizabethan thought, he was to be summarily condemned,

for it was in this way that civilized man might forfeit his claim
to humanity and descend the scale of being to the level of the
beasts. There was no doubt in the minds of most Elizabethans
that post-lapsarian man needed watching and restraint, that fallen
Nature required the discipline of Art and the gift of Grace.

Since the ambivalent image of the Savage Man is implicitly
an expression of the controversy over Nature and Art, the themes
of the Noble and Ignoble Savage represent in effect opposing
interpretations of the division between the two terms. The
copious voyage literature of the fourteenth to seventeenth centuries, especially in its tales of savage men, intensified concern
with the old issue of Nature versus Art, with the result that the
commonplace views about the terms were revivified by contact
with fresh experience. Montaigne is worth quoting at some
length here to illustrate these generalizations, to show how the
theme of the Noble Savage, the myth of the Golden Age, and
the division between Nature and Art might fuse together, might
combine inextricably, in discussing a new and different kind of
man, in this case the cannibal.

There is ever perfect religion, perfect policie, perfect and compleat
use of all things. They are even savage, as we call those fruits wilde,
which nature of her selfe, and of her ordinarie progresse hath produced: whereas indeed, they are those which our selves have altered
by our artificiall devices, and diverted from their common order, we
should rather terme savage. In those are the true and most profitable
vertues, and naturall properties most lively and vigorous, which in
these we have bastardized, applying them to the pleasure of our
corrupted taste. . . . there is no reason, art should gaine the point
of honour of our great and puissant mother Nature. . . . Those nations seeme therefore [to] have received very little fashion from humane wit, and are yet neere their originall naturalitie. The lawes of
nature doe yet command them, which are but little bastardized by
ours. . . . I am sorie, Lycurgus and Plato had [no knowledge of these
nations]: for me seemeth that what in those nations we see by experi-

ence, doth not only exceed all the pictures wherewith licentious Poesie hath proudly imbellished the golden age, and all her quaint inventions to faine a happy condition of man, but also the conception and desire of Philosophy. They could not . . . beleeve our societie might be maintained with so little art.[29]

The passage utilizes all the usual themes and commonplaces in a frontal attack on one of the chief tenets of Christian humanism —the identification of Reason and Nature; all the bulwarks of conservative thought are reduced with calculated effect. Montaigne's aim, on one level at least, is simply to shock the conservative reader. Nature is not only praised, but praised at the expense of Art, of the products of human reason, of civilization itself.

The orthodox view naturally remained less tolerant of cannibalism and those who practiced it. The Preface to Martyr's *Decades of the Newe Worlde* justifies Spanish exploitation by pointing to the ungovernable cruelty of the cannibals, to savage's inhumanity to savage:

Theyr bondage is suche as is much rather to be desired then theyr former libertie which was to the cruell Canibales rather a horrible licenciousnesse then a libertie, and to the innocent so terrible a bondage, that . . . they were euer in daunger.[30]

It is this orthodox view that Montaigne opposes, not so much (perhaps) because of his feelings one way or another about cannibals, but rather because of his feelings about orthodoxy and what it takes to live the good or "natural" life. The cannibals are for him little more than a fascinating convenience, a subject of topical interest that provides an illustration for his general views of human nature. The cannibals focus concerns that occupy his mind on other—perhaps most other—occasions. The myth of the Golden Age, the law of nature and the ideal of reason, the horticultural analogy, the division between Nature and Art that represents the central contrast of the passage—all these traditional elements are for the moment concentrated on the subject of the cannibals, and Montaigne characteristically makes the most of the occasion by systematically inverting the values orthodox thinking assigned to Nature and Art. The division between Nature and Art, present but defunct in the medieval period, has suddenly acquired new vitality. The relationship between Nature and Art has regained its status as a controversial issue.

Some recapitulation may be welcome at this point. Viewed in the broadest possible way, the division between Nature and Art reached the Renaissance through two main channels. On the one hand, there exists a fairly direct line of transmission through the Latin Middle Ages. During medieval times the habitual tendency to pair Nature and Art was held in suspension—present but not tangent to the immediate problems of the age. The division was preserved in refrigerated blocks of classical learning and provided commonplace material for Jean de Meun, Chaucer, the *Pearl* poet, and many others. As early as John of Salisbury, however, writers once more began to think with and about the terms, and this tendency was accelerated by a new emphasis on man and his works as it appears in the voyage literature of the Renaissance. During the Middle Ages the old problems had not disappeared but only lain dormant—implicitly in travel literature and explicitly in commonplace form—until the Renaissance once again began to use Nature and Art as instruments of controversy. On the other hand, the division between the terms reached the Renaissance directly through the recovery of classical texts. Renewed interest in antiquity meant necessarily renewed concern with the division between Nature and Art, meant necessarily the assimilation and use of classical vocabulary, so that terms such as Nature and Art were adopted along with the texts and the philosophical problems with which the words were first associated. In so far, then, as the Renaissance represents a displacement of interest from the order of grace toward greater emphasis on the order of nature, the division between Nature and Art was conveniently at hand to be used in analyzing the activities of man *qua* man in relation to the natural world.

Recalling points made earlier will provide the perspective necessary for understanding how the Middle Ages transformed the meaning and function of the pastoral form. From its inception a sophisticated genre, pastoral is the literary result of the poet's insights into the differences between rural and urban values, the (mainly) social differences between Nature and Art. In Theocritus the tension between Nature and Art was never resolved but neither was it ever exploited as a moral opposition. In Vergil, however, the aesthetic organization of primitivist attitudes approaches closely the condition of moral antithesis; the opposition of Nature to Art, latent in all pastoral poetry, has begun to take on moral force and direction. The creation of Arcadia, the literary expression of the myth of the Golden Age, is in effect the creation of an ideal world in which Nature has no need of Art. Longus took the further step. In *Daphnis and Chloe* the aesthetic structure recommended by the example of Vergil possesses clear moral implications; the natural values of the green world oppose the artificial values of sophisticated society, so that the ethical preferences of the story grow out of an acknowledgment of an opposition between Nature and Art. It remained for the Middle Ages to make the pastoral opposition acceptable to Renaissance orthodoxy, which in most areas preferred balance rather than conflict between Nature and Art.

During the medieval period the pastoral genre was "Christianized" by understanding its pagan elements allegorically. Of course the genre had revealed "allegorical" tendencies very early, even as early as Theocritus, who is said to have introduced himself and some of his fellow poets into the Seventh Idyl. And yet the techniques of personal and political allusion that appear in pastoral from Vergil to Milton do not suggest the extent of allegorical practice in the Middle Ages. During this time the entire genre became a metaphor, an elaborate method for talking about almost anything and still using shepherds and sheep as counters. Although one hesitates to suggest that medieval pastoral ought to become an object of popular scrutiny, what happened to the genre during the Latin Middle Ages seems crucial for an understanding of Renaissance pastoral. It was then that the pastoral developed the use summarized by Puttenham in 1589 when he pointed out that the eclogue attempts not simply "to counterfait or represent the rusticall manner of loues and communication: but vnder the vaile of homely persons, and in rude speeches to insinuate and glaunce at greater matters."[31] During the Middle Ages the pastoral becomes a vehicle, a form for talking about almost anything but strictly bucolic notions. Although the conventions of the genre remained superficially the same, their meaning and function were altered radically to conform to the Christian universe.

Full justification of these statements about the allegorical reading of pastoral probably requires a systematic survey of the extant Latin eclogues. Unfortunately none is available.[32] W. W. Greg devotes a few pages to the medieval pastoralists—to some few of them anyway—and sums up his investigation in this way: "It would hardly be worth recording these . . . undistinguished writers . . . were it not that they show how the memory at least of the classical pastoral survived amid the ruins of the ancient learning."[33] Greg's chief interest lies in the decorative tradition of pastoral, but had he done more than "record" the survival of pastoral in the Middle Ages, he might have seen that the "undistinguished writers" of that time not only preserved the "memory" of antiquity but also turned the pastoral to uses never dreamt of in the philosophy of Theocritus. It was, furthermore, the medieval modifications of the tradition that insured the survival of the form into the Renaissance and eventually, in combination with Vergil and Longus, produced a kind of pastoral that was equipped to deal in Christian terms with the division between Nature and Art.

There are, of course, pastoral poems in the Middle Ages that are simply uninspired imitations of what I have called, in the introduction, the "decorative" tradition: all the usual pastoral furniture clutters the form—correspondences between old age and autumn, youth and spring; clean sheep and fine, strong shepherds; a liberal use of the pathetic fallacy. Even when the pattern is repeated with enthusiasm, as in the "Conflictus Veris et Hiemis," [34] the medieval poet cannot be described as developing the range of the form. The "Conflictus" is a kind of *lis*, a debate on the Theocritean pattern between Spring and Winter. The shepherds Dafnis and Palemon are present, and after a number of pleasant exchanges the victory is awarded to Spring. The effect is agreeable, though highly artificial; we are not, however, in the presence of anything new.

But there are a number of eclogues in the Carolingian period, and even before,[35] that have suffered radical changes under the general medieval tendency toward allegory. Such, for example, is the "Carmen" of Radbertus, Abbot of Corbie in the ninth century. In a prose prologue Radbertus explicitly acknowledges that his pastoral characters have another meaning; he therefore obliges the reader with a skeleton key to the eclogue. Fillis and Galathea are the speakers in a pastoral lament for the former Abbot, Adalhard; they represent, we are told, the old monastery of Corbie and the new one founded by Adalhard in Germany.[36] Pastoral terms and pastoral conventions fuse with the pastoral imagery of the Bible to produce what may be described as an "allegorical" effect.[37] Adalhard in l. 59 is *sanctissime pastor*, and Heaven in l. 151 recalls the familiar Elysian fields of pastoral: *Ethereis pascamur eo quam perpete campis*. The vocabulary at the close of the poem illustrates neatly enough the admixture of pastoral and religious statement:

"Desine plura," soror tum, "mater," ait Galathea,
"Ista quidem inspecta melius tum forte canemus,
Cum paradysus ovans nobis quoque sorte virebit.
Actenus agrorum flores et lilia carpe,
Donec alleluiatica circum gaudia stridant.
Sparge viam violis, virtutum floribus arvam,
Pinge rosis callem, plateis lilia sterne." [38]

Similar are Modoin's eclogues,[39] two ninth-century pastorals
of which the second will serve as an illustration here. In ll. 6
and 9 of the Prologue, Naso (Modoin's poetical pseudonym) tells
us explicitly that his poem is *carmine velato* and that he writes
with hidden meanings in mind: *Arguet archanis aliquis mea
carmina dictis.* In the poem Micon and Nectilus recline in the
shade, a kind of *locus amoenus* familiar to readers of pastoral;
and they sing with the beasts listening all about them in the
approved pastoral tradition. A song is found, carved into a tree,
written in praise of the sun that casts its rays over all the earth,
bringing peace and prosperity and a return of the Golden Age:
the sun, we discover, is the Emperor Charles who rules the world,
and Micon has celebrated his achievements under the *nomen* of
the sun (ll. 115 ff.):

Caesareo populum Carolus gentesque coercet
Tegmine, cuncta regit terrarum regna per orbem,
Imperioque pio toto dominabitur orbi.
Hunc ego iamdudum memini sub nomine solis,
Qui nitet in totum claro vibramine mundum.[40]

This poem is an example of what Hamblin calls "court pastoral," [41] where the poet's main concern is praise of some court
figure—presumably a more or less delicate way of recommending
oneself for preferment. Allegorical in a different way from the
spiritual pastoral of Radbertus, it nevertheless exhibits the same
tendency—and is radically different from the personifications
in the "Conflictus Veris et Hiemis."

Yet another variant of the same type is "Theoduli Ecloga," one of the most widely read works of the Middle Ages. Curtius remarks its importance many times,[42] showing that it entered the medieval canon as early as Conrad of Hirsau (*ca.* 1070–*ca.* 1150); and G. L. Hamilton has pointed to its use as one of the primary textbooks of the Middle Ages.[43] Theodulus has replaced the usual pastoral figures with personified abstractions, going one step further than the "Conflictus Veris et Hiemis." Pseustis (Liar) and Alithia (Truth) represent paganism and Christianity in a kind of pastoral flyting or singing match. Pseustis, hailing from Athens, recites mythological stories; while Alithia, descendant of David, the first pastoral singer, presents counter-examples from the Old Testament. Phronesis is the judge, and the victory goes of course to Alithia. In the medieval canon, pagan and Christian authors were usually ranged side by side, and Theodulus reacted against this lack of proper discrimination by creating a pedagogical corrective cast in the fiction of a pastoral debate. "Theoduli Ecloga" remained a part of the curriculum as late as the sixteenth century.[44]

The reasons that the eclogue became a highly formalized device for talking about almost anything in terms of shepherds are clearly too complex to be easily summarized, but it is possible to speculate with some exactness about the kind of forces that were at work. It seems germane to recall that pastoral has rarely occupied itself entirely with shepherds, shepherdesses, and sheep. Pastoral is revery over rusticity, not rusticity itself; as Empson says somewhere, pastoral assumes that one can tell all about civilized, urban man by talking about his rural counterpart. Further, we have seen that pastoral developed as a literary response to the perception that Nature differs from Art, that pastoral became the literary reflex of a philosophical controversy. But to recall the sophisticated origins of pastoral does not explain Modoin or Theodulus; such speculations do not take us far enough.

Works like Longus' *Daphnis and Chloe,* for example, are simply not "allegorical" in the sense that Modoin's or Radbertus' eclogues are. The philosophical implications are there, rightly enough, deeply involved in all the pastoral machinery, but the philosophical concepts of Nature and Art have been almost completely assimilated to a literary form that is itself based ultimately on the opposition of the natural and the artificial. Thus the concepts are virtually indistinguishable from the form. Nor are Vergil and Theocritus "allegorical" in the same way as the medieval pastoralists. Although F. R. Hamblin points out political, social, and literary allusions in classical pastoral,[45] neither Vergil nor Theocritus merely *uses* the form to talk about something else. Even if Theocritus introduced himself and his fellow poets into the Seventh Idyl as shepherds, his chief interest nevertheless attaches to Sicilian peasant life and scenery, employing Doric dialect and similar devices for a more realistic effect. So also with the eclogues of Vergil. Although they are about as highly allusive in diction and cadence as any poetry, they still do not approach the medieval uses of pastoral. Despite the political and other implications of his work, especially in the Fourth Eclogue, Vergil remains preoccupied with his own feelings in relation to the traditional content of pastoral. The medieval eclogue, however, has shifted the center of gravity, so that the importance of pastoral machinery lies in its analogical value (*ethereis . . . campis*), and the significance of the form resides in its "allegorical" potentiality. The medieval writer is interested not so much in Thestylis and Ametas as he is in God, the Emperor Charles, and the curriculum.

Why this shift in emphasis? and how was it accomplished? Except in the case of men like Jerome, the Christian could not even try to ignore the heritage of pagan writing. In regard to poetry, in particular, the medieval attitude toward pagan learning may be discerned in outline as early as Macrobius:[46] the classics are already The Ancients—at least those among the classical authors who could in some way be regarded as universal authorities on everything from religion to natural science—and their works were subjected in this light to an appallingly thorough allegorical scrutiny. Allegorical exegesis became a standard method of literary criticism, with the result that the Fourth Eclogue was applied to the birth of Christ as early as Constantine and the Golden Age spoken of in pastoral poetry was identified with Eden as early as Lactantius. These methods reached their culmination in the twelfth and thirteenth centuries, when the masters at Paris taught Vergil's *Georgics* and *Eclogues,* even Ovid's *Metamorphoses,* as "fables" that revealed Christian truth to the initiated.[47]

It was against this tendency toward such industrious allegorizing that Jerome reacted, and out of the conflict generated in this way we may speculate on the kinds of opportunity open to the Christian who was also a poet. He could write hymns and ascend to heaven, or he could write pagan poetry and go to hell. Fortunately, there were still other (more palatable) alternatives to the apparent disjunction between pagan literature and Christian faith. Curtius points out, for example, that Prudentius managed to avoid the problem by creating a specifically Christian poetry that availed itself of purely Christian subjects—the sanctity of work, the cult of the martyrs, the Trinity, the origin of sin, the battle of the virtues and vices—and at the same time refused to fall into the standard categories of classical genre.[48] Yet Prudentius appears to have been an isolated case, and most Christian poets turned to still another solution of their dilemma. Juvencus, who came to terms with antique literary theory in the fourth century, defines a position that attained general force during the medieval period:

By God's will all earthly things are subject to mortality. Yet countless men, because of their deeds and their virtues, live on in the praise of poets, as in the noble songs of Homer, in the sweet art (*dulcedo*) of Virgil. And these poets themselves are also sure of eternal fame, although they weave lies [i.e., mythology] into the deeds of past times.

How much more will my poem outlive ages, for it sings the deeds of Christ and perhaps will yet save me at the Last Judgment. May the Holy Ghost assist me and lave my mind in the water of Jordan.[49]

Juvencus' justification allowed the Christian poet to appropriate the antique system of genres while at the same time rejecting the philosophic and religious bases of classical thought. The result was to be, ideally, a union of Christian content and classical form.

The pastoral form was in particular a singularly attractive partner for such a union, because its content had to undergo relatively few changes to be acceptable within the Christian system. Among the different kinds of prefigurative correspondences elaborated by the Middle Ages, doubtless those of the Song of Songs are the most important in connection with pastoral. The canticles were, at least for the Middle Ages and the Renaissance, eclogues communicating such mysteries as Christ's love for His Church. When regarded as an allegorical dream-pastoral, the Song of Songs provided a biblical precedent for the group of ideas and emotions associated with classical pastoral. The words of Solomon, who was shepherd as well as king, charged them with new meanings, so that the same things could be written, yet understood differently.

The pastoral idea of a Golden Age, for instance, was easily assimilated into specifically Christian eclogues; one simply understood by it a reference to the Garden of Eden, where man did not toil, where there was no greed, and where man lived in harmony with nature. The shepherd, too, was a figure that easily made the transition: in particular there was David, the singer-shepherd, and in general there was the whole range of biblical parable, sermon, and story that lent an allegorical significance to the shepherd, the pastor faithful of men's souls. Of collateral importance to the adoption of a Christian pastoral was the general feeling that the classical genres were somehow rooted in nature, that they were discovered, not invented, by the ancients. Pastoral, to be sure, was not the highest of the genres, but nevertheless it was a *kind,* and the poet who violated its rules thereby violated decorum, that is, committed an offense against nature. For such reasons as these the classical eclogue passed virtually unchanged in form *and* content into the Middle Ages.

Yet the content of pastoral had remained unchanged only in a literal sense. Although the rustic observations of Theocritus had hardened into the most formalized of literary conventions, they now echoed with new and different meanings. And there had developed a corpus of criticism that explicitly sanctioned ulterior meanings and gave intellectual justification to religious and other allusions. The Carolingian pastorals we examined are one result, which is itself a stage in the development of pastoral toward the Renaissance uses of the form. These three eclogues illustrate a single thesis from three quite different points of view. Radbertus, Abbot of Corbie, intends to praise and lament his predecessor, Adalhard: he is concerned with monasteries and their place in the secular world, with the prospect of heaven and the life of the monk. Modoin is interested in the reign of Charles, the new Golden Age, in political affairs and matters of preferment. Theodulus is a kind of pedagogue, concerned with teaching mythology but at the same time seeing that the half-truths of the ancients are placed in proper Christian perspective. What all three share in common is the eclogue form and the pastoral furniture that goes back at least to Theocritus. And what seems necessary to emphasize is simply this: The pastoral has become a *vehicle* in a very strict sense, a form for the allegorical expression of a variety of different subjects. This use of pastoral was of immense importance for the Renaissance: there behind the traditional locutions lay the truths of Revelation, and the most conventional phrases reverberated with biblical overtones.

The late Middle Ages and the Renaissance therefore found the form obligingly elastic.[50] When Dante and John of Bologna (Giovanni del Vergilio) exchanged Latin epistles, neither writer apparently felt any sense of incongruity in casting his news, polite invitations, and literary gossip in the form of the eclogue. Petrarch's *Eglogae* include, among a variety of "extra-pastoral" subjects, a debate between two shepherds that becomes St. Peter's denunciation of the Pope. Boccaccio in one eclogue speaks of a dead daughter, a lost Pearl, who brings him news of the afterlife. But the best example for our purposes is perhaps Baptista Spagnuoli (1448–1516), the "good old Mantuan" of *Love's Labour's Lost* who wrote ten Latin eclogues familiar to every Renaissance schoolboy. These pastorals address themselves to love and marriage, to the difference between love and lust, to satirical fulminations against womankind, to the way the rich fail to patronize learning, to satire of city life, to a quasi-religious vision of worldly corruption, to a pastoral virgin who turns out to be the Virgin, to satire on Rome, and to a pastoral *débat* between the Conventuals and the Discalced Carmelites. To the Renaissance the form must have seemed almost infinitely flexible by definition, and poets responded by accommodating the genre to a variety of ends.

One consequence of this radical flexibility, a consequence of fundamental importance for my thesis, was the creation of a new sub-genre of allegorical pastoral in which the entire form tends toward metaphor. The green world, freed almost entirely by the medieval pastoralists from the demands of realistic fiction, became invested with an aura of magical benevolence. Even so late as *Pilgrim's Progress* Bunyan affirms in doggerel verse the sense of arcane mystery that had become associated with the Arcadian dream world:

> Thus by the Shepherds secrets are revealed,
> Which from all other men are kept concealed.
> Come to the Shepherds then, if you would see
> Things deep, things hid, and that mysterious be.[51]

We are dealing here with a potentiality of the form that differs fundamentally from the technique of allegorical allusion that appears, say, in the ecclesiastical eclogues of Petrarch or Boccaccio. It is the difference between using the form for topical reference and regarding the entire genre as a kind of trope. In this latter view the pastoral world becomes an infinitely suggestive ideal, a trope for Eden, in which Nature, free of the "hereditary imposition" of the Fall, retains its first integrity and may therefore be observed under its universal aspect.

Thus the "Christianization" of pastoral has immense importance as well for the history of Nature and Art. Specifically it solves the moral problem of pagan literature: How can poets accept a literary convention that praises Nature to the exclusion of Art? Pastoral, at least as it exists in antiquity and in Italy before Guarini, seems often to recommend a "naturalistic" or *libertin* ethic that runs directly counter to orthodox Elizabethan morality. It is the old question, debated by so many Puritan moralists: What has Christ to do with Apollo? With particular reference to pastoral, however, the question becomes, What has Christ to do with Pan? and the answer is, The two are one and the same. As solemn "E.K." puts it in his gloss on the May eclogue of *The Shepheardes Calender:*

Great Pan is Christ, the very God of all shepheards, which calleth himselfe the greate and good shepherd. The name is most rightly (me thinkes) applyed to him, for Pan signifieth all, or omnipotent, which is onely the Lord Jesus.[52]

"E.K." has many more learned remarks to make, but the educated reader of the Renaissance was already prepared to see the natural man in a shepherd, Christ in Pan, and Eden in the Golden Age.[53] Of these equivalences, these symbolic counters, the identification of the Golden Age with Eden has most relevance to Nature and Art.

Under the allegorical pressure of the Middle Ages the ideal landscape of pastoral fused with the Christian Garden of Eden. Arcadia, early linked to the Golden Age in Vergil, coalesced with

Eden to form a new whole—the Christian landscape of Renaissance pastoral.[54] To the Renaissance the identification of the pastoral fields with the biblical Garden was perfectly commonplace, leading, where it is not simply assumed, to the sort of rhetorical question found in Golding's Ovid (1565–67):

> Moreouer by the golden age what other thing is ment,
> Than Adams tyme in Paradyse, who beeing innocent
> Did lead a blist and happy lyfe untill that thurrough sin
> He fell from God? [55]

Golding soberly asserts this in connection with Ovid! Such assertions meant not only the moralizing of Ovid but also the legitimizing of the pastoral tendency to exalt Nature and ignore or condemn Art. To prefer Nature before Art in the Golden Age might be a plea for sexual "naturalism" as in Tasso or an argument against the equation of Reason and Nature as in Montaigne. But the same preference in Eden is merely an acknowledgment of scriptural fact: unfallen Nature is by definition good and stands "above Rule or Art." Milton's Garden before the Fall is

> A Wilderness of sweets; for Nature here
> Wantond as in her prime, and plaid at will
> Her Virgin Fancies, pouring forth more sweet,
> Wild above Rule or Art; enormous bliss.
>
> (V.294–97)

The implications for pastoral are obvious. Its hedonistic connotations could be canceled by reading the genre allegorically, by finding meaning for the "naturalistic" elements of pastoral in relation to the ideal Nature of the Garden of Eden. Whether this attempt to decontaminate pastoral was altogether justified or "sincere" cannot be answered with a single statement, but it is safe to say that it is impossible fully to understand, and hence to judge, important parts of Spenser, Shakespeare, and Marvell without first understanding the effort to quarantine pastoral within a specific moment of scriptural history.

Plainly by the time of the Renaissance the ideal Nature of pastoral poetry had come to signify religious perfection in addition to the Vergilian perfection of sensibility, so that pastoral nostalgia for the Golden Age became intensified and transformed by religious yearning for Eden. To put it another way, one kind of pastoral had become a theological showcase in which the ideal relationship between Nature and Art, realized only partially and sporadically in the post-lapsarian world, could be exhibited as it was supposed to have functioned in the Garden of Eden. The Nature of the post-lapsarian world was for the Renaissance poet quite another matter:

> Man is compos'd here of a two-fold part;
> The first of Nature, and the next of Art:
> Art presupposes Nature; Nature shee
> Prepares the way to mans docility.[56]

Fallen man had need of Art to help repair the ruin of his first parents: the integrity of Nature had been impaired by the Fall, but it seemed to many that man might exercise his reason for his own betterment. Indeed, moralists from Seneca to Milton conceived it a positive duty to exercise the God-given faculty of reason, "For Nature giueth not vertue; it is an art to be made good." But such generalizations do not apply to the Nature exhibited in religious eclogues: in the green world of pastoral the myths of Eden and the Golden Age coalesce, and the pristine excellence of the result lies beyond the reach of all but literary Art.

CHAPTER IV

Spenser's Legend of Courtesy

Book VI of Spenser's *The Faerie Queene* illustrates the way critical misunderstanding can arise from neglect or ignorance of the history of pastoral in relation to Nature and Art. Quite generally it is supposed that the last books of *The Faerie Queene* betray progressive deterioration from the high standards of the first two. The critics of Book VI, perhaps in unconscious recognition of its numerical distance from the heights, seem particularly ready to accept the assumption of decline. B. E. C. Davis' *Edmund Spenser* remains typical of this attitude, for in his argument against the lack of unity in the Legend of Courtesy—its "detached sketches, interspersed with much that is purely romantic" —he quotes Strachey's well-known opinion of Shakespeare's last plays: "It is difficult to resist the conclusion that he was getting bored with himself. Bored with people, bored with real life, bored with drama, bored, in fact, with everything except poetry and poetical dreams." [1] The implication is that Spenser has similarly forsaken his earlier dedication to a serious purpose, that the once sharp outline of his thought has blurred into poetical daydreams.

Book VI does indeed appear to offer evidence to support such views, for it might be argued that Spenser's treatment of "salvage men" is fundamentally inconsistent, that the book is hopelessly episodic, that the lack of theological allegory betrays diminishing interest on the part of the poet, and that the pastoral interlude represents cavalier disregard for the moral intention. It is difficult, however, to rest entirely secure in the belief that Spenser and Shakespeare did their writing out of senile ennui. It seems possible, for example, that both poets were simply manipulating conventions of which we are ignorant, that they were drawing on kinds of experience, literary and other, that are no longer available to us.

The intellectual milieu in which Spenser and Shakespeare wrote has been pretty thoroughly investigated, especially in regard to theology and moral philosophy, but the material of the previous chapters has suggested that the work of regaining an imaginative awareness of Renaissance literature remains incomplete in at least one important area. My uneasiness in the presence of Strachey's remarks arises, then, not so much from his use or abuse of the "intentional fallacy" as from his calm assumption that his understanding of what constitutes artistic unity and serious purpose must necessarily coincide with Shakespeare's (or Spenser's).

In the matter of Book VI such criticism springs, I believe, from a failure to appreciate the whole of Spenser's purpose, from a failure to grasp imaginatively the categories—Nature and Art— in which Spenser, in common with many men of his age, habitu- ally thought. Book VI is not, to be sure, a philosophical docu- ment. It is a pastoral romance in the tradition of *Daphnis and Chloe* and Sidney's *Arcadia*. In addition, it is moral allegory, the quest of true courtesy in the person of Calidore for love and fame in despite of defamation, slander, backbiting, and false rumor, represented by the Blatant Beast; the contrasting behavior of knights (Calepine versus Turpine) and ladies (Serena versus Blandina) offers a panoramic view of manners and morals, span- ning the entire range from true courtesy to complete baseness. Book VI is more than this. Although not philosophy, it is in- formed by a moral view that takes its strength, like Longus' *Daphnis and Chloe,* from the philosophical division between Nature and Art. Spenser not only exhibits the workings of courtesy in the activities of his knights and ladies but also displays the origin and place of the virtue within the order of nature.

When Spenser, for example, whimsically declines to commit himself on the origin of Blandina's false courtesy, his speculations fall (perhaps only half-consciously) into the terms of the traditional division between Nature ("kynd") and Art:

> Whether such grace were given her by kynd,
> As women wont their guilefull wits to guyde,
> Or learn'd the art to please, I doe not fynd.[2]
>
> (vi.43)

In *Amoretti* XXI Spenser wonders whether the "feature of her face" was the "worke of Nature or of Art," and the same formula recurs throughout his poetry, usually repeated a little mechanically in connection with painting or gardening. But we have seen that the pairing of Nature with Art might point to something more than a literary tic or "commonplace" reflex. Readers of Spenser will think instantly in this connection of the Garden of Adonis and the Bower of Bliss where the moral judgment, expressed primarily in terms of Nature and Art, is neither commonplace nor mechanical. The controversy over what is to be rendered unto Nature and what unto Art was particularly intriguing in Spenser's time; and by assuming for a moment that the controversy was important to Spenser himself we may grant to Book VI a serious purpose that would otherwise escape our understanding.

Courtesy is by definition appropriately considered in the order of nature—it is not a theological virtue—but the fact that there exists a division in the order of nature requires the poet to deal with certain established conventions. Specifically the task remains of placing the virtue within the order of nature itself. Is it given by Nature or made by Art? or is it perhaps the result of some subtle combination of both? Since questions such as these can be treated both in philosophy and in literature, Spenser had two main traditions on which to draw in examining courtesy or, for that matter, anything else that belonged primarily to the order of nature. Besides the philosophical tradition of Nature and Art there was the literary tradition of pastoral, and in Book VI Spenser uses the two of them in close conjunction to achieve his purpose of defining true courtesy.

Although Spenser, with a trace of amused misogyny, confesses his inability to "fynd" whether Blandina's false courtesy derives from "kynd" or "art," he cannot afford to show hesitation in regard to the central figure of the book. Accordingly he begins to commit himself immediately in describing Calidore, the Knight of Courtesy,

> In whom it seemes that gentlenesse of spright
> And manners mylde were planted naturall.
>
> (i.2)

The observation does not, of course, imply an egalitarian attitude. Spenser was quite unencumbered by the democratic sentiments that cluster around our own references to "natural" values. Far from anticipating Thomas Paine, Spenser looks back over some two thousand years of investigation into the relationship of Nature to Art. The poet knew perfectly well that nobility of birth does not invariably issue in noble action, but he would have agreed with most courtesy books in thinking that blood will out and breeding will tell. Courtesy for him held much wider connotations than it does today; there was for Spenser no "fayrer flowre" among all the virtues than the "bloosme of comely Courtesie" (Proem iv). The virtue encompasses morals as well as manners, forming the basis for civilization itself as it "spreds it selfe through all civilitie."

The reason for Spenser's attributing so much importance to courtesy is quite simple. For him it was the virtue by which a man knew who and where he was, the virtue that conferred a sense of degree or of hierarchy. And this sense of hierarchy, whatever else it might be, was usually felt by Renaissance man to be supremely "natural." Thus Spenser, in explaining that "curtesie" is the "vertue" that allows men "to beare themselves aright/ To all of each degree" (ii.1), explicitly adds that man's chief aid is Dame Nature:

> Thereto great helpe Dame Nature selfe doth lend:
> For some so goodly gratious are by kind,
> That every action doth them much commend,
> And in the eyes of men great liking find;
> Which others, that have greater skill in mind,
> Though they enforce themselves, cannot attaine.
> For everie thing, to which one is inclin'd,
> Doth best become, and greatest grace doth gaine:
> Yet praise likewise deserve good thewes, enforst with paine.
>
> (ii.2)

Although praise should also be accorded those who achieve a proper appreciation of degree through the exercise of conscious effort, through Art or "skill," Spenser's prejudice in favor of Nature is obvious.

Noble birth and noble Nature were closely associated in most Renaissance minds. Spenser (in the person of Sir Calidore) so admires the wit of courteous Tristram that "sure he weend him borne of noble blood" (ii.24); and lo, he is in fact the son of good King Meliogras! This is by no means an isolated instance. Pastorella and even, it is hinted, the Savage Man turn out to have the proper blood lines. Although there exists no *necessary* connection between blood and virtue, Spenser's general position remains firmly aristocratic:

> For a man by nothing is so well bewrayd
> As by his manners, in which plaine is showne
> Of what degree and what race he is growne.
> For seldome seene, a trotting stalion get
> An ambling colt, that is his proper owne:
> So seldome seene, that one in basenesse set
> Doth noble courage shew, with curteous manners met.
>
> (iii.1)

Spenser assumes, then, that virtue is mainly a matter of proper breeding, that true courtesy must be considered chiefly the gift of Nature, and that Art may in certain instances offer a praiseworthy substitute ("good thewes, enforst with paine") for the real thing.[3]

Such generalizations about Nature and Art do not, however, represent Spenser's position with sufficient nicety. They fail to take account of the ways in which Book VI *dramatizes*—perhaps "allegorizes" would be a better word—the division in the order of nature. Since Spenser is not writing a courtesy book, an examination of his explicit statements does not take us very far into Book VI as a work of art. As Spenser himself admits in the Letter to Raleigh, there are "some" to whom his "methode will seeme displeasaunt, which had rather have good discipline delivered plainly in way of precepts, or sermoned at large."[4] Those preferring the "darke conceit" to what is "sermoned at large" will immediately appreciate that it is not only in his explicit, conceptual statements but also in his descriptions of "salvage men" and shepherds, traditional exemplars of the division between Nature and Art, that Spenser conveys the full complexity of his response to the ancient debate.

In the Proem Spenser informs us that courtesy,

> though it on a lowly stalke doe bowre,
> Yet brancheth forth in brave nobilitie,
> And spreds it selfe through all civilitie. (iv)

To exhibit courtesy as a natural virtue, then, will be to display its origins and relationships within the order of nature as it "spreds" from its lowest manifestation to the highest degree of "civilitie." It is to this end that Spenser presents us with the contrast between two kinds of "lowly stalke"—the Savage Nation and the Savage Man. Although both are superficially intended to represent man in a state of nature, Spenser actually uses the contrast to discriminate between Art and two kinds of Nature. The savage or wild man is particularly apt for Spenser's purpose since he occupies an intermediate position on the scale of being, between rational man and the rest of the animal kingdom. As a moral example he may be used in two ways: as a direct warning (to this end man may come if he forsake his rational nature) and as a satirical thrust (look how much more civilized the savage is than the courtier with all his supposed advantages).

The Savage Nation he describes as an unlovely assortment of bestial lechers, altogether similar to that "wilde and salvage man" of Book IV, who was "overgrowne with haire" and "liv'd all on ravin and on rape" (vii.5). They survey the sleeping Serena, Calepine's lady, with lecherous eyes—in Spenser a sure indication that something particularly nasty is in the offing—and resolve to devour her; suggesting in these and other ways how it is possible to commit a "monstrous cruelty gainst course of kynde" (viii.36), to commit an offense against Nature as moral and ethical norm.

This is man in a state of nature—but clearly post-lapsarian nature. The Savage Nation is a nation of "cruell Canibales" whose "horrible licenciousnesse" was familiar to most, if not all, voyagers to the "Newe Worlde." [5] This kind of natural man, for Spenser if not for Montaigne, might be corrupted by false Art and false religion, as Spenser ironically demonstrates by allowing the cannibals to attribute their capture of Serena to "heavenly grace" (viii.37). The logical and religious travesty of the next stanza emphasizes the lesson:

> That since by grace of God she there was sent,
> Unto their god they would her sacrifize,
> Whose share, her guiltlesse bloud, they would present;
> But of her dainty flesh they did devize
> To make a common feast.

Spenser's account of the Savage Nation doubtless owes a great deal to travel literature, yet obviously he has interpreted his materials differently than, say, Montaigne. [6] In "Of the Caniballes," as we have seen, Montaigne asserts that the "terme savage" should really be applied to the way civilized man alters Nature by Art and points to the noble "Caniballe" to prove that there is "no reason" why "art should gaine the point of honour of our great and puissant mother Nature." [7] Spenser's interpretation, though conducted in terms of the same division between Art and Nature, probably impresses us as less naïve. Since whatever natural dignity his savages may have possessed has been corrupted through the worship of false gods, it appears that for Spenser the Nature of "salvage men" may be perverted by false Art just as surely and easily as that of Montaigne's civilized man. To Montaigne (in "Of the Caniballes," but not elsewhere) the dichotomy between Art and Nature is absolute; for Spenser the matter is apparently more complicated. Courtesy, wherever else it may grow, clearly does not flourish on this particular "lowly stalke."

The Savage Man, on the other hand, typifies Nature in an entirely different sense, recalling the natural and untutored virtue of Sir Satyrane as he is represented in Book I. This way of organizing toward a didactic end, this method of contrasting good and bad examples of the same thing, is characteristic of Spenser. Even this key distinction between the Savage Man and the Savage Nation has been emphasized in earlier books of *The Faerie Queene.* To cite only the well-known examples, it is reflected again in the contrast between Hellenore's "natural" Satyrs, who are depicted simply as bestial lechers, and Una's, who are represented more favorably because Spenser needs a "good" example of how natural man ought to receive revealed truth. Clearly Spenser is doing much the same thing with the contrast developed between the Savage Nation and the Savage Man; the link between the two is Serena, and the conduct of the Savage Man toward her is emphatically different from that of the Savage Nation.

The Savage Man rescues Serena and Sir Calepine from that "discourteous craven" (iv.2), Sir Turpine; for his "ruder hart" has been moved to compassion (iv.3) by the sight of Turpine's ungallant conduct. After the Savage Man impressively disposes of Turpine, he turns to Serena, who is at first understandably fearful of his intentions.

> But the wyld man, contrarie to her feare,
> Came to her creeping like a fawning hound,
> And by rude tokens made to her appeare
> His deepe compassion of her dolefull stound,
> Kissing his hands, and crouching to the ground;
> For other language had he none, nor speach,
> But a soft murmure, and confused sound
> Of senselesse words, which Nature did him teach,
> T'expresse his passions, which his reason did empeach.
>
> (iv.11)

Entirely artless, the Savage Man nevertheless embodies "lowly" courtesy by Nature. Although he befriends Serena and Calepine, his hospitality and life, "obaying Natures first beheast," leave something to be desired:

> But the bare ground, with hoarie mosse bestrowed,
> Must be their bed, their pillow was unsowed,
> And the frutes of the forrest was their feast:
> For their bad stuard neither plough'd nor sowed,
> Ne fed on flesh, ne ever of wyld beast
> Did taste the bloud, obaying Natures first beheast.
>
> (iv.14)

Those who had read of the "West Indies" would identify this "bad stuard" easily enough. He was the "wyld man" who in "olde tyme lyued in the golden age":

There are certayne wild men, which liue in the caues and dennes of the mountaynes, contented only with wylde fruites. . . . They lyue without any certayne dwelling places, and without tyllage or culturyng of the grounde, as wee reade of them whiche in olde tyme

lyued in the golden age. They say also that these men are without
any certayne language.[8]

Unlike the Savage Nation, who clearly live in the Iron Age, this
"wyld man" has resisted the corrupting influence of Art because
he is entirely artless and because "gentle bloud" (Spenser assumes
he must have "gentle bloud")

> howsoever it may grow mis-shapt,
> Like this wyld man, being undisciplynd,
> That to all vertue it may seeme unapt,
> Yet will it shew some sparkes of gentle mynd,
> And at the last breake forth in his owne proper kynd.
>
> (v.1)

But obviously the Savage Man is also a "bad stuard," intended
to exemplify courtesy only imperfectly: he suggests a limit to the
efficacy of "undisciplynd" Nature. (Spenser is of course working
within the order of nature and does not intend the limit to be
understood as referring to the division between Nature and
Grace.) The Savage Man, though innocent of false Art, also remains ignorant of the ways in which Art may complement Nature,[9] as happens earlier, for example, in the Garden of Venus.

> For all that Nature by her mother wit
> Could frame in earth, and forme of substance base,
> Was there, and all that Nature did omit,
> Art, playing second Natures part, supplyed it.
>
> (IV.x.21)

Although courtesy is still to be thought of as chiefly a natural
endowment, the contrast between the Savage Man and the Savage Nation dramatizes (or "allegorizes") further distinctions: it
teaches us that the Nature of courtesy may be either perfected
or perverted by Art. Thus Mirabella, who is "deckt with won-
drous giftes of Natures grace" (vii.28), is punished for using Art

to deny her womanhood, which is "soft and tender . . . by kynde" (viii.2). But natural endowment has been improved by Art in the hermit who has withdrawn himself from the false artificiality of court.[10] Like the Savage Man

> he them full faire did entertaine,
> Not with such forged showes, as fitter beene
> For courting fooles, that curtesies would faine,
> But with entire affection and appearaunce plaine.
>
> (v.38)

Unlike the Savage Man he has learned the Art of treating each according to degree,

> That could his good to all, and well did weene,
> How each to entertaine with curt'sie well beseene.
>
> (v.36)

True Art may therefore dress Nature to advantage.

The pastoral episode treats the division between Nature and Art from yet another point of view, offering the reader still another concept of Nature as a basis for comparison. This time Spenser ignores the accounts of the voyagers and draws instead on purely literary tradition, on the traditional view of Nature and Art in pastoral literature. Among Spenser's shepherds lies the green world of ideal Nature, the only area of Faerie Land that remains unravaged by the Blatant Beast. As Sidney says of his own Arcadia, "Here wrong's name is unheard: slander a monster is." [11] The sixteenth-century reader would no doubt expect the green world to retain its innocent purity, and not because both he and the poet were unattentive to such details.[12] The ideal landscape of pastoral is meant to recall the harmony of Eden, the moment in scriptural history when Nature operated without impediment and had no need of Art to attain perfection. We have seen that the complex evolution of pastoral could provide the Renaissance poet with, among other things, a kind of theological showcase in which is displayed the true and original relationship of Nature to Art. Thus, if the Savage Nation represents the reality of fallen Nature, Spenser's world of pastoral displays the other side of the coin: *natura naturata* still, but now recalling its pristine, prelapsarian state. Spenser had, ready to his hand, a literary form that was traditionally used not only to explore the relation of Nature to Art but also to symbolize Nature in the ideal sense.

Sir Calidore enters the green world and accepts the "gentle offer" of the shepherds, who though they "despise the dainties of the towne" nevertheless treat the knight with proper courtesy (ix.7). The knight has entered the kind of pastoral universe in which Longus had so long ago placed his Daphnis and Chloe. Indeed, *Daphnis and Chloe* is among the sources in pastoral romance that Spenser has drawn upon for the foundling motif seen in Pastorella and, less obviously, for the implied contrast between Nature and Art. Old Meliboe, the foster-father of fair Pastorella, expatiates in the fashion of conventional pastoral on the advantages of living according to Nature—not Art: *Nec mirum, quod divina natura dedit agros, ars humana aedificavit urbes.*[13] The "worlds gay showes" cause only unhappiness and envy, but he who is "taught of nature" remains "contented" (ix.20–22). Gold, in the best pastoral manner, is thought of as that "mucky masse, the cause of mens decay," the artificial product of courtly complexity, of a way of life far inferior to the "simple sort of life, that shepheards lead" (ix.33).

All the customary deprecations of Art are there, together with the corresponding praises of untouched Nature—with this qualification: Meliboe's wholesale condemnation of Art, to which Calidore at first gives his assent (ix.26), must be understood to apply only to the ideal Nature of the pastoral world. This is the lesson Sidney teaches through the moral truancy of Basilius in the *Arcadia*.[14] The Garden is closed to man, and he must assume his proper responsibilities in the fallen world, where the dichot-

omy between Art and Nature is not absolute. It is Meliboe himself who points the moral. When Calidore expresses the wish that
the "heavens so much had graced mee,/ As graunt me live [among
the shepherds] in like condition" (ix.28), the old man objects:

> But fittest is, that all contented rest
> With that they hold. (29)

Calidore may thus abandon the "manner of his loftie looke" and
doff his "bright armes" (ix.36) to win the fair Pastorella—Art is
superfluous in the green world; but he must assume again the
"manner" appropriate to a knight when they both return to the
world of fallen nature.[15] For beyond the charmed circle of the
shepherds the Blatant Beast runs amok, the untutored Nature of
the Savage Man is insufficient, and Art may either improve
upon or aggravate the deficiencies of Nature.

The dance of the Graces on Mount Acidale represents a typi-
cally Spenserian departure from conventional pastoral, yet the
exact significance of the innovation is perhaps undefinable. What
may be understood without difficulty is its relevance to Spenser's
view of courtesy. The *locus amoenus* of Mount Acidale, the finest
example of Nature's work, appears in the center of the green
world.

> For all that ever was by Natures skill
> Devized to worke delight was gathered there,
> And there by her were poured forth at fill,
> As if, this to adorne, she all the rest did pill. (x.5)

It is here that Sir Calidore catches a glimpse of the Graces, those
"daughters of delight," upon the "open greene":

> An hundred naked maidens lilly white,
> All raunged in a ring, and dauncing in delight. (x.11)

The image is extraordinary, not only because of its elegant nudity but also because of the rhetorical and metrical balance of the lines; and this glimpse of ordered beauty, the result of disciplined rhetoric, seems to have represented for Spenser the imaginative center of Book VI.

Unfortunately the Graces have caused critics a certain amount of uneasiness, for it seems that Spenser has here touched on some area of the imagination more or less inaccessible to exact discourse. The most persuasive spokesman for this area of the mind is C. S. Lewis, who is perhaps for that reason one of the few critics who hazard an interpretation of the Graces.[16] Lewis argues that the dancing maidens represent "inspiration" in the widest sense, as the key to all human activities: "To Spenser, in fact, as to Shelley or Plato, there is no essential difference between poetic beauty and the beauty of characters, institutions, and behaviour, and all alike come from the 'daughters of sky-ruling Jove' [the Graces]."[17] And Lewis may be right—at least the size of the generalization precludes his being entirely wrong. But what is really needed is a generalization that takes in less and hence explains more precisely how the Graces relate to the rest of Book VI.

It may be that the Graces do in fact symbolize something more specific than Lewis suggests and that they do indeed possess more precise imaginative connections with the rest of the book than has been supposed. In their orderly dance, and especially in their function as teachers of men, the Graces seem to signify "disciplynd" Nature—the perfect "curtesie" that forms the ground for all "civility":

> These three on men all gracious gifts bestow,
> Which decke the body or adorne the mynde,
> To make them lovely or well favoured show,
> As comely carriage, entertainement kynde,
> Sweete semblaunt, friendly offices that bynde,
> And all the complements of curtesie:

They teach us, how to each degree and kynde
We should our selves demeane, to low, to hie,
To friends, to foes; which skill men call civility.

(x.23)

If the Graces do symbolize "disciplynd" Nature, the natural art of "civility," Spenser's use of them for this purpose would not have escaped his readers. The poet is no more recondite than his sources—Cooper's *Thesavrvs* and Cartari's *Imagines Deorum*— which were to be found in the grammar schools. There is, moreover, little doubt that Spenser used Cartari, who emphasizes the civilizing role of the Graces, without whose gifts men lapse into animality.[18]

In Spenser the Graces are associated with both the art of the poet and his natural gifts. To all mankind they "teach" the art of due observance of degree as well as "bestow" on them the natural "complements of curtesie." But such statements restrict unduly the total meaning of the Graces, whose final significance resists conceptual formulation because it lies, finally, at the center of that extraordinary image of naked naturality "dauncing in delight." Which is not to say that Spenser's image is meaningless. Unlike Symbolist imagery, which is often intentionally opaque, Spenser's images have an intellectual basis that may be suggested (not of course precisely defined) in prose. Consider the dance. It is "natural" but not in the sense of "unformed," "spontaneous," or "inchoate." The point is worth emphasis. Because the dance of the "naked maidens" is a vision not only of "delight" but of symmetrical delight ("All raunged in a ring . . ."), it perfectly images *ordered* beauty or Nature "disciplynd." Proportion, symmetry, order, harmony—these form, for Spenser as for most Renaissance poets, the indispensable ground of beauty and Nature seen as the Art of God. Art has undressed these maidens to advantage. The Graces thus symbolize preoccupations that Spenser elsewhere expresses less richly in conceptual terms, examines less completely in "emblems" like the Savage Man, and personifies in Calidore, the Knight of Courtesy himself. The Graces suggest, in short, the ideal union of Nature and Art that is the height of courteous civility, and they are therefore viewed appropriately as the culminating image of Book VI.

To think of the Graces as the symbol of the ideal union of Art and Nature explains as much as or more than does the theory of "inspiration" and in thinking so we incidentally pay Spenser the compliment of attributing to him a unified imagination. I have been suggesting throughout, in fact, that Book VI as a whole is the result of a more purposeful and unified imagination than most readers suppose.

In general, the Legend of Courtesy reveals Spenser's concern with a question of great theoretical importance for the Renaissance. In particular, this legend fulfills a purpose other than the obvious one of illustrating the workings of courtesy in the activities of knights and ladies, for it elucidates as well the origins and place of the virtue in the order of nature. Spenser seems to have gone about this theoretical investigation in a characteristic manner: through the presentation of contrasting pairs that serve as "philosophical" foci, lending shape and direction to the book as a whole.

At hand was the popular and fairly extensive literature of travel, which either saw the savage as living nobly with simple dignity in a modern Golden Age or described him as nasty, unappealing, and brutish—an example of fallen Nature, unredeemed by the truths of Revelation. At hand lay also the pastoral tradition; because of its association with the prelapsarian Nature of Eden, it was another convenient means of investigating the relation of man to Art and Nature. In the Savage Man against the Savage Nation and in pastoral simplicity against courtly complexity, Spenser develops his individual literary response to courtesy in relation to Nature and Art.

Although the precise quality of Spenser's response to the division in the order of nature is doubtless not reducible to a systematic exposition, certain key distinctions need to be made. Courtesy should above all be considered as chiefly the product of Nature rather than Art, particularly when Art is viewed as the false revelation of the Savage Nation or the insincere manners of courtly society, both of which represent the misuse of human reason. Yet Art, provided it is not overly complex, may complement and even perfect the noble but untutored Nature of such as the Savage Man. Calidore himself embodies *civilized* courtesy, the best combination of Nature and Art possible in the order of nature. Although courtesy is "planted naturall" in him, he has added "comely" manners and deportment, "gracious speach," and knightly attributes "approv'd in batteilous affray" (i.2)—all products of Art that are superfluous in the green world of ideal Nature but obviously important elsewhere.

All this is simply to reassert in other terms the Renaissance commonplace that man is confronted with a choice within the order of nature: he may elect so to combine the benefits of Art and Nature that even in a fallen world he will realize his rank as the *rational* animal, or he may choose to lapse into bestiality through ignorance and the misuse of Art. In brief, Spenser's double attitude toward Art turns ultimately on a particular view of man and the value of human reason, a view much closer to Hooker's than Montaigne's. For Spenser the courteous man "hath . . . learnd him selfe first to subdew" (i.41); Calidore is strong because "his own thought he knew most cleare from wite" (iii.16). As Boethius has it:

Since, then, this is the condition of human nature, that it surpasses other classes only when it realizes what is in itself; as soon as it ceases to know itself, it must be reduced to a lower rank than the beasts. To other animals ignorance of themselves is natural; in men it is a fault.[19]

Accordingly, the knight-hermit must inform Serena and Timias that the bite of the Blatant Beast can be cured only through self-definition and consequent subjugation of the will: "For in your selfe your onely helpe doth lie" (vi.7). Man must first understand himself, so that he may then perceive his place in the order of nature. And courtesy, like other natural virtues, will involve a proper appreciation of degree. So also with Art. If only it is based upon a true perception of the given limits as well as the given potentialities of human reason Art will be used to perfect and not to pervert Nature.

Spenser's use of Art and Nature as controlling terms in his definition of courtesy has also a certain amount of relevance to the other legends of *The Faerie Queene*. To choose the most convenient and important example outside Book VI, the contrast between the Bower of Bliss and the Garden of Adonis evolves out of the division between Nature and Art. C. S. Lewis investigates this matter at some length, concluding that the division is ultimately between "reality" and "imitation," so that he has "stumbled on another of those great antitheses which run through" the whole poem: "Like Life and Death, or Light and Darkness, the opposition of natural and artificial, naive and sophisticated, genuine and spurious, meets us at every turn."[20] Lewis' intuitive appreciation of the division characterizes his sympathetic reading, yet it fails to do justice to the complexity of Spenser's treatment.[21] It is in fact tantamount to asserting—and Lewis would assuredly never maintain it in these terms—that Spenser is a primitivist for whom all use of human reason is misuse. The antithesis indubitably exists in Spenser and is certainly present throughout the poem, but it is inaccurate and misleading to assume that it expresses absolute opposition.

The example of Book VI requires us to remember that untutored or unenlightened Nature may be condemned and that Art, when it is not needlessly complicated,[22] when it does not shade into the Faustian vice of *curiositas,* may enhance and complement Nature. Even in Plato, where Lewis begins, the contrast is not absolute; although Plato, like Aristotle, is preoccupied with the division, the implied opposition between the two terms is in the last analysis resolved by both philosophers. The Renaissance attitude is generally quite similar, though of course the reconciliation proceeds from different assumptions. Witness Sir Thomas Browne: "Now Nature is not at variance with Art, nor Art with Nature, they being both servants of his Providence." For Browne the apparent antithesis of the order of nature was finally resolved in the order of grace: "for Nature is the Art of God." [23] And for Spenser, if not for Montaigne, a partial reconciliation was possible, even necessary, within the order of nature itself.

CHAPTER V

Shakespeare's The Winter's Tale

The Winter's Tale, like Book VI of *The Faerie Queene,* exhibits a specialized use of the traditional materials of pastoral in conjunction with an explicit interest in the philosophical problem of Nature versus Art. Discussion must involve, at least initially and briefly, some reference to Shakespeare's earlier work and then to *Cymbeline* and *The Tempest,* both from his last period; for these later works, in particular, share many of the same intellectual concerns as well as the romance form. The last plays suffered a period of criticism in which, like Spenser's Legend of Courtesy, they were dismissed because they resembled insufficiently the work of The Poet's Serious Period. After the sentimental pleasure nineteenth-century critics like Dowden took in visualizing Shakespeare On The Heights in his last years at Stratford, the reaction, led by Lytton Strachey, took the romances in one way or another as evidence of senile decay. Shakespeare's powers were declining; like Spenser he was being bored to death by life and art. In the past twenty years, however, the last plays have received favorable attention from such writers as G. Wilson Knight and E. M. W. Tillyard, who have come to regard the romances as organic extensions of Shakespeare's earlier preoccupations, as complementary to his earlier tragic concerns.

In one way or another the writers of recent criticism have endeavored to lend the last plays dignity by arguing that Shakespeare had more on his mind than cranking out remunerative romances. The verse, in its range and intensity, seems to support the idea that these plays have depths beyond what is usually allowed to the genre of romance. In *Cymbeline,* for example, the generally wooden Posthumus, at long last united to Imogen, exclaims in the moment of their embrace:

> Hang there like fruit, my soul,
> Till the tree die!   (V.v.263–64) [1]

The sudden power of lines such as these appears to point to a degree of seriousness that seems incompatible with the form of dramatic romance, and in *The Winter's Tale* and *The Tempest* the percentage of such lines increases.

A convenient example of the kind of intensity of which Shakespeare was capable at this time occurs in *The Winter's Tale* when Leontes describes his state of mind at discovering his wife's supposed infidelity:

> How blest am I
> In my just censure, in my true opinion!
> Alack for lesser knowledge! how accurs'd
> In being so blest! There may be in the cup
> A spider steep'd, and one may drink, depart,
> And yet partake no venom, for his knowledge
> Is not infected; but if one present
> Th' abhorr'd ingredient to his eye, make known
> How he hath drunk, he cracks his gorge, his sides,
> With violent hefts. I have drunk, and seen the spider.
>   (II.i.36–45)

We are of course at liberty to see the rhetorical mastery and violent strength of verse like this as melodramatic; what is harder is to see it as appropriate to romance. Accordingly, recent criticism has quite properly tried to find "symbolic" and "mythic" undercurrents beneath a "superficial" surface of romance and pastoral elements. D. A. Traversi, for example, maintains that the "plot of *The Winter's Tale* is a perfect example of the symbolic technique perfected by Shakespeare in his last plays. It is the story of the division created in love and friendship by the passage of time and by the action of 'blood,' and of the healing of these divisions through penitence and renewed personal devotion."[2]

Granting it seems unwise to dismiss the genre of romance without having scrutinized it at all closely, most of us will nevertheless sympathize with such attempts to lend the last plays a serious purpose, if only because we are dissatisfied with the picture of Shakespeare as an elderly romanticist yawning his way through imitations of Beaumont and Fletcher. The tendency is to seek this serious purpose at some "mythic" or "symbolic" level because the romantic and pastoral elements are generally regarded as merely entertaining.

Putting aside for a moment the knowledge that pastoral does not preclude philosophy, the fact remains that the improbable plots of the last plays invite symbolic interpretation. In each of the plays a royal father loses his offspring through his own passionate excess, so that an initial atmosphere of prosperity and tranquillity precedes a time of confusion and suffering. In each the lost child is restored after living for a time among shepherds or in the wilderness, so that after the period of suffering, and out of the green world, emerges a new atmosphere of prosperity and tranquillity. This symbolic pattern is, however, so overlaid with the highly stylized elements of traditional romance—sublimely faithful love and excessive jealousy, complex incident and intrigue, puppet characterization, mistaken identity, disguisings, coincidence, innocuous poisons, white magic, amiable savages, and the like—that the pattern is hard to discern and harder still to exhibit as part of Shakespeare's conscious or unconscious intention.[3]

Although *The Winter's Tale* reveals a particularly complete and intense formulation of the "mythic" or "symbolic" pattern that critics suppose to be characteristic of the last plays, this underlying configuration is of such a comprehensive type that it has proved susceptible of translation into a variety of different terms:

it may be a derivative pattern of a quasi-psychological kind, as in Tillyard's theory that the last plays represent a vital extension of concerns revealed by Shakespeare during his tragic phase; or it may be an anthropological pattern, a sophisticated vegetation myth, its ultimate meanings looking back on folk ritual;[4] or it may even be, despite the elements of romance, a theological pattern of sin, atonement, and redemption.[5] So far as *The Winter's Tale* is concerned, the problem is not so much whether the under-lying pattern exists, but how it is to be theorized about.

The language and imagery of the play, remarkably rich in allusions, seem to offer justification for psychological, theological, anthropological, and other interpretations, but my own conviction is that we are not likely to settle anything through appeals to different systems of abstraction; all such systems appear to be so comprehensive as to include the fundamental story elements of which the romances are compounded. My own contribution, in any case, is not to offer a new system of abstractions (for I intend to describe the underlying pattern in as neutral language as possible), but to point out that a fundamental part of the pattern reveals Shakespeare's literary and philosophical concern with Nature and Art. In other words, the "symbolic" pattern of *The Winter's Tale,* turning on images of the seasons, of birth and death, of the sea as destroyer and savior, works together with the conceptual pattern of Nature and Art.

The division between Nature and Art occupied Shakespeare throughout his career. It is implicit in the pastoral episodes of *As You Like It,* and even as early as *Venus and Adonis* he is toying with the conventional notion of strife between Nature and Art in painting:

> Look, when a painter would surpass the life
> In limning out a well-proportioned steed,
> His art with nature's workmanship at strife,
> As if the dead the living should exceed.
>
> (ll. 289–92)

And in reference to a painting of the siege of Troy in *The Rape of Lucrece:*

> A thousand lamentable objects there,
> In scorn of nature, art gave liveless life.
>   (ll. 1373–74)

The association of "art" with death and "nature" with life persists even so far as the "dead likeness" of Hermione in *The Winter's Tale;* and the commonplace pairing of Nature and Art is alluded to in play after play, reappearing at some length in *Timon of Athens,* shortly before the writing of the last romances. In the opening scene that advertises the main concerns of that play, the Poet and the Painter are discussing an example of the Painter's work, and the Poet is amiably self-important in traditional terms:

> I will say of it,
> It tutors nature. Artificial strife
> Lives in these touches, livelier than life.
>   (I.i.36–38)

Such statements are commonplace, and despite some attempt at variation the similarity of wording implies that Shakespeare produced such literary detritus from his memory on demand, without thought and without effort, as the appropriate occasion presented itself.

Although Shakespeare's use of the division in his allusions to the fine arts is entirely traditional, Nature and Art represented a vital and living problem for him in the ethical speculations of the last plays. In *Cymbeline* the beginnings of what is to be an intense preoccupation may be glimpsed in one of the major ethical contrasts of the play—between the King's stepson, Cloten, and his real sons, Guiderius and Arviragus. Cloten is the product of the "art o' th' court" that Belarius, the guardian of the real sons, continually disparages. Guiderius and Arviragus, having been brought up in savage surroundings apart from the court,

represent the triumph of Nature untutored by Art. As Belarius
explains it:

> O thou goddess,
> Thou divine Nature, how thyself thou blazon'st
> In these two princely boys! They are as gentle
> As zephyrs blowing below the violet,
> Not wagging his sweet head; and yet as rough,
> (Their royal blood enchaf'd) as the rud'st wind
> That by the top doth take the mountain pine
> And make him stoop to th' vale. 'Tis wonder
> That an invisible instinct should frame them
> To royalty unlearn'd, honour untaught,
> Civility not seen from other, valour
> That wildly grows in them but yields a crop
> As if it had been sow'd.   (IV.ii.169–81)

The opposition between Nature and Art is not absolute for
Shakespeare—he allows the Princes to express an awareness that
courts may be in many respects superior to caves—but throughout the terms have been manipulated in such a way as to provide
a main theme of the romance. As far as the Princes are concerned, Shakespeare agrees with Spenser and the courtesy books
in making Nature more powerful than nurture; and thus it is
appropriate that Nature unaided by Art should figure in the
reconciliation scene at the end of the play. Granted the thematic
value of the terms, remarks like those of Belarius' attain in context a force beyond that which may be assigned to a commonplace. In *Cymbeline* statements about Nature and Art have become part of the dramatic design, so that they function, perhaps
a little creakily, as part of the plot and not merely as isolated
allusions.

By the time of *The Tempest* the process has been developed
and intensified, passing from the relatively derivative use of the
division to a more subtle and skillfully articulated study of the

traditional opposition of Nature to Art. Frank Kermode's elegant Introduction to *The Tempest* takes full account of Nature and Art and there is no need to rehearse his arguments here; although one may grow restive at his identification of Caliban as the central figure of the play, against which all the other characters are measured, it nevertheless seems clear that Kermode is right in contending that the "main opposition is between the worlds of Prospero's Art, and Caliban's Nature." [6] Hence there is little to be gained by pursuing this survey: enough has been said to establish Shakespeare's interest, early and late, in Nature and Art and to provide a context for detailed consideration of *The Winter's Tale,* the play that exploits most fully the relationship between the philosophical division and the pastoral genre.

Beneath the romance trappings of *The Winter's Tale* the critics have seen a pattern that, reduced to its essentials and stated in relatively neutral language, is based on cycles or alternations of harmony and alienation, of integration and disruption.[7] Harmony, symbolized in the friendship of Leontes and Polixenes, receives initial emphasis in the first scene as Camillo remarks, perhaps a little ambiguously: "They were train'd together in their childhoods; and there rooted betwixt them then such an affection which cannot choose but branch now." In the next scene Polixenes sounds the same note as he recalls for Hermione what it was like to be "boy eternal" with her husband, Leontes.

> We were as twinn'd lambs that did frisk i' th' sun
> And bleat the one at th' other. What we chang'd
> Was innocence for innocence; we knew not
> The doctrine of ill-doing, nor dream'd
> That any did. Had we pursu'd that life,
> And our weak spirits ne'er been higher rear'd
> With stronger blood, we should have answer'd heaven
> Boldly, "Not guilty," the imposition clear'd
> Hereditary ours.   (I.ii.67–75)

The idea of carefree harmony and the connotations of spring and birth are in this particular passage subordinated to the theological terms. The harmony recalled by Polixenes is a vision of the integrity of man in Eden, free of the taint of original sin—an association reinforced by the wit of the following lines as he and Hermione joke about the boys having "first sinn'd with" the queens, the implication being that the innocence of former days was lost because of woman.

This is not allegory, of course, nor is *The Winter's Tale* a covert recapitulation of the Fall of Man. But the web of allusion in these lines provides a frame of reference within which the main events of the play can receive meaning: the speech introduces the vision of the green world, the ideal of past harmony, and associates it with birth, innocence, spring, even with the Garden of Eden. To speak technically, this is the "integrity" of Nature before the Fall.

The vision of the Garden, however, is brief and not easily sustained. As Shakespeare's audience was well aware, the harmony of Eden had been lost to man so that his "stronger blood" was no longer free of the hereditary "imposition." Consequently the Elizabethan audience was better prepared than Shakespeare's modern critics for Leontes' sudden and unmotivated jealousy, the towering excess of passion that, appearing in the same scene with Polixenes' speech of remembered bliss, obliterates the initial mood of harmony and introduces the chaos and death for which Leontes is finally to do penance.

Leontes is a man, his Nature impaired by the Fall, so that he is *non posse non peccare,* not able not to err. The terrible consequences of Leontes' passion—alienation from Polixenes and Camillo, the death of his son, the death of Antigonus, the apparent deaths of his daughter and wife—form the main burden of the play until the Chorus of Time that introduces Act IV. Meanwhile the members of Shakespeare's audience have seen the result of an excess of passion and have been able to judge the action in the terms, moral and theological, most meaningful to them. The first phase of the cycle is complete; harmony and integration have been replaced by alienation and disruption.

The pivotal point of the play lies where it should, toward the end of Act III; as in *Pericles* and *The Tempest* it involves a storm at sea, the archetypal image of birth and death. The young shepherd (the clown) witnesses the destruction of the ship and the death of Antigonus, but at the same time the old shepherd comes across the living babe whose restoration figures in the fulfillment of the oracle. The scene thus recalls the disruption and chaos of the earlier action and at the same time anticipates the restoration of harmony in the last act. As the old shepherd puts it, saying more than he understands: "Now bless thyself! thou met'st with things dying, I with things new-born" (III.iii.116–18).

Act IV includes the pastoral interlude and, as we have come to expect, the main references to the controversy over Nature and Art. Florizel, the son of Polixenes, has fallen in love with the shepherdess Perdita whom we know to be the daughter of Leontes, marooned by his order during a transport of jealousy. The child has grown up without benefit of Art, and yet her demeanor, like that of the Princes in *Cymbeline*, reflects the irrefragable excellence of royal blood. Throughout the word "queen" is applied to her, for as Florizel says:

> Each your doing,
> So singular in each particular,
> Crowns what you are doing in the present deed,
> That all your acts are queens.   (IV.iv.143–46)

Both royal children are for the moment disguised as shepherds, the difference being that Florizel knows his true birth whereas Perdita does not. And while they masquerade as pastoral figures, Shakespeare takes care to have us associate the children with more than purity of blood.

Florizel's name—it does not appear in Shakespeare's source—

is clearly allegorical, and the association with Flora receives further emphasis in the Prince's description of Perdita in her role as queen of the sheepshearing:

> These your unusual weeds to each part of you
> Do give a life—no shepherdess, but Flora
> Peering in April's front! This your sheep-shearing
> Is as a meeting of the petty gods,
> And you the queen on't.   (IV.iv.1–5)

Despite the wide difference in (apparent) birth, Shakespeare makes it clear that there is no intention of exercising *droit du seigneur;* Florizel's "youth" and "blood" are as idyllic and pure as his pastoral surroundings, as Perdita herself recognizes even when his praise of her is so extravagant as to seem suspicious:

> Your praises are too large. But that your youth,
> And the true blood which peeps so fairly through't,
> Do plainly give you out an unstain'd shepherd,
> With wisdom I might fear, my Doricles [i.e., Florizel],
> You woo'd me the false way.   (IV.iv.147–51)

Florizel makes it explicit:

>   my desires
> Run not before mine honour, nor my lusts
> Burn hotter than my faith.
>   (IV.iv.33–35)

In short, Shakespeare has taken care to lend Florizel and Perdita the qualities that his audience associated with pastoral figures—idyllic innocence and artless Nature.

The value of Perdita's artlessness is particularly emphasized. Her intellectual simplicity cleaves directly to the heart of a problem, a quality that leads Camillo to acknowledge that he

>   cannot say 'tis pity
> She lacks instructions, for she seems a mistress
> To most that teach.   (IV.iv.592–94)

And her modest demeanor does not prevent her from making the pastoral comparison between country and court explicit in referring to Polixenes' rage at discovering his son in love with a "shepherdess":

> I was not much afeard; for once or twice
> I was about to speak, and tell him plainly
> The selfsame sun that shines upon his court
> Hides not his visage from our cottage, but
> Looks on alike.   (IV.iv.453–57)

Even this satiric cut—it is in no sense "democratic"[8]—is of the kind common in pastoral. So far in Shakespeare there is no more than what may be expected from the bucolic tradition: spring, youth, innocence, idyllic love, and the assumption that Nature is superior to Art. But when we have understood the exact function of the pastoral episode in relation to the play as a whole, in relation to its dramatic structure and to its underlying alternation of harmony and disintegration, we will be in a better position to see the individual uses to which Shakespeare has put the traditional materials of Nature and Art.

The pastoral episode immediately precedes the last act, the time of reconciliation and reintegration. The court of Sicily—where the action of the play began—is now the scene of an elaborate series of discoveries in which poetic and other justice is rendered all around. A number of exchanges between Paulina and Leontes have assured the audience that the king is truly repentant; the theological note, sounded so persistently and quietly throughout the play, once more assumes a prominent function, as in the words of Cleomenes:

> Sir, you have done enough, and have perform'd
> A saint like sorrow. No fault could you make
> Which you have not redeem'd; indeed, paid down
> More penitence than done trespass. At the last,
> Do as the heavens have done: forget your evil;
> With them, forgive yourself.   (V.i.1–6)

Redemption is indeed at hand.

Florizel and Perdita, fleeing Bohemia and the anger of Polixenes, appear at the Sicilian court; and Leontes, in words that recall the pastoral interlude, welcomes the lovers as a change from the winter of his discontent: "Welcome hither / As is the spring to th' earth" (V.i.151–52). The "unstain'd" youth of Florizel and Perdita, their "true blood," symbolizes the restoration of harmony, the coming of spring to the wasteland, and the purification of the "stronger blood" of their fathers that is impaired by the stain of original sin. Perdita, she who was lost, is found, and discovered to be the daughter of the King; Leontes and Polixenes are once more united in friendship; the way is cleared for the young lovers; Hermione is restored to Leontes during the famous (or notorious) statue scene; and the extraordinary network of repeated words and phrases—youth and age, spring and winter, Nature and Art, birth and death, innocence and sin, Nature and Grace, blood and infection, and so on—is resolved in a series of brilliant puns, in the paradoxical wit of the last scenes. The second phase of the cycle of alienation and harmony, of disruption and reintegration, has been completed.

Enough has been said so that the function of the pastoral scenes in this cycle of—to put it theologically—Fall and Redemption is perhaps obvious. Without these scenes the play would be structurally and symbolically defective, for they reflect, at the appropriate point in the action, the harmony with which the play began: the qualities that Leontes and Polixenes were said to have had as boys are those which Shakespeare gives in turn to Perdita and Florizel. And even the imagery of "twinn'd lambs," together with the assumption of innocence unimpaired by original sin, that Shakespeare uses in describing the young princes accurately reflects pastoral conventions; Shakespeare chose appropriately if not "originally" in this respect.

The imaginative force of the paradisiacal intimacy that once existed between Polixenes and Leontes is therefore essentially similar to the pastoral harmony that is now associated with Perdita and Florizel, and it is therefore proper that the two moments in the Garden balance each other structurally, the one preceding disruption and the other preceding integration. Moreover, the two moments serve a similar moral function in the play. In the cycle of disruption and integration the moments of childhood innocence and pastoral integrity provide the audience, in essentially similar ways, with visions of ideal order in terms of which the rest of the action may be meaningfully understood. The pastoral episode is consequently not merely a decorative interlude but the structural and symbolic prelude to the restoration of harmony in the last act.

Shakespeare's use of pastoral as the expression of an ethical ideal, of a simple world by which the more complex one might be judged, is strictly traditional, and yet it is a little more complicated than my statements so far might imply. Shakespeare's idealization of shepherd life, for example, does not extend much beyond Perdita who is, like Pastorella in *The Faerie Queene,* of shepherd nurture but not of shepherd nature. And while the old shepherd, that "weather-bitten conduit of many kings' reigns" (V.ii.61–62), is allowed to display a certain amount of rude dignity, the Mopsas and Dorcases of Shakespeare's pastoral world are bumpkins, foils for that snapper-up of unconsidered trifles, Autolycus. Perdita's royal blood manifests itself despite her surroundings and not because of them. For Shakespeare, then, shepherds may serve as exemplars of virtue if they are royal shepherds, and Nature may do without the civilizing influence of Art if it is royal Nature. Toward ordinary shepherds Shakespeare's attitude is realistic and gently satirical; his tolerant humor recalls Theocritus but is a long way from Vergil's delicate enthusiasms.

Shakespeare's attitude toward the division between Nature and Art is at least as complicated, but analysis begins most conveniently with his knowledge of traditional materials. Certainly he was aware of the long-standing association of pastoral with Nature and Art, for his pastoral episode includes a fairly thorough debate on the subject. Camillo and Polixenes, disguised, appear at the sheepshearing to investigate the truth of the rumored liaison between Florizel and some humble shepherdess. Polixenes and Perdita discuss flowers, but matters of cultural propriety are always near the surface of what is ostensibly a horticultural argument.

These speeches are worth quoting at length because of their explicit relevance to my thesis, their complex character, and their importance as conceptual statements of the ethical concerns of the play. Perdita begins by apologizing for presenting these men of "middle age" with winter flowers; she has no fall flowers because she will not grow "nature's bastards," and the discussion immediately turns into a highly technical debate on Nature and Art.

> *Per.*   Sir, the year growing ancient,
> Not yet on summer's death nor on the birth
> Of trembling winter, the fairest flow'rs o' th' season
> Are our carnations and streak'd gillyvors,
> Which some call nature's bastards. Of that kind
> Our rustic garden's barren, and I care not
> To get slips of them.
> *Pol.*   Wherefore, gentle maiden,
> Do you neglect them?
> *Per.*   For I have heard it said
> There is an art which in their piedness shares
> With great creating nature.
> *Pol.*   Say there be.
> Yet nature is made better by no mean
> But nature makes that mean. So, over that art
> Which you say adds to nature, is an art
> That nature makes. You see, sweet maid, we marry
> A gentler scion to the wildest stock
> And make conceive a bark of baser kind
> By bud of nobler race. This is an art

Which does mend nature—change it rather; but
The art itself is nature.
  Per.   So it is.
  Pol.   Then make your garden rich in gillyvors,
And do not call them bastards.
  Per.   I'll not put
The dibble in earth to set one slip of them;
No more than, were I painted, I would wish
This youth should say 'twere well, and only therefore
Desire to breed by me.   (IV.iv.79–103)

The speeches are obviously meant to be significant in relation to the entire action of the play; they are not merely decorative commonplaces, but their function has never been fully explained.

There is a possibility that Shakespeare intended the actor portraying Polixenes to speak his lines in such a way that the audience will take the horticultural reasoning as a trap, as a device by which Polixenes hopes to expose Perdita as a scheming wench who is after that "bud of nobler race," Florizel. But it is Perdita who first commits herself against "nature's bastards," and Polixenes' tone, now deliberative, now authoritative, does not appear to support such an interpretation. The King seems pretty clearly to be reasoning in earnest.

Admittedly, the contention that an Art that changes Nature is in fact Nature may seem at first blush sophistical, calculated to make a young girl betray her desires for the "gentler scion." Yet Polixenes' stand is perhaps the most dignified and carefully argued in the whole history of possible opposition between Nature and Art. Like Aristotle and Plato, Polixenes points out that the "art itself is nature." Aristotle had argued in the *Physics* that when we claim that Art perfects Nature we do in fact mean in the last analysis that Nature perfects herself: "The best illustration is a doctor doctoring himself: nature is like that." [9] And Plato in the tenth book of the *Laws* had maintained that the good legislator "ought to support the law and also art, and acknowledge that both alike exist by nature, and no less than nature."[10] Although Polixenes' argument may appear sophistical, it is in fact an orthodox statement of the "real" significance of the ancient opposition.

There is of course nothing new in the mixture of horticultural and social vocabularies either, but the implications of the mixture in Polixenes' argument are shockingly unorthodox:

> You see, sweet maid, we marry
> A gentler scion to the wildest stock
> And make conceive a bark of baser kind
> By bud of nobler race.

Translated into purely social terms—Shakespeare's equivocal vocabulary forces the audience to consider the social implications—the argument of Polixenes seems to call for a program of egalitarian eugenics, a program equally shocking, one suspects, to Polixenes and to the Elizabethan audience. Especially in the given dramatic situation, for the King is at this moment disguised as a shepherd expressly to prevent his "gentler scion" from marrying a "bark of baser kind."

Perdita has throughout revealed a Spenserian appreciation of "degree," and now her reply to Polixenes rejects his (implied) social radicalism along with his horticultural orthodoxy:

> I'll not put
> The dibble in earth to set one slip of them;
> No more than, were I painted, I would wish
> This youth [Florizel] should say 'twere well, and only therefore
> Desire to breed by me.

Perdita's uneasiness in her "borrowed flaunts" (IV.iv.23), her modest conviction that she is, "poor lowly maid,/ Most goddesslike prank'd up" (IV.iv.9–10), has culminated in her final identification of Art with deceit, with false imitation, with "painted" womanhood—a kind of Art morally and otherwise inferior to Nature. Her position is, indeed, as venerable as that of Polixenes, appearing in such diverse places as Plato's concept of imitation in the fine arts, in Castiglione's view of cosmetics,[11] and in virtually the whole of the pastoral tradition. Yet neither Polixenes nor Perdita may be taken to represent Shakespeare's final word on the division between Nature and Art.[12] The two traditions are both philosophically "respectable"; dramatic propriety alone requires that Polixenes maintain the court position and Perdita hold to the pastoral belief in the absolute dichotomy between the two terms.

If Shakespeare's "own" position must remain for the moment conjectural, it is at least possible to understand what he is doing with the ancient division between Nature and Art. Clearly he is using it *dramatically,* as an oblique commentary on the action of the play. Less obvious is his use of the conceptual terms of the division to reflect the major ethical concerns of the play, using them to sum up with dramatic irony the ethical and social questions of *The Winter's Tale.*

With Perdita, for example, the debate becomes a comment on the way Shakespeare has characterized her. She is given to us as the creation of Nature who, despite her lack of Art, is "mistress/ To most that teach"; she is completely incapable of deceit, and her charming sensuousness is tempered by a clear perception of decorum, of her proper place in the order of things. At the same time her role in the sheepshearing is the creation of Art; her "unusual weeds" make her a "goddess," a "queen," but since these "borrowed flaunts" are deceitful, she resolves finally to "queen it no inch farther" (IV.iv.460). Thus Perdita's stand on the ancient debate accurately reflects her character; it is perfectly consistent with the manner in which she is dramatized. It is this and more. In addition it anticipates ironically the discoveries of the last act, for although Perdita at this point appears to be arguing (in horticultural terms) against a marriage with Florizel, her words describe unwittingly but exactly the final situation of the two lovers: in the last act it will be revealed that Perdita is a "queen" by Nature rather than by Art, that her "borrowed flaunts" are hers by right. At the time when she takes her stand on the question of Nature versus Art, she is by Nature what she conceives herself to be by Art.

Her speech to Polixenes is therefore effective in two main ways: on the one hand it accents her pastoral status as a figure of Nature, free of the corruption and taint of Art, suggesting the Nature of Eden; on the other hand the speech anticipates obliquely the last act of the play in which she and the other characters (the spectator is of course already aware of the dramatic irony of her speech) will understand that Florizel's metaphorical praise —"all your acts are queens"—represents truth on the literal as well as the figurative level.

Polixenes' argument similarly sets up reverberations far beyond the limits of his speech and the immediate context. Polixenes, like Perdita, seemingly argues against his own best interests, for his resolution of the opposition between Nature and Art apparently sanctions the marriage of a noble to a commoner, the "bud of nobler race" to a "bark of baser kind." Thus, as far as Shakespeare and the audience are concerned, it is still another opportunity for dramatic irony; again the spectator is aware of more in a character's words than the character himself. Polixenes appears conscious only of the horticultural application of his words while the spectator is in a position to see that, in the case of Perdita, the "art itself *is* nature." Thus, Polixenes is also "right," even in the social sense of his words, though he cannot yet see that the queenliness of Perdita's "nature is made better by no mean/ But nature makes that mean." It is only in the last act that the disagreement between Perdita and Polixenes is transcended and resolved in the general restoration of harmony.

The last act is worth looking at in connection with Nature and Art because Shakespeare returns to the subject, this time in the sphere of the fine arts, in an attempt to resolve the paradoxical contrarieties generated out of the debate between Perdita and

Polixenes. That which was lost has been found in the person of Perdita, and the two kings are reunited. All that remains is for the dead to rise as in *Pericles:* the "dead" Hermione is still lost to Leontes. Her improbable restoration in the statue scene has been condemned as a vulgar concession to popular taste and cited as an example of the triviality of the romance form. Such criticism quite misses the point, for it ignores the ground swell of harmony and alienation that informs the play and, even more pertinently, it neglects Shakespeare's preoccupation with Nature and Art.

Properly assessed, the "unrealistic" quality of the statue scene is beside the point. Here as elsewhere in the last romances Shakespeare's respect for "truth" lies in the intensity of his verse and in the underlying pattern of the plays. If the statue scene is improbable, it nevertheless conforms with fidelity to the cycle of alienation and harmony, and the verse of this scene possesses a rare imaginative integrity. All the crucial words of the play—summer and winter, "infancy and grace," Nature and Art, life and death —come together in the last scenes in a series of reckless paradoxes. Paulina speaks to the statue:

> Bequeath to death your numbness, for from him
> Dear life redeems you.   (V.iii.102–3)

The time of Hermione's "better grace" has arrived; her stepping down from the pedestal means harmony, forgiveness, restoration, redemption.

The role played by Nature and Art in this larger resolution is perhaps obvious. Clearly a statue represents Art, and in this case the statue represents living Art,[13] or Nature. Such distinctions were equally clear to Shakespeare, and his language shows that he also expected his audience to have in mind the traditional opposition between the terms. We first hear of the statue from the Third Gentleman, whose description is marked by the ancient division and avails itself of the ancient analogy:

. . . a piece many years in doing, and now newly perform'd, by that rare Italian master, Julio Romano, who, had he himself eternity and could put breath into his work, would beguile Nature of her custom, so perfectly he is her ape.   (V.ii.103–8)

The artist is the ape of Nature, his imitation practiced so perfectly that he almost outdoes Nature, his final aim being *naturam vincere.* We have already seen the same notion in *Venus and Adonis,* the *Rape of Lucrece,* and *Timon;* it is the cliché of iconic poetry of the period, summed up in Cardinal Bembo's epitaph on Raphael: "Nature feared that she would be conquered while he lived, and would die when he died." [14] It is in this tradition of friendly contest between Art and Nature that Paulina invites praise of her "statue":

> Prepare
> To see the life as lively mock'd as ever
> Still sleep mock'd death,
>   (V.iii.18–20)

and it is in this tradition that Leontes praises it:

> The fixure of her eye has motion in't,
> As we are mock'd with art.
>   (V.iii.67–68)

Art has successfully imitated Nature, or so it seems to those who do not know that Paulina has preserved Hermione alive.

The symbolic value of the scene is clear: as with Perdita, the imitation or "mock" of Nature turns out finally to be Nature after all. What seems to be Art is in fact Nature, fulfilling Polixenes' assertion that the "art itself is nature" and confirming Perdita's belief in the supremacy of "great creating nature." The statue scene is with all its improbability a dramatic embodiment of Shakespeare's preoccupation with Nature and Art; it transcends the earlier disagreement between Perdita and Polixenes, for the opposition between Nature and Art dissolves in the pageantry of the statue's descent.

The traditional division lies at the center of *The Winter's Tale.* It is used conceptually and as an instrument of dramatic irony in the pastoral episode, and it appears symbolically as part of the total resolution of Act V. Nevertheless, Shakespeare does not seem to be as far committed to the division as Spenser. Although both poets take full advantage of the association of the literary genre with the philosophical division and although both use the pastoral as "an element in the harmonious solution of a longer story" [15] about the court, in Shakespeare the division lacks much of the didactic immediacy it possesses in Spenser. The virtue of courtesy must be placed properly in the order of nature, and Spenser uses Nature and Art to achieve this didactic end; he is thinking *with* the established terms more than he is *about* them. Perhaps because *The Winter's Tale* is less obtrusively didactic, Shakespeare thinks *about* the terms more than he does *with* them, finding in Nature and Art opportunities for witty debate and verbal paradox; perhaps because of his lack of absolute commitment he can afford to extract from various and conflicting interpretations the full dramatic value of the philosophical division. In *The Winter's Tale* the traditional terms represent, through dramatic irony, a conceptual summation of the ethical and social interests of the play, and in the last act they form a main part of the elaborate series of paradoxes culminating in the statue scene—the pun made flesh.

CHAPTER VI

Marvell's Garden of the Mind

The significance of Andrew Marvell's experiments in the pastoral genre must be carefully assessed if we are to understand the emotional and intellectual concerns that give purpose and weight to his finest lyrics. For Marvell was not much given to direct statement, his considerable virtues being of an ironic, allusive kind. As a consequence his poems, taken singly and without regard for the conventions of their genre, are more open to appreciation than analysis,

> Annihilating all that's made
> To a green Thought in a green Shade.

Although the body of his lyric verse is small, attempts to discern continuity and regularity, to define basic assumptions and deep commitments, have been frustrated by his reliance on a semiprivate vocabulary, by his attitude of urbane detachment, and by a group of brilliant but apparently random poetic experiments. In his pastoral poems, however, Marvell for once explored the possibilities in a particular genre and developed the implications of a single theme: it is here, revealed by his modifications of the pastoral *kind* and by his personal response to the paired terms of Nature and Art, that we possess the clearest indication of attitudes elsewhere concealed by ironic wit.

Marvell wrote a number of poems that are clearly a part of the pastoral tradition, and there is considerable variation in his treatment of them within the genre. Variety has always been characteristic of the genre itself; despite—perhaps even because of—its stereotyped conventions, the form has lent itself to a remarkably wide range of poetic and other intentions. Marvell's use of the genre is no exception, although some of his experiments, such as "Two Songs at the Marriage of the Lord Fauconberg and the Lady Mary Cromwell," [1] remain comparatively uninteresting not only because of their occasional nature but also because the simple Hobbinols and rustic Thomalins are vehicles for little more than courtly compliment.

Marvell's best pastorals, however, depart radically from such relatively unambitious themes and purposes: situations are no longer simple, man is no longer artless, and feelings become quite complicated. The traditional lover of pastoral is replaced by the Mower, a figure at once cheerfully ingenuous and darkly mysterious, whose relationship to Nature seems complex and ambiguous and who suffers strangely at the hands of an unusual shepherdess. In short, Marvell's intentions become much more ambitious, growing in both scope and intensity, but the pastoral *kind* remains to provide a form in which the maturer interests may be expressed.

"Ametas and Thestylis Making Hay-Ropes" (46) and "Daphnis and Chloe" (33) are possibly among the first of Marvell's pastoral experiments; at least they show no hint of his more serious concerns. Possibly among the first . . . There is no way of determining exactly when most of the "Miscellaneous Poems" were written.[2] In any case, precise knowledge of chronological order would have absolute value only if we could depend on a poet to exhibit straight-line progress toward a particular goal. But success may be lost as well as found, and poets, like other men, commit themselves to a variety of ends, sometimes returning with new understanding to an old problem only after a number of years, so that later work may bear the sediment of early efforts. If "Ametas and Thestylis" and "Daphnis and Chloe" are not chronologically early, they are nevertheless experiments that did not lead to additional poems of the same type. They are poems of the fashionable world in the tradition of the love-debate *pastourelle*. Marvell adopts the ethics of this tradition, probably influenced by the French *libertins* of the seventeenth century, and attempts to make the pastoral form sustain some fairly sophisticated arguments about love.

In "Ametas and Thestylis" the witty debate closes quickly with the usual gesture:

> Then let's both lay by our Rope,
> And go kiss within the Hay.

In "Daphnis and Chloe," where a similar theme is attenuated through approximately eight times as many lines, Marvell may have realized that he had extended himself in this direction about as far as he could go. Although there is no doubt that the shepherdess this time remains virtuous, the last stanzas show that the two poems exhibit essentially the same attitude:

> But hence Virgins all beware.
> Last night he with Phlogis slept;
> This night for Dorinda kept;
> And but rid to take the Air.

> Yet he does himself excuse;
> Nor indeed without a Cause.
> For, according to the Lawes,
> Why did Chloe once refuse?

These are obviously poems addressed to something very like court society, perhaps the small circle of literati at Appleton House, who might be relied upon to appreciate both the wit and the delicious excitement of the naturalistic ethics. To Marvell at this time, as to Tasso in *Aminta,* it seems that "what pleased was proper," according "to the Lawes" of *libertin* naturalism.

"Clorinda and Damon" (18) and "A Dialogue between

Thyrsis and Dorinda" (19) may be viewed as transitional poems. Although Marvell's most central and characteristic preoccupations do not yet appear, the poems imply movement in the direction of the best pastorals through their explicit rejection of "naturalistic" or *libertin* ethics. What pleases is no longer necessarily proper; Marvell even begins to use the pastoral form to discuss religious matters. Such a use was of course not at all uncommon, either in the Middle Ages or in the Renaissance. We have seen that it had behind it the putative foreshadowing of Christ in Vergil's Fourth or Messianic Eclogue, the mystical glosses on the pastoral Song of Songs, the shepherds of the Gospels, the medieval uses of the genre, and numerous Renaissance "imitations," so that Sidney could assert confidently in his *Apologie for Poetrie* that the genre, "under the prettie tales of Wolves and Sheepe, can include the whole considerations of wrong dooing."[3] Puttenham similarly emphasizes that the genre does not simply attempt to "represent the rusticall manner of loues and communication: but vnder the vaile of homely persons, and in rude speeches to insinuate and glaunce at greater matters."[4] But the poetical and critical traditions notwithstanding, Marvell apparently at first found it hard to "insinuate and glaunce at greater matters."

Marvell's problem was one of technique: How is it possible to write on complex, civilized themes while still retaining all the baggage of traditional pastoral? As we have seen, the answer lies in the allegorical potentialities of the form. Puttenham alludes to this solution with the words "insinuate and glaunce," but Marvell in "Thyrsis and Dorinda" attempts to discuss "greater matters" more or less directly. The speakers are therefore so ingenuous in relation to the subject matter that even rustic charm cannot save the piece. Although Dorinda has reservations about Death, being unsure where she will "go," Thyrsis assures her it merely means a new home in Elizium. Dorinda remains only partially satisfied, and presents her swain with a question he could not hope to answer directly and still retain his rustic character:

> But in Elizium how do they
> Pass Eternity away?

Thyrsis' rejoinder conflates planetary music, English sheep dogs, and allusions to the Golden Age in an attempt to reassure the shepherd lass:

> Oh, ther's, neither hope nor fear
> Ther's no Wolf, no Fox, nor Bear.
> No need of Dog to fetch our stray,
> Our Lightfoot we may give away;
> No Oat-pipe's needfull, there thine Ears
> May feast with Musick of the Spheres.

This answer so intrigues Dorinda that she persuades her swain to share "poppies" with her, thus "smoothly pass away in sleep," and arrive in Elizium ahead of schedule.

Is the poem a religious allegory? Perhaps. Elizium is a land of "Everlasting day," the inevitable resting place of the "Chast Soul": "Heaven's the Center of the Soul." But these religious allusions do not form a consistent pattern, nor are they meaningful additions to the dramatic situation of this dialogue between a shepherd and his lass. The subject seems to be, ultimately, the attractiveness of heaven, but if the pastoral is Christian in this sense, its message—that one may anticipate the joys of heaven with a suicidal "poppy"—is distinctly un-Christian. If the poem is allegorical, its dark conceit leaves a reader in obscurity. Since Marvell was a sophisticated man, an urban wit, he could not have found the convention—admittedly often broken—of rustic speakers and rude diction entirely to his taste; and he had apparently not yet learned to use the pastoral form successfully to hint at complicated notions, to "insinuate and glaunce at greater matters."

Marvell himself wrote a kind of poetic commentary on the difficulty of expressing complex matters through the simple diction of unsophisticated shepherds and shepherdesses. "Clorinda and Damon" resembles "Thyrsis and Dorinda" in its concern with Christian rather than "naturalistic" values, but in "Clorinda and Damon" the rejection of *libertin* ethics has become the main dramatic issue of the poem. It is more successful poetry than "Thyrsis and Dorinda," mainly because its religious burden nowhere conflicts with the pastoral situation and vocabulary; the pastoral form has become a vehicle for "greater matters" that deepen without distorting the literal meaning of the pastoral dialogue. Clorinda represents the *libertine* shepherdess, dedicated to natural pleasure on the nearest "grassy Scutcheon," but Damon, mysteriously armed against her Marlovian blandishments, declines to live with her and be her love:

> C. Seize the short Joyes then, ere they vade.
> Seest thou that unfrequented Cave?
> D. That den? C. Loves Shrine. D. But Virtue's Grave.
> C. In whose cool bosome we may lye
> Safe from the Sun. D. not Heaven's Eye.
> C. Near this, a Fountaines liquid Bell
> Tinkles within the concave Shell.
> D. Might a Soul bath there and be clean,
> Or slake its Drought?

Damon explains that "Pastures, Caves, and Springs" no longer entice him, for the "other day" he encountered Pan:

> C. What did great Pan say?
> D. Words that transcend poor Shepherds skill,
> But He ere since my Songs does fill.

Not the Pan of woodland and stream, of riggish dance and goatish desire, but the Great Pan of *The Shepheardes Calender* and *The Nativitie Ode* whose ethics and words indeed "transcend poor Shepherds skill." This Pan is Christ, and thus what

began as a relatively slight pastoral lyric has become the vehicle
for a weighty event in scriptural history: the impact of Christ's
Revelation on natural man. And Marvell has been notably successful in communicating these "greater matters" without using
"Words that transcend poor Shepherds skill."

Presumably a man of Marvell's ironic disposition would find
techniques of indirection and allusion particularly congenial, but
there are obvious dangers in the use of such methods. Most obviously, there is the possibility that readers may misinterpret, or
even entirely overlook, the significance of a reference such as
that to "great Pan." The word, after all, is the same; it is the
meaning that has changed. Less obviously, and perhaps for that
reason more common, there is the danger of misunderstanding
what the poet intends to accomplish through the use of a particular allusion at a particular time: a single allusion, however suggestive, does not invariably mean that the poem is a detailed
allegory. It is this last danger that seems to have complicated
exegesis of "The Nymph Complaining for the Death of Her
Faun" (22), where the Faun—to mention only one of the controversial figures—may be presumed to represent everything from
Christ to the Church of England.[5]

"The Nymph Complaining" is admittedly thick with classical
and Christian allusions, and they lend an effect of depth and
solidity to a work that could otherwise have been maudlin and
melodramatic in tone. But it will not do to mistake the function
of these allusions.

The Nymph's Garden can hardly fail to suggest the Garden
of Eden, and the Faun itself—"Lillies without, Roses within"—
clearly stands for a kind of Edenic harmony with Nature, the
original purity and innocence. Difficulties appear, however, when
the reader tries to anchor such symbolic overtones to a detailed,
inclusive interpretation. Consider the lines in which the Nymph
accuses the "wanton Troopers" of their crime:

> Though they should wash their guilty hands
> In this warm life-blood, which doth part
> From thine, and wound me to the Heart,
> Yet could they not be clean: their Stain
> Is dy'd in such a Purple Grain.

I think it is safe to say that Marvell nowhere wrote a sentimental line, but there is in the Nymph's words an emotional excess that lies just this side of the maudlin—until suddenly in the following two lines it is channeled into a spiritual context in which such language is entirely appropriate to its object, the Crucifixion:

> There is not such another in
> The World, to offer for their Sin.

If we now felt inclined, we might possibly see the poem in the following way: the Faun is Christ, the Nymph is the Virgin Mary, Sylvio is the God alienated by the Fall, the Garden is Eden, and what is really a very fine poem has become absurd. There is no doubt that this exegetical activity "enriches" one's experience of the poem, but surely it does the work a disservice to see a simple equation in such consciously oblique references. We are not dealing with one-to-one allegory but a technique of allusion almost random in nature:

> O help! O help! I see it faint:
> And dye as calmely as a Saint.
> See how it weeps. The Tears do come
> Sad, slowly dropping like a Gumme.
> So weeps the wounded Balsome: so
> The holy Frankincense doth flow.
> The brotherless Heliades
> Melt in such Amber Tears as these.

By establishing connections, at strategic points, between the simple dramatic situation and scriptural or other history, Marvell has transformed the traditional pastoral epicedium into an intense

experience; and although its intensity cannot be adequately accounted for in terms of the death of a faun, it seems equally
clear that the poem is not to be read as a detailed allegory.

For the moment, however, reading "The Nymph Complain-
ing" is perhaps less interesting than the difficulties in reading it.
Marvell was to make use of this technique of allusion in his
most unusual group of poems, those concerned with that strange
figure the Mower. Reminiscences of classical and Christian literature everywhere deepen the texture of these poems, yet the function of Marvell's oblique references remains obscure. And their
obscurity assumes greater importance in connection with the
Mower, for the poems in which he appears offer problems even
on the literal level, problems that seem to require an allegorical
solution. In the Mower episode of "Upon Appleton House, to
My Lord Fairfax" (59) the reader finds himself beset by difficulties
resembling those in "The Nymph Complaining." There is, however, this difference: the literal action, the basic dramatic situation, of the Mower episode seems completely intelligible only
through reference to another level of meaning.

In the Mower episode [6] the traditional shepherd is replaced by
the Mower, a figure who reflects something of the pastoral convention and something of what his name suggests. On the one
hand, the Mowers exhibit the usual idyllic charm of rural life;
from their sea of "unfathomable Grass" they "bring up Flow'rs,"
and their dances illustrate their simple, close relationship with
Nature:

> Where every Mowers wholesome Heat
> Smells like an Alexanders sweat.
> Their Females fragrant as the Mead
> Which they in Fairy Circles tread:
> When at their Dances End they kiss,
> Their new-made Hay not sweeter is.
>
> (ll. 427–32)

Yet their idyllic harmony with Nature may be shattered with incredible rapidity:

> With whistling Sithe, and Elbow strong,
> These Massacre the Grass along:
> While one, unknowing, carves the Rail,
> Whose yet unfeather'd Quils her fail.
> The Edge all bloody from its Breast
> He draws, and does his stroke detest;
> Fearing the Flesh untimely mow'd
> To him a Fate as black forebode.
>
> (ll. 393–400)

Viewed against the usual sentiments of the pastoral tradition, the incident is quite extraordinary: the moment of violence suddenly obliterates the mood of pastoral calm.

Thestylis, conventionally the simple shepherdess (often the simple shepherd!), is referred to as "bloody," her actions vulture-like: "Greedy as Kites has trust it up." "Death-Trumpets creak" in the throats of the parent birds, and the meadows suddenly become a "Camp of Battail," "quilted ore with Bodies slain." The entire incident has occupied only four stanzas (L–LIII), but the reader acquainted with pastoral conventions will want to know why it is there at all. What are we to make of it? The language is too forceful and violent to be dismissed as a fanciful conceit provoked by the sight of a few hayricks: the accident of the "bloody . . . stroke" seems to possess some significance above and beyond the literal level of the action. Unlike "The Nymph Complaining," however, this episode does not seem to allude to an area of experience in which the appropriateness of the violent language may be appreciated.

Of course, there are in the episode, as elsewhere in Marvell, many literary and historical allusions, and yet they seem to illuminate only the passage at hand and not the accident of the "bloody . . . stroke." But perhaps the pun on "Levellers" repre-

sents a covert allusion to the Puritans, so that "the Field" is the
field of Civil War, the Mower is Cromwell, and the "Rail" is
Charles? Or maybe the Mower is Fairfax . . . This kind of
reading, though variations of it have appeared persuasively in print,
seems to me to depend primarily on rare ingenuity and a real ability to confuse vehicle and tenor; it also requires a reader to attend
to one system of allusions while resolutely refusing to think about
others. What does one do with the references to "Roman Camps,"
"Desert Memphis Sand," "Pyramids," "Manna," "Marriners,"
and "Israalites"? Is Marvell warning his countrymen against the
menace of Israeli seamen operating out of Egypt? Note what happens when we actually *pursue* an allusion—those "Levellers," for
example. In Stanza LVI the "levell'd space" after the harvest
is described in a highly suggestive conceit:

> The World when first created sure
> Was such a Table rase and pure.

But if we are disposed to view this comparison as an attempt to
make the meadows symbolize the world at a certain moment
in history, we are quickly disabused in the next two lines where
Marvell draws on his knowledge of bullfighting to find a more
apt simile:

> Or rather such is the Toril
> Ere the Bulls enter at Madril.

Like the Nymph's Faun the Mower reveals a capacity for
harmony with nature, but as always in Marvell the relationship
of man and Nature is precarious, liable to be lost in a moment.
This double attitude will be familiar to readers of "The Picture
of Little T.C. in a Prospect of Flowers" (38), where the Nymph
"reforms" the "errours of the Spring" but is warned that an
offense against course of *kind* will shatter the idyllic relationship:

> But O young beauty of the Woods,
> Whom Nature courts with fruits and flow'rs,

> Gather the Flow'rs, but spare the Buds;
> Lest Flora angry at thy crime,
> To kill her Infants in their prime,
> Do quickly make th' Example Yours;
>   And, ere we see,
> Nip in the blossome all our hopes and Thee.

Such hints as this of darker depths in Nature are focused in the Mower, where they form a strong contrast to the more conventional tone of traditional pastoral.

Although the allusions in "Upon Appleton House" offer perhaps even more difficulties than those of "The Nymph Complaining," it at least seems clear that the accident of the "bloody . . . stroke" possesses considerable emotional significance for Marvell. Indeed, in "Damon the Mower" (41) the "bloody" interlude is repeated, this time within the convention of the pastoral love complaint. Damon, pining for the love of Juliana, reflects on his harmony with nature:

> And, if at Noon my toil me heat,
> The Sun himself licks off my Sweat.
> While, going home, the Ev'ning sweet
> In cowslip-water bathes my feet.

But Juliana is the source of "unusual Heats," all Nature wilts, and the "Massacre" of "Upon Appleton House" reappears with more serious consequences. Again all grass is flesh:

> While thus he threw his Elbow round,
> Depopulating all the Ground,
> And, with his whistling Sythe, does cut
> Each stroke between the Earth and Root,
> The edged Stele by careless chance
> Did into his own Ankle glance;
> And there among the Grass fell down,
> By his own Sythe, the Mower mown.

Again the reader of "decorative" pastoral is unprepared for the sharply detailed, realistic moment of violence, and again he does not quite know what to make of it. Although the commonplaces of pastoral hyperbole have become strangely serious, there is no real explanation for the darker implications of the piece, suggested but undefined:

> Only for him no Cure is found,
> Whom Julianas Eyes do wound.
> 'Tis death alone that this must do:
> For Death thou art a Mower too.

Surely the significance of the Mower would have been clear to Fairfax's circle at Appleton House, but to the modern reader there may seem to be a lack of awareness on Marvell's part that in the Mower he has created an ambiguous figure. At least, in contrast to "The Nymph Complaining," there is no technique to show the reader, more or less precisely, what the ambiguity means. Although it is evident that the Mower possesses considerable emotional meaning for Marvell, above and beyond the figure's literal significance, there is no context in which the "bloody" incidents are seen as purposeful excess, in which the force of the language is justified, or in which the capacity of the Mower for both harmony and conflict with Nature is resolved. The central tenet of pastoral verse, the idyllic correspondence between man and Nature known as the pathetic fallacy, has apparently been deliberately violated, and yet there is no overt explanation of why Marvell departed so radically from the pattern of traditional pastoral. The significance of these departures can be appreciated fully only in the context of the other Mower poems, only as we compare context with context in order to make private meanings public.

"The Mower to the Glo-Worms" (44) is a pretty little lyric that has no obscurities for someone not overcurious about the last stanza. The first three stanzas invoke the Glo-Worms, whose function it is to guide the "wandring Mowers." In the fourth and last stanza the "unusual" Juliana reappears, the Mower's harmony with Nature is again lost, and the whole affair is given an intellectual emphasis oddly at variance with the conventions of pastoral love lyrics:

> Your courteous Lights in vain you wast,
> Since Juliana here is come,
> For She my Mind hath so displac'd
> That I shall never find my home.

By ignoring the other Mower poems we could probably find a place for this lyric in the tradition of the pastoral love complaint —even though love is not explicitly mentioned in the poem. Certainly this "displacement" of the mind seems to be far less serious than the accident of the "bloody . . . stroke." And yet another poem in the series, "The Mower's Song," suggests that Marvell's use of the word "Mind" was anything but casual.

"The Mower's Song" (45) also concerns Juliana and the mind, and again Marvell adventures from the pastoral theme of harmony with Nature:

> My Mind was once the true survey
> Of all these Medows fresh and gay;
> And in the greenness of the Grass
> Did see its Hopes as in a Glass;
> When Juliana came, and She
> What I do to the Grass, does to my Thoughts and Me.

The pastoral harmony between the Mower and Nature no longer exists; the correspondence is in the past tense. As in "The Mower to the Glo-Worms," moreover, Marvell sees the lost harmony, the "true survey," as having had its basis in a particular condition of the mind, now lost with the coming of Juliana. Her presence —the word "love" is again absent from the poem—has dark implications for the Mower. The refrain,

> When Juliana came, and She
> What I do to the Grass, does to my Thoughts and Me,

recalls the violence of the "bloody . . . stroke" and once again demonstrates an imaginative refashioning of Isaiah's proposition: for the Mower all flesh is grass, all grass flesh.

Stanza II emphasizes the Mower's alienation from Nature and explicitly jettisons the convention of attributing human emotions to Nature by exactly reversing the terms of the pathetic fallacy:

> But these, while I with Sorrow pine,
> Grew more luxuriant still and fine;
> That not one Blade of Grass you spy'd,
> But had a Flower on either side.

The word "luxuriant," because of the ambiguous antecedent of "these," may be read as a significant pun: if the antecedent of "these" is taken to be "Medows," as the context requires, then "luxuriant" simply denotes exuberant growth; if, however, "these" is taken to refer to "Thoughts," its immediate grammatical antecedent, "luxuriant," then includes a pun on its old meaning of "lascivious." For it will presently appear that this poem and also the next to be considered—"The Mower against Gardens," beginning "Luxurious Man, to bring his Vice in use"—are about how man gets and employs his lascivious thoughts.

In Stanza III the Mower reproaches the "Unthankful Medows" that could a "fellowship so true forego," and then, in the next stanza, he turns to threats of "luxuriant" proportions:

> But what you in Compassion ought,
> Shall now by my Revenge be wrought:
> And Flow'rs, and Grass, and I and all,
> Will in one common Ruine fall.
> For Juliana comes, and She
> What I do to the Grass, does to my Thoughts and Me.

Ostensibly, the Mower's motive for revenge is the betrayal of the meadows that meet in their "gawdy May-games" while he and his "Thoughts" suffer from Juliana.

Although such an explanation seems more satisfactory than any derived from the literal action of "Upon Appleton House" or "Damon the Mower," it still fails to account for the darker undertones of the whole poem or the emotional metre and diction of this stanza, especially in the refrain, and in the third and fourth lines whose three commas and repeated connectives accentuate the slow, impressive movement of a heroic style. Granted that the intensity of such threats is common, if not to real lovers, then at least to their literary counterparts, it remains difficult to find a place for the Mower's threat in the pastoral tradition. Not only has the original correspondence between the Mower and Nature been lost, but now the Mower seems determined to contribute to his own alienation from the "true survey." Pastoral harmony has become pastoral discord.

But if we pause for a moment to examine the poem in more abstract terms, the situation may be summed up in such a way as to explain Marvell's modifications of the pastoral *kind* and to provide some answers to the questions I have been raising throughout. Man once existed in an ideal correspondence and harmony with Nature: the appearance of woman resulted in the loss of the ideal state, in the awareness of mortality, in the inclination to sin. This is, of course, the Christian story of the Fall of Man from the pastoral harmony of Eden.

The Mower, to be sure, is not Adam nor is Juliana Eve; the poem must be read with at least as much literary tact as is required by "The Nymph Complaining." It is not accurate to say that "The Mower's Song" is an allegory of the Fall of Man, but neither is it sufficient to plead that this is a very complex poem that new critics (from Puttenham on) should be assiduous to read on a minimum of two levels. The reader has been led to consider a pastoral love complaint in relation to an event in scriptural history, but the exact poise or balance that Marvell has achieved remains hard to state explicitly: genre becomes trope.

In "The Mower's Song" Marvell has avoided the limitations

of conventional pastoral almost entirely, and avoided them successfully, despite the fact that he is perhaps most oblique and indirect here. Since the poem is more subtle and carefully articulated than the Mower episode of "Upon Appleton House" or "Damon the Mower," a reader appreciates the significance of another area of experience, one that "transcend[s] poor Shepherds skill," without being confused by suggestive but irrelevant, or only momentarily relevant, terms; that is, by allusions and comparisons which, while they may throw light on the passage at hand, yet fail to form a consistent group amongst themselves.

There is in "The Mower's Song" a simultaneous blending of kinds of experience as Marvell accommodates the literary technique of pastoral to scriptural history. With the exception of one key word—"fall"—he does not even use terms ambiguously suggestive of scriptural events. Instead, he has made the plot or action of the poem significant in itself; the organization of the action and the relationship of the Mower to Nature are in themselves expressive of the Fall of Man. Even though the Fall is barely suggested by the plot, the diffuse connection established in the reader's mind is enough to provide an explanation of the characterization of Juliana and to reveal the basis for the Mower's ambiguous relationship with Nature. Genre has merged with scriptural history, as indeed it often had before during the Middle Ages and Renaissance. The genre that had always described *an* Eden here describes *the* Eden, the theological "home" of "The Mower to the Glo-Worms," from which man lapsed with the coming of woman: "For She my Mind hath so displac'd. . . ." As Golding's Ovid has it,

> Moreouer by the golden age what other thing is ment,
> Than Adams tyme in Paradyse.[7]

Which is not to imply that Marvell is "traditional" in any restricted sense; he draws on earlier pastoral, but he is not indistinguishable from the tradition. By manipulating the traditional form of the pastoral, Marvell has managed to make it an adequate vehicle for his own attitudes toward Christian history, for clearly he has not limited himself to a simple retelling of the story of the Fall.

Marvell sees the Fall primarily as a change that occurred in the mind of man, as a change in the way man looks at or thinks about Nature, because he carefully distinguishes between "Thoughts and Me" and takes pains to emphasize the role of the mind: "My Mind was once the true survey. . . ." The fifth and last stanza of "The Mower's Song" illustrates the attitude:

> And thus, ye Meadows, which have been
> Companions of my thoughts more green,
> Shall now the Heraldry become
> With which I shall adorn my Tomb;
> For Juliana comes, and She
> What I do to the Grass, does to my Thoughts and Me.

The grammatical structure of the refrain refuses to let the reader regard man's experience with Nature and man's experience of himself and his "Thoughts" as separate or unconnected. The Fall is seen as a change in the response of the mind to Nature: "Companions of my thoughts more green." Man's present spiritual condition is a tomb with Nature figuring as its decorative heraldry. Thus man's inability to think "thoughts more green" corresponds to his alienation from the "true survey" of Nature that he formerly enjoyed, from the Edenlike state of mind that allowed him to exist in harmony with a "companionable" and "compassionate" Nature.

The remaining poem in this group, "The Mower against Gardens" (40), reinforces the conclusions derived from "The Mower's Song," and provides even more explicit statements of Marvell's attitude toward the mind of man, the Fall, and Nature —all of which permit us to see that Marvell was engaged in the traditional Nature-Art controversy that we have examined earlier.[8] The lapsed, corrupted mind of man is the subject of the poem, the theological time is post-Fall:

> Luxurious Man, to bring his Vice in use,
> Did after him the World seduce.

Although the poem bristles with horticultural puns and theological allusions, the main theme is clear: Man, through the activities of his "double . . . Mind," corrupts the meadows—"Where Nature was most plain and pure"—and fulfills the threat of "The Mower's Song" ("Will in one common Ruine fall"). Theologically speaking, the fallen mind possesses for most religious thinkers some knowledge of good as well as evil, but here Marvell restricts himself to man in his knowledge of evil. He is represented as having overreached his natural limits and succumbed to the medieval vice of *curiositas:*

> And yet these Rarities might be allow'd,
> To Man, that sov'raign thing and proud;
> Had he not dealt between the Bark and Tree,
> Forbidden mixtures there to see.

Marvell communicates his theme by developing a contrast between the natural, untouched meadows and the artificial garden. The meadows are "sweet Fields" where Nature is free to impart a "wild and fragrant Innocence." [9] On the other hand, the activities involved in making the garden—that "dead and standing pool of Air"—are expressed in witty vice-metaphors: the bastard plant no longer knows the "Stock from which it came"; grafting produces an "uncertain and adult'rate fruit"; the emasculated cherry (stoneless) is induced to "procreate without a Sex"—for this "green Seraglio has its Eunuchs too." Thus two worlds are presented in opposition: one, the world created by man, is expressed in metaphors of "luxuriant" illegitimacy; the other, a world of fauns and gods, is the preferred state, where "presence" rather than "skill" is the ideal agent.

Man's emphasis on "skill" has led to a corresponding neglect of the innocence to be had from the "sweet Fields" of Nature. Nature, then, when not deformed by "Forbidden mixtures," still preserves something of the intercourse between heaven and earth that man forfeited through the Fall. Man's "double . . . Mind," on the other hand, has attempted to recreate, out of its knowledge of evil, the Garden of Eden—and the result is Acrasia's Bower.[10] Art has corrupted Nature.

I have been trying to define some of Marvell's fundamental commitments by pointing out a development in his thought and literary technique from the highly derivative and naturalistic pastorals of the fashionable world, to a criticism, especially in "Clorinda and Damon," of *libertin* ethics, and finally to the use of the pastoral form as a vehicle for the expression of his more mature concerns. Marvell was not of course unique in using the pastoral form for Christian ends; in fact, our historical perspective makes such a use seem almost inevitable. Given the "Christianization" of Vergil's Fourth Eclogue, the shepherds of the Gospels, the mystical glosses on the Canticles, and the medieval and Renaissance tendency toward allegory, it is hard to see how readers and writers could fail to identify a conception like that of the Golden Age, where a bountiful, beneficent Nature literally dropped food into men's laps, with the Christian idea of the Garden of Eden. Nor was Marvell unique in using pastoral as a way of responding to the division between Nature and Art. Given our knowledge of the tradition, such a use, again, seems almost inevitable. But if Marvell's use of pastoral is not unusual, his particular modifications of the tradition are, and it is here that the poet reveals himself and his philosophy of man most clearly.

The way Marvell manipulates the most venerable pastoral convention, that of man in idyllic sympathy with Nature, leaves no doubt that he was deeply preoccupied with man's double estate—his capacity both for harmony with, and alienation from,

Nature. This attitude toward man in relation to Nature is, moreover, not simply a matter of temperament; it has a firm, precise theological basis in the scriptural fact of the Fall from Eden and the consequences that may be supposed to have proceeded from it.

Thus three main traditions are necessary for an understanding of Marvell's poetry: the literary tradition of pastoral; the philosophical tradition of Nature and Art that has always been associated with pastoral; and the Christian tradition, which gives a particular shape and meaning to the other two. In the more poetic (and private) terms with which I have been working, Marvell sees the Fall as having produced a "double . . . Mind," one that possesses both the Mower's capacity for the harmony of the "true survey" and the alienation of the "bloody . . . stroke"; for Innocence and Vice; for Nature and Art.

Art or "skill" is the immoral activity of a "double . . . Mind" as it deals in "Forbidden mixtures." Marvell makes the matter most explicit in "Upon Appleton House," where the activities of "Man unrul'd" contrast unfavorably with the instinctively good behavior of birds and beasts (Stanza II). Stated in the conceptual terms with which we are familiar:

> But Nature here hath been so free
> As if she said leave this to me.
> Art would more neatly have defac'd
> What she had laid so sweetly wast;
> In fragrant Gardens, shaddy Woods,
> Deep Meadows, and transparent Floods.
> (Stanza X)

Nature, "orderly and near" (IV), produces Fairfax's garden, which is not artful but nevertheless "in order grows" (XXXIX). For Marvell the *locus amoenus* is, like Milton's Eden, the result not of "nice Art" but "Nature boon." Art is, in short, a principle of corruption, of false rather than true order, the instrument of man's further alienation from Nature and hence from God, whose Book of the Creatures human Art has deformed.

The Mower in these terms becomes a much more comprehensible figure. Clearly he is Marvell's symbol of fallen man, the lowest of the angels and the highest of the beasts, made in the image of his God and yet capable of the depths of depravity. The Bible notes that God made man upright, but he has sought out many devices, like Marvell's "Luxurious Man" who, "to bring his Vice in use,/ Did after him the World seduce." The result is the Mower, the natural man who displays a faculty for both harmony and alienation, a faculty possibly shared by all men in all times in relation to Nature. And yet Marvell's Nature is not Wordsworth's, because the one is ordered where the other is spontaneous. Similarly, the Mower is symbolic but not Symbolist, for the meanings clustered around Marvell's mysterious figure, while in the last analysis indefinable, are in an important sense neither vague nor illimitable but retain by association something of the firm outline characteristic of their theological formulation. Nor is the Mower's ambiguous relationship with Nature in any way Empsonian; the ambiguity is limited, defined, by scriptural history, and it may finally be resolved through reference to the theological fact of the Fall.

The themes of harmony and alienation, most clearly articulated in connection with the Mower figure, appear to be similarly, though less obviously, present in the ironic wit of most of Marvell's best lyrics, lending these deceptively casual verses the weight and precision derived from a specific view of man and the universe. There seems to be little doubt, for example, that "The Picture of Little T.C." would be an extremely slight effort if it were not for the last stanza, where the dark moral undercuts the courtly posturings of the preceding lines. The same is true of the concluding lines of "A Dialogue between the Soul and Body" (20):

What but a Soul could have the wit
To build me up for Sin so fit?
So Architects do square and hew,
Green Trees that in the Forest grew.

Here a knowledge of Marvell's general attitude toward Nature and Art permits us to appreciate the full force of the Body's wry comparison; the Soul is like the architect not only in its amoral capacity to "build" but also in its immoral capacity to use Art to deface "green" Nature. Marvell's language, perhaps to a greater degree than that of most poets, reveals its full resonance only in relation to the entire body of his lyric verse, which is the reason that T. S. Eliot has done the poet a disservice in suggesting that the critical task in the "case" of Marvell is "to squeeze the drops of the essence of two or three poems": "The fact that of all Marvell's verse, which is itself not a great quantity, the really valuable part consists of a very few poems indicates that the [distinguishing] quality of [his verse] is probably a literary rather than a personal quality." [11] It has seemed to me, rather, that the literary quality of this individual talent is, despite its traditional elements, highly personal.

Even the more explicitly religious poems are difficult to appreciate in isolation. "The Coronet" (14), for example, may appear at first glance to be a purely religious meditation, but it is to be read as a pastoral. The "I" of the poem speaks of his "Shepherdess," and a whole dimension of the poem vanishes if we are inattentive to what is involved when Marvell represents his "I" as a singer-shepherd. The poem is a paradigm of conversion, a dramatization, like Herbert's "The Collar," of the need for Grace through the deliberate cultivation and then rejection of blasphemous or religiously mistaken thoughts. Marvell's shepherd begins by announcing his intention to reform, to replace his Saviour's crown of "Thorns" with a "Chaplet" of flowers (his "fruits are only flow'rs" [12]):

> Dismantling all the fragrant Towers
> That once adorn'd my Shepherdesses head.

But he is forced to reject these thoughts, for he finds that pride, the "Serpent old," has become part of the "Chaplet" with "wreaths of Fame and Interest." (Chaplet means prayer as well as wreath, and therefore also refers to the song of the shepherd.) The ascent, as St. Bernard says, is through humility rather than pride; and thus the shepherd begs God to "disintangle" the "winding Snare" of Satan "Or shatter too with him my curious frame,"

> Though set with Skill and chosen out with Care.
> That they, while Thou on both their Spoils dost tread,
> May crown thy Feet, that could not crown thy Head.

The little Augustinian drama is complete, the progress from sinner to saved that so absorbed the seventeenth century ("The Collar," Walton's life of Donne, or Donne's "If poisonous minerals . . .") has been reenacted in the poem with great concentration of meaning. A good example of the concentration possible in this kind of pastoral may be found in the "curious frame" of line twenty-two: it refers first to the artful chaplet (poem and prayer and wreath) that is "set with Skill," the "skill" or Art that deformed the "Meadows" in "The Mower against Gardens"; but it is also refers to the human being, that overly curious creature whose Art may obscure the divine Nature within; and finally it refers to the poem itself, an object of curious Art that must be "disentangled" from human "Fame and Interest" in order to become a pure chaplet or psalm in praise of the "king of Glory." By the end of the poem the sinner has been saved, and the pagan shepherd-poet has become a David, that shepherd-poet who danced before the Ark of God.

Even in the poems of human love the theme of alienation from Nature through Art gives Marvell's tone a distinctive toughness, setting such a lyric as "To His Coy Mistress" (26) clearly apart from others of its kind. Whereas the lovers of Donne's "The Sunne Rising" are identified, in half-ironic hyperbole, with the universe, the sun being advised to

> Shine here to us, and thou art every where;
> This bed thy center is, these walls, thy sphere,

Marvell's "am'rous birds of prey" gain our attention through their isolation, their defiant opposition to the world:

> And tear our Pleasures with rough strife,
> Thorough the Iron gates of Life.
> Thus, though we cannot make our Sun
> Stand still, yet we will make him run.

This attitude of ironic defiance, the tough determination to live with one's nature though it is somehow out of joint with the world, has been much admired. Yet we have seen that Marvell's attitude is only superficially admirable in modern terms, for it stems not from the metaphysical disillusionment of the twentieth century but from the theological conviction that man fell from the ideal harmony of the Garden of Eden. In contrast to that of the Underground Man, Marvell's malaise has a cure within the terms of the system that defines the nature of his illness.

The fact is that Marvell, unlike most of his modern readers, thought it possible to recover the lost harmony with Nature, which before the Fall man had possessed in the Garden. There is more than a hint of the possibility in the ordered innocence of the Fairfax garden of "Upon Appleton House," where the recovery is linked to contemplative retirement. In the "Horatian Ode" Cromwell leaves his "private Gardens" and joins "wiser Art" to "Nature," so becoming the union of active and contemplative or the "Man . . . that does both act and know." But the clearest illustration appears in the contemplative lesson of "The Garden" (48), probably Marvell's most famous and variously read poem. The themes of alienation and harmony, of Art and Nature, are present in "The Garden," and probably it could be demonstrated that they are as sure a guide to the total attitude of the poem as any of the numerous influences already brought to bear on its richly suggestive verses. But here my purpose is only to round out this discussion of Marvell's pastoral experiments, to sketch the workings of man's "double . . . Mind" in its knowledge of good rather than evil. It is in this sense that "The Garden" offers a solution to the desperate condition of man implied by "The Mower against Gardens" and "The Mower's Song."

The speaker of the poem withdraws from the "busie Companies of Men" into the solitude and innocence of the garden, finding there what the reader of pastoral will recognize as an elegant condensation of the "soft" primitivism associated with the Golden Age:

> What wond'rous Life in this I lead!
> Ripe Apples drop about my head;
> The Luscious Clusters of the Vine
> Upon my Mouth do crush their Wine.

Doubtless these lines are sensuous, but sexual, hence sensual, connotations are more easily kept where they belong, in the background, if we remember that this is an account of what Nature really *was* during the Golden Age, animated in Marvell by a Christian neo-Platonism that saw the landscape tremulous with divinity. This garden is neither the Acrasia's Bower of "The Mower against Gardens" nor the spiritual tomb of "The Mower's Song." There Nature had been corrupted by the overcurious Art of man's "double . . . Mind," but here the intimacy of the speaker with Nature is meant to recall the harmony of the Garden of Eden. Here intimacy precedes the purification of the mind:

> Mean while the Mind, from pleasure less,
> Withdraws into its happiness:
> The Mind, that Ocean where each kind

> Does streight its own resemblance find;
> Yet it creates, transcending these,
> Far other Worlds, and other Seas;
> Annihilating all that's made
> To a green Thought in a green Shade.

The withdrawal of the mind, creating an inner world of Nature and annihilating the outer world corrupted by Art, precedes the illumination of the soul in the next stanza; thus for a moment the poet, translating physical into spiritual geography, recovers the "true survey" of "The Mower's Song."

Through the process of "annihilation" the speaker has managed to think "thoughts more green" in a world seduced by the Art of "Luxurious Man." Art, or "all that's made" by the mind of man, has been transformed into Nature, or the "green Thought in a green Shade." Within himself the speaker has formed a garden, a paradise notably free of dainty devices: this is the *hortus conclusus* of the mind, established within not by Art but by the other impulse of that "double . . . Mind," by "Annihilating all that's made/ To a green Thought in a green Shade." The Mower has, after all, found his "home," the spiritual residence of Adam's sons located in the dark backward and abysm of theological time, and his return has fulfilled the promise of Milton's angel:

> then wilt thou not be loth
> To leave this Paradise, but shalt possess
> A Paradise within thee, happier far.

To us Marvell's attitude toward Nature and Art perhaps seems primitivist, even rigidly anti-intellectual, and yet his intention probably extended no farther than the effort of the moralist to put matters in proper perspective: so that salvation might be attained, so that the lost pastoral innocence, the paradisiacal integrity of Nature, might be reconstituted with the aid alone of literary Art in the garden of the mind.

Epilogue

This has been an inquiry into the origins and literary consequences of those two "vast and all-comprehending Dominions
of Nature and Art." I have sought to write not a history of Nature and Art nor even a comprehensive analysis of pastoral, but
rather to explore the more notable moments of interaction between the "all-comprehending Dominions" and the particular
species of allegorical pastoral that is tropical instead of topical.
Despite these limitations it may be hoped that the investigation
lends new significance to an old aspect of Renaissance thought,
and may therefore be taken as a plea for greater flexibility in our
understanding of what scholarship has accustomed us to call the
Elizabethan World Picture. It is not that the "Dominions of
Nature and Art" cannot be assimilated to what we already know
—Chapter I, I believe, makes that amply clear; it is rather that
a reader needs always to be aware that the Renaissance had at its
disposal significant ways of categorizing experience, of organizing thought, that cannot be immediately understood through
recourse, say, to the great chain of being. The need for vigilance
becomes particularly acute as we proceed, for in the late sixteenth
and early seventeenth centuries the divided and distinguished
worlds of Nature and Grace, together with the further division
into Nature and Art, began to assume, especially in Puritan controversy and scientific discourse, progressively greater importance: in line with the prevailing tendency of the period the
vocabulary created by antiquity and the Middle Ages was being
directed to new ends.

Western man had early developed a sophisticated awareness
of the differences that may be perceived between what was made

(Nature) and what he himself made (Art), between what was spontaneous and unreflective in himself (Nature) and what was the result of conscious intellection and acquired habit (Art). Even in the myths of Prometheus and the Golden Age there are unmistakable traces of the attempt to make the stories subserve one or another attitude toward the "true" relationship of Nature to Art. Later ages expressed their awareness of the division in pastoral literature, which assimilated the myth of the Golden Age, and in philosophic controversy, which brought myth into the purview of logical discourse. But it was not until the Renaissance that philosophy fused with poetry to provide the circumstances necessary for Book VI of *The Faerie Queene, The Winter's Tale,* and Marvell's allusive verse. Although the pastoral genre had always mirrored implicitly the division between Nature and Art that philosophy debated explicitly, it was necessary for the genre to develop fully its allegorical potentiality before there could occur the striking cross-fertilization of the sixteenth and seventeenth centuries.

If, as seems certain, Theocritus alluded to himself and to his fellow poets under the guise of shepherds in at least some of the Idyls, it is plain that in one sense pastoral has possessed allegorical tendencies from its recorded beginnings. It is essentially the same kind of allegory that reappears in much of Renaissance poetry, as when Spenser anagrammatically alludes in *The Shepheardes Calender* to Grindal under the name of Algrind or when Milton uses "Lycidas" to speak of Edward King. Considered precisely, this kind of thing is less an art of allegory than a technique of allusion: it could lead to complicated political satire and learned animadversions upon a corrupt clergy, but it must be recognized that here lie only the most remote origins of the use of pastoral in literature like *The Winter's Tale.* Before reaching Spenser and Shakespeare it was necessary that the entire form become "allegorical," an emblem or trope of the world at a particular moment in spiritual history: genre had to become metaphor.

In this view the process of development really begins in Vergil. Theocritus had succeeded in maintaining a kind of balance between the possibly conflicting claims of the natural and the artificial, but with Vergil's fabrication of an emotional landscape in his Arcadian eclogues the genre entered upon a new phase: the country of Arcadia, once peopled ungraciously with "acorn-eating swine," began to assume the shape of an unattainable ideal, inhabited by shepherds whose natural delicacy tended to issue in harmonious lyrics. Each eclogue, like most of the lives it depicted, became a rounded whole, fit vehicle for a new range of emotion that included dignified nostalgia for a time of lost innocence. And yet even in Vergil there is nothing like the philosophic debate that engaged the attention of Shakespeare's Perdita and Polixenes; nor is there anything that could fairly be called the doctrinal preference for Nature unspoiled by Art that informs so much of Renaissance poetry. The case is a little different with *Daphnis and Chloe*. In Longus, Vergil's aesthetic ordering of experience assumes a moral cast that verges on the doctrinal: the distinctive quality of the green world, where Daphnis and Chloe are brought up and to which they elect to return, betrays Longus' tendency to identify evil with Art and Nature with benevolence, with the result that the pastoral romance embodies quasi-philosophical principles that later proved attractive to the Renaissance.

But the example of Longus, or at least the example of the position he more than half adopted, could not be immediately acceptable to most Christian writers. Pauline Christianity had imbued many of its adherents with a deep-seated distrust of Nature, so that it was first necessary somehow to decontaminate the genre before acceding fully to the kind of philosophic bias it possessed, at least by implication, in *Daphnis and Chloe*. Fortunately the medieval or Renaissance poet had two distinct traditions of pastoral on which to draw, and it happened that the one was allowed to neutralize the pagan implications of the other. Having ample precedent not only in classical but also in Christian antiquity, he could recall with the Psalmist that the Lord was his shepherd; that according to Peter he might hope to receive, when the chief Shepherd shall appear, a crown of glory that fadeth not away; that the Gospels relied extensively upon pastoral imagery; that David, the type of the shepherd-singer, had used his gifts to dance before the very Ark of God; that Solomon had given himself to the writing of a dream pastoral figuring forth the love of the Church for Christ; and that consequently it might be argued that even Vergil in his Fourth Eclogue had soared with no middle wing to prefigure the Nativity of the chief Shepherd. Thus both the form and the content of pastoral submitted to the allegorical impulse of medieval Christianity; in the hands of its Carolingian practitioners the genre, despite its heavy reliance on traditional devices, became a vehicle or trope for whole ranges of experience having little or nothing directly to do with the care of sheep. The same vocabulary was used—but differently understood: to describe the Golden Age was to portray Eden, to speak of Great Pan was to tell of Christ, to admire a virgin shepherdess was to adore the Virgin, and to indulge the pathetic fallacy was to depict with verisimilitude man's prelapsarian condition.

The landscape of classical Arcadia, associated with the Golden Age as early as Vergil, coalesced with Eden to shape from traditional materials a new whole incandescent with mystery: the Christian landscape of Renaissance pastoral. By no means all pastoral, of course, admits such specialized and oblique resonances; yet the tradition was sufficiently felt to allow writers like Spenser, Shakespeare, and Marvell to bend the genre to their distinctive literary aims. The green world could become a microcosm of the world as it should be or had been before the

Fall; within such a charmed circle divine Nature had no need of human Art, for there the providential basis of the universe was to be exhibited in its essential clarity, undimmed by the realities of a Black Plague or a London fire.

The topography of fallen Nature excited demonstrably different feelings, for the greater number of Renaissance moralists followed their classical guides in maintaining that since (fallen) Nature does not bestow virtue it is an Art to be made good. The opposition between the terms, initially linguistic, had very early begun to trouble the surface of Greek thought; and by the time of Plato the pairing of Nature and Art was not only an analytical convenience, a way of organizing experience, but also a philosophical "problem" in the grand debate between primitivist and anti-primitivist strains in antique philosophy. In Aristotle, Seneca, and Cicero, as well as in Plato, there may be observed a tendency to ascribe normative function to Nature; consequently there are passages in all these writers susceptible of primitivistic or even "naturalistic" interpretation. But when such passages are assessed in context it appears that each of these representative thinkers finally resists the idea of fundamental conflict between the terms. In line with the primarily ethical bent of their philosophies they would have found much of themselves in Herrick's epigram "Upon Man":

> Man is compos'd here of a two-fold part;
> The first of Nature, and the next of Art:
> Art presupposes Nature; Nature shee
> Prepares the way to mans docility.

Because of the medieval emphasis on the order of grace rather than the order of nature, the division between Nature and Art gradually relinquished much of the philosophical immediacy it had possessed for the writers of classical antiquity. Nevertheless, the use of the terms persisted, not only in the deep storage of the medieval encyclopedists but also in the work of poets like

Jean de Meun and philosophers like John of Salisbury. Thus when the writers of the Renaissance felt called upon to describe new experiences, as for example the Natural Man of the New World, there lay close to hand, both through the recovery of classical texts and through medieval modifications, the ancient and perennially useful division between Nature and Art.

The terms exercised a particularly seductive fascination on the writers of the Renaissance, for the renewed emphasis on the order of nature invited a return to many of the classical methods of dealing with experience. Fludd's "mirror of Nature and image of Art" offers a convenient way of visualizing the result: a universe governed ultimately by God but ordered most immediately by the two efficient causes of *Natura* and her ape *Ars*. When used together the terms represented an almost infinitely flexible and yet "real" principle of classification that might be used to define the most fundamental relationships within the order of nature. Consequently it is not surprising that writers so diverse as Montaigne and Hooker had recourse to the division in expressing their awareness of themselves and the world in which they lived. Although interpretations of the relative importance of Nature and Art differed radically, even within the same writers, the division itself remained a constant in discourse about subjects so apparently unrelated as gardening, education, elegiac criticism, and cosmetics.

Spenser and Shakespeare relied on this background they shared with their readers in making the philosophical division serve literary ends. In many ways the two poets are remarkably similar in their use of Nature and Art as an integral part of the pastoral form. Both accept the venerable association of the literary genre with the philosophical division as a collaboration that lies quite within the bounds of decorum. Both rely on the symbolic possibilities of the pastoral as an element of resolution in plots that involve the court as well as the country; in both writers the pastoral episode is not merely decorative but has structural function and symbolizes ideal, even prelapsarian, Nature. Both poets pursue the implications of the division in several areas of human endeavor—fine arts, horticulture, manners and morals. Both reveal considerable mastery of what is historically a tricky opposition; and the complexity of their treatment, despite the utterly conventional quality of the materials employed, implies that their readers possessed in common an easy familiarity with the pastoral uses of Nature and Art. For neither poet is the reliance upon the terms merely a result of verbal habit; although both are on occasion quite prepared to reiterate the commonplace rejectamenta of tradition, Book VI of *The Faerie Queene* and *The Winter's Tale* reveal a disposition to use the genre and the division to construct vital fictions, to think with and about the terms.

By the time of the writing of *The Winter's Tale,* however, the new philosophies had already begun to call the old in doubt, so that it may fairly be questioned whether Shakespeare's handling of the ancient themes differs, where it does differ, from Spenser's only because of the temperamental and aesthetic differences that separate the two men. Shakespeare, for example, appears more self-conscious in his artistry, in the sense that he is more disposed to explain and less ready to take for granted; it is only superficially paradoxical that he allows Perdita and Polixenes to express more overt "philosophy" and at the same time reveals throughout less implicit faith in the importance of assigning "right" or absolute values to Nature and Art. One may think here of A. N. Whitehead's famous advice in *Science and the Modern World;* when the object is the criticism of the philosophy of an age, attention should not be directed chiefly to the positions explicitly defended but to those fundamental assumptions that even adherents of diverse philosophies unconsciously presuppose: "Such assumptions appear so obvious that people do not know what they are assuming because no other way of putting things has ever occurred to them." Where Spenser's attempt to place "courtesy" accurately within the order of nature slips into an almost unconscious reliance on the terms, Shakespeare's use of the division is explicitly the occasion for dramatic irony and philosophical debate; where one can afford to assume, the other, apparently, must assert and explain.

Clearly, however, there are so many imponderables—the most obvious being Shakespeare's and Spenser's genius for resisting easy generalization—that it would be simple-minded to give much credence to these historical speculations. And yet the example of Andrew Marvell makes it difficult to ignore the possibility that the historical circumstances propitious for the union of Nature and Art were in the process of change and decay. It is at least unmistakable that Marvell extends the tradition and brings it to a close; beyond this point it would have been hazardous to venture because it would mean the abandonment of all respect for public meaning. His pastorals, the best of which were probably written to intrigue a small circle of literati at Fairfax's Appleton House, modify the tradition with unexampled subtlety. The poet's detached wit and oblique allusiveness exploit the capacity of the genre to become a metaphor or emblem of man's condition at specific moments in scriptural history; suffused with disciplined nostalgia for the lost integrity of the Garden, his poems mark a point in the history of pastoral and of Nature and Art that was to be misunderstood by even the next literary generation.

It was not that poets no longer wrote pastorals, nor even that philosophers no longer debated the relative excellence of Nature and Art. Pope not only wrote elegant pastoral verse; he also advised his readers (in a manner reminiscent of Dante and Sir Thomas Browne) that "All Nature is but Art unknown to thee." But his pastorals, ruled by a newly awakened sense of decorum, were unencumbered by those "irreverend combinations" that discomfited Dr. Johnson in the presence of "Lycidas"; and the *Essay on Man,* its epigrams resonant with traditional phrasing, harbored the spirit of Leibnitz rather than Hooker. Even before the death of Marvell, Hobbes had begun his *Leviathan* with Browne's premise that "Nature" is the "Art whereby God hath made and governes the World," but the passage that immediately follows makes the traditional phrasing serve heterodox opinion:

Art goes yet further, imitating that Rationall and most excellent worke of Nature, Man. For by Art is created that great LEVIATHAN called a COMMON-WEALTH or STATE, (in latine CIVITAS) which is but an Artificiall Man.

The crucial inversion—that the state is a creation of Art rather than Nature—symbolizes in the political sphere the obliteration of Fludd's universe, the universe of Spenser, Shakespeare, and Marvell. During the following centuries, as writers first realized in verse the ideals of neoclassical decorum and then professed to sing in "profuse strains of unpremeditated art," the pastoral genre and the philosophical terms persisted, though as diminished things, all the while acquiring new meanings, new methods, new aims. The shepherd was no longer *personnage régnant,* no longer a compelling focus for the refracted aspirations of the age. In the sixteenth century the bucolic hero had preempted the place of Everyman, the pilgrim of medieval life; and it was now the shepherd's turn to swell the progress of a literary line—first The True Wit, then The Man of Feeling—that more nearly embodied the sentiments and ideas of succeeding generations. The particular alliance of genre and philosophy that informed a significant portion of Renaissance literature was never to be recovered.

For a moment in history reliance on those two "vast and all-comprehending Dominions of Nature and Art" had been so complete that the terms could dictate as well as express thought. It is widely appreciated that the intimate connection between language and thought may work either to the detriment or advantage of a writer, and professors are quite properly accustomed to emphasize the detrimental aspects of the connection, if only because it is easy for a student to believe he is thinking when he is actually soothing sore muscles in a tub of tepid phrases. Yet within certain limits stereotyped language may be held to possess a use and validity of its own. Even Dr. Johnson admitted that we may speak cant so long as we do not think it, acknowledging in effect that many events, such as breakfast, simply ought not to require a fresh response to the universe. In the interest of politeness, economy, or easy comprehension we automatically affix the conventional epithet to the commonplace occurrence. Doubtless we do not live each day so intensely as Thoreau, but when night comes we have had less trouble with the tax collector. The commonplace division between Nature and Art—sometimes antithetical, sometimes complementary—afforded minor writers a chance to deal clearly if not distinctively with life, to square their universe momentarily to human dimensions. And to greater men, Nature and Art, shared with an audience sensitive to their manifold import and to the symbolic uses of pastoral, offered the means to strike an arrestingly beautiful line of purpose across experience.

Notes

INTRODUCTION

1. See M. H. Abrams, *The Mirror and the Lamp* (New York, 1958), pp. 103–24, esp. p. 122.

2. "Nature, of course, and her Ape, which we call Art." The quotation comes from Robert Fludd, *De macrocosmi historia,* Vol. I of *Utriusque cosmi maioris scilicet et minoris metaphysica, physica atque technica historia* (Oppenheim, 1617), p. 7. The illustration appears on pp. 4–5.

3. *Commentaires et annotations sur la sepmaine de la creation dv monde de Gvillavme de Saluste Seigneur du Bartas* (Paris, 1583), p. 12.

4. A. O. Lovejoy and George Boas, *Primitivism and Related Ideas in Antiquity* (Baltimore, 1935), pp. 447–56.

5. From the dedicatory epistle to his translation of Gassendi's life of Peiresc. *The Mirrour of True Nobility & Gentility: Being the Life of the Renowned Nicolaus Claudius Fabricius, Lord of Peiresk* (London, 1657), sig. A3^v.

6. For the slippery task of treating ideas in relation to literature, see A. O. Lovejoy, *The Great Chain of Being* (Cambridge, Mass., 1936), pp. 3–23; Lionel Trilling, *The Liberal Imagination* (New York, 1953), pp. 268–87; and R. S. Crane, "Literature, Philosophy, and the History of Ideas," *MP,* LII (1954), 73 ff.

7. Frank Kermode's stimulating Introduction to *English Pastoral Poetry* (London, 1952) emphasizes, so far as I know for the first time, the relation of pastoral to Nature and Art.

8. Most modern writers on the pastoral accept this distinction. The standard history in English is W. W. Greg, *Pastoral Poetry and Pastoral Drama* (London, 1906). A fine short account is that of E. K. Chambers, "The English Pastoral," *Sir Thomas Wyatt: And Some Collected Studies* (London, 1933), pp. 146–80, available also as the introduction to his edition of *English Pastorals* (London, n.d.). The account to which I am most indebted is Frank Kermode's Introduction to *English Pastoral Poetry*. But see also William Empson, *Some Versions of Pastoral* (London, 1935), for an analysis that sees pastoral not as a literary *kind* in the strict sense but more as a manner of perceiving the world. For an account aimed

almost exclusively at Italian, French, and Spanish pastoral, see *La Pastorale: Essai d'analyse littérature* (Assen, 1950) by the Dutch scholar Mia Irene Gerhardt, also published under the title *Essai d'analyse littéraire de la pastorale dans les littératures italienne, espagnole et française* (Assen, 1950).

9. *England's Helicon,* ed. Hugh MacDonald (Cambridge, Mass., 1950), p. 34.

10. When Dr. Johnson *did* scent "allegory" in "Lycidas" he supposed it to produce "irreverend combinations." He was, as one might suspect, almost consistently anti-pastoral. On "Lycidas": "Its form is that of a pastoral: easy, vulgar, and, therefore, disgusting." "Milton," *Lives of the Poets,* Vol. VIII of *Works,* Literary Club Edition from Type (New York, 1903), pp. 85 ff. Pertinent comment occurs also in *Adventurer* No. 92; *Rasselas,* Ch. XIX; in the lives of Pope and Ambrose Philips; and in Nos. 36 and 37 of the *Rambler.*

11. *The Allegory of Love* (London, 1936), p. 352. Lewis does of course recognize the "allegorical" potentialities of the pastoral. Here I use him only to indicate the kind of opposition that may be provoked by men like the commonsensical, and eternally dangerous, Dr. Johnson.

CHAPTER I: *Renaissance Uses of Nature and Art*

1. Thomas Ravenscroft, *A Briefe Discourse . . . , 1614,* "Of Ale and Tobacco," *English Madrigal Verse,* ed. E. H. Fellowes (2d ed.; Oxford, 1929), p. 189.

2. *Poems on Several Occasions* (Antwerp, 1680), facsimile edition, ed. James Thorpe (Princeton Studies in English, No. 30; Princeton, 1950), p. 95.

3. *Ben Jonson,* ed. C. H. Herford and Percy Simpson, V (Oxford, 1937), 66–67.

4. Sir Thomas Eliot, trans., *The Education or Bringinge Vp of Children* (London , n.d.), sig. A4^v. Cf. Plutarch, *Moralia* 4b.

5. Ed. G. H. Mair from the 1560 edition (Oxford, 1909), p. 5.

6. Ed. Edward Arber (English Reprints; London, 1869), pp. 126, 41. Cf. Richard Taverner, *Proverbes or Adagies with Newe Addicions Gathered out of the Chiliades of Erasmus* (London, 1539), fol. xliiii^v–xlv^r: "Thurst out nature wyth a croche, yet woll she styll runne backe agayne. . . . A croked bough of a tree, be it neuer so much dryuen an other waye wyth a forke, or crotch, yet yf thou ones take awaye the forke, anone it returneth to that owne nature & course agayne. So in lyke wyse, yf man. . . ."

Erasmus is glossing Horace's "Naturam expellas furca, tamen usque recurret."

7. Ed. L. C. Martin, *The Poetical Works of Robert Herrick* (Oxford, 1956), p. 224. For similar sentiments in the same terms, this time on dress, see "Art above Nature, to Julia," p. 202: "I must confesse, mine eye and heart/ Dotes less on Nature, then on Art." Cf. Jonson's famous "Such sweet neglect more taketh me/ Than all th' adulteries of art."

8. "The Hovsholders Philosophie," *The Works of Thomas Kyd*, ed. F. S. Boas (2d ed.; Oxford, 1955), p. 256.

9. *The Civile Conversation of M. Steeven Guazzo*, first 3 books trans. George Pettie (1581), 4th book trans. Bartholomew Young (1586), ed. Charles Whibley (Tudor Translations, Second Series; New York, 1925), II, 12.

10. *The Anatomy of Melancholy*, III.ii.2.3. Ed. Floyd Dell and Paul Jordan-Smith (New York, 1955), p. 689.

11. J[ohn] B[ulwer], *Anthropometamorphosis: Man Transform'd. . . . the Native and Nationall Monstrosities That Have Appeared to Disfigure the Humane Fabrick* (London, 1653), p. 263.

12. *Flora: seu, De florum cultura. Or, a Complete Florilege* (London, 1665), p. 1.

13. *Essays, Plays and Sundry Verses,* ed. A. R. Waller (Cambridge, 1906), pp. 457 and 395. For Shirley's "The Garden," where "art" attempts to "purchase Nature," see *The Poems of James Shirley,* ed. Ray Livingstone Armstrong (New York, 1941), p. 16.

14. P. 5, as quoted in Harold S. Wilson, " 'Nature and Art' in *Winter's Tale,* IV.iv.86 ff.," *Shakespeare Association Bulletin*, XVIII (1943), 116.

15. Ed. G. D. Willcock and Alice Walker (Cambridge, 1936), pp. 303–4.

16. Reprinted from 3d ed. (1626) by Eleanour S. Rohde (London, 1937), pp. 39 and 36.

17. Trans. Ben Jonson, *Ben Jonson,* ed. C. H. Herford, Percy and Evelyn Simpson, VIII (Oxford, 1947), 331–33, ll. 581–86. Horace (ll. 408–11) runs:

> Naturâ fieret laudabile carmen, an arte,
> Quaesitum est. Ego nec studium sine divite vena,
> Nec rude quid prosit video ingenium; alterius sic
> Altera poscit opem res, & conjurat amicè.

18. *The Works,* ed. J. William Hebel, II (Oxford, 1932), 358.

19. *Poems and Translations; with the Sophy, a Tragedy* (London, 1709), pp. 85–86.

20. *Ad Lucilium epistulae morales* xc.44–45: "Non enim dat natura virtutem; ars est bonum fieri." *The Workes of Lvcivs Annaevs Seneca, Newly Inlarged and Corrected,* trans. Thomas Lodge (London, 1620), p. 379. Cf. the translation by Richard M. Gummere (Loeb Classical Library; London, 1920), II, 429.

21. Usury, for example: "It is also said by *Aristotle* that God is *animal sempiternum et optimum,* of whom both heauen and Nature doe depend; which nature is imitated of our arte as much as may be, for arte depending vpon Nature, shee is as it were her Chylde, and *per consequence* Gods Neipce. So that offending Nature we immediatly offende God, and he that offendeth arte offendeth God touching the hurt or annoyaunce of Nature; but the Vsurer offendeth Nature, for it is not naturall that money should beget or bring forth money without corruption." Thomas Kyd, "The Hovsholders Philosophie," *Works,* ed. Boas, p. 281.

Or the rhetorical debates between poet and painter where Nature and Art are almost invariably the crucial terms. See the account of the *paragone* between Nature and Art in J. H. Hagstrum's *The Sister Arts* (Chicago, 1958).

Or for a definition of occult philosophy that relies on the terms, see Henry Cornelius Agrippa, *Three Books of Occult Philosophy,* trans. J. F. (London, 1651), pp. 73 f.

For more respectable science, consider the program of the Royal Society, which aspired to make "Records of all the Works of Nature, or Art." Thomas Sprat, *History of the Royal-Society of London* (London, 1702), p. 61. See also Charles R. Weld, *A History of the Royal Society with Memoires of the Presidents* (London, 1848), I, 146: "In order to the compiling of a complete system of solid philosophy for explicating all phenomena produced by nature or art. . . ." Cowley, in the last lines of "To the Royal Society," lauds its history (*Poems,* ed. A. R. Waller [Cambridge, 1905], p. 453):

> T'has all the Beauties Nature can impart,
> And all the comely Dress without the paint of Art.

Or magic: "The works of Magick are nothing else but the works of Nature, whose dutiful hand-maid Magick is. For if she find any want in the affinity of Nature, that it is not strong enough, she doth supply such defects at convenient seasons, by the help of vapours, and by observing due measures and proportions; as in Husbandry, it is Nature that brings forth corn and herbs, but it is Art that prepares and makes way for them. Hence it was that *Antipho* the Poet said, *That we overcome those things by Art, wherein*

Nature doth overcome us; and *Plotinus* calls a Magician such a One as works by the help of Nature onely, and not by the help of Art." John Baptista Porta, *Natural Magick* (London, 1658), p. 2.

22. The seminal work is probably A. O. Lovejoy's *Great Chain of Being* (Cambridge, Mass., 1936), comprising the William James Lectures delivered at Harvard in 1933, but accounts perhaps more immediately useful to students of the Renaissance appear in Hardin Craig, *The Enchanted Glass* (New York, 1936), E. M. W. Tillyard, *The Elizabethan World Picture* (New York, 1944), Marjorie Nicolson, *The Breaking of the Circle* (Evanston, Ill., 1950), Leo Spitzer, "Classical and Christian Ideas of World Harmony," *Traditio*, II (1944), 409–65; III (1945), 307–64, and Theodore Spencer, *Shakespeare and the Nature of Man* (New York, 1955), which first appeared in the early 1940s about the same time as Tillyard's work. Here I closely follow Spencer in particular because his emphasis falls finally where mine does—on man—and because I believe his brief account retains sufficient balance to avoid such attacks on scholarly orthodoxy as Hiram Haydn's *The Counter-Renaissance* (New York, 1950). My own thesis, however, does not require a choice between Haydn and, say, Douglas Bush.

23. This brief exposition will have served to remind the reader of the idea of order as it appears in Raleigh's Preface to the *History of the World*, the first book of Hooker's *Laws of Ecclesiastical Polity*, the speech on degree in Shakespeare's *Troilus and Cressida*, the church homily *Of Obedience*, Sir John Davies' *Orchestra*, the *Book of the Governor* by Elyot, and, explicitly or implicitly, throughout most of Renaissance literature.

24. The labels given currency by A. S. P. Woodhouse. My exposition closely follows his concise formulation in "Nature and Grace in the *Faerie Queene*," ELH, XVI (1949), 195. *Vide* also "The Argument of Milton's *Comus*," *University of Toronto Quarterly*, XI (1941), 46–71. Mr. Theodor Gang has challenged Mr. Woodhouse, "Nature and Grace in the *Faerie Queene*: The Problem Revisited," *ELH*, XXVI (1959), 1–22, claiming that the distinction between Nature and Grace has no poetic significance. Mr. Woodhouse, "Spenser, Nature and Grace: Mr. Gang's Mode of Argument Reviewed," *ELH*, XXVII (1960), 1–15, replies that Mr. Gang's distinctions have no significance, poetic or other. My own argument does not require one to attribute "poetic" significance to Nature and Grace, just plain significance will do.

25. *History of the World* I.ii.5, *Works*, ed. Oldys and Birch (London, 1829), II, 58.

26. *The Nature of Man: A Learned and Usefull Tract Written in Greek* by Nemesius, trans. George Wither (London, 1636), pp. 20–21.

27. *Ibid.*, Wither's Preface, a justification of the study of the order of nature, sigs. A2ᵛ and A5.

28. From William Rand's dedicatory epistle to his translation of Gassendi's life of Peiresc. The phrase defines the object of Peiresc's enquiring mind. *The Mirrour of True Nobility & Gentility: Being the Life of the Renowned Nicolaus Claudius Fabricius, Lord of Peiresk* (London, 1657), sig. A3ᵛ.

29. *Works*, ed. Martin, p. 153. "Docility" here retains the sense of the Latin root: teachableness, educability.

30. "Description of the Intellectual Globe," *The Works of Francis Bacon*, ed. James Spedding, Robert Leslie Ellis, and Douglas Denon Heath, V (London, 1889), 507, 506.

31. *Anatomy of Melancholy*, III.ii.2.3, p. 683.

32. *De legibus* i.12, trans. C. W. Keyes (Loeb Classical Library; London, 1928), p. 333.

33. *Arte of English Poesie*, ed. Willcock and Walker, p. 303.

34. Cooper's *Thesavrvs* (London, 1584; first ed., 1565) offers the following synonyms in the "Ars, artis" entry: "Crafte: subtiltie: cunning: gyle: deceite. . . ."

35. Ch. 7 of "Voyage to the Houyhnhnms," *Gulliver's Travels*, ed. Arthur E. Case (New York, 1938), p. 286.

36. *Essays*, III.xii, trans. John Florio (1603), ed. W. E. Henley, introd. George Saintsbury (Tudor Translations; London, 1892–93), III, 322.

37. Pierre Charron, *Of Wisdome*, trans. Samson Lennard (London, 1640), pp. 273–74.

38. Apuleius, *The Golden Ass* ii.4. Cf. the 1566 trans. of W. Adlington, revised by Stephen Gaselee (Loeb Classical Library; London, 1947), p. 55, where *ars aemula naturae* is rendered "art envying nature."

39. *The Civile Conversation of M. Steeven Guazzo*, trans. Pettie, I, 124.

40. Sir Hugh Plat, *Delightes for Ladies, to Adorne Their Persons, Tables, Closets, and Distillatories*, first printed 1602, reprinted from ed. of 1627 by Violet and H. W. Trovillion (Herrin, Ill., 1942), p. xvii.

41. Hiram Haydn, *The Counter-Renaissance*, pp. 468–97, *passim*, seeks to associate the complementary relationship between Nature and Art with the "Christian humanists," the antithetical relationship with the "Renaissance naturalists." The generalization oversimplifies because it ignores the fact that Nature and Art mark a division in the order of nature, hence are broadly applicable, and therefore capable of different inter-

pretation not only by different writers but also by the same writers in different contexts.

42. *Epitaphes, Epigrams, Songs and Sonets* (London, 1567), fols. 102ʳ–103ʳ.

43. My purpose in what follows is schematic rather than historical. For the sake of managing simply a seemingly endless number of complications I treat "Nature" as if it were neutral and inert in combination with Art, invariably acted upon, as in Turbervile's poem, rather than interacting with Art. Needless to say, this is not always historically the case.

44. Thomas Underdowne's trans. (1587) of Heliodorus, *An Aethiopian History,* ed. W. E. Henley, introd. Charles Whibley (Tudor Translations; London, 1895), pp. 93–94.

45. No translator given (London, 1685), p. 9.

46. *Arte of English Poesie,* pp. 303–4.

47. St. Ambrose, *On the Duties of the Clergy* I.xviii.75. See *S. Ambrosii episcopi mediol. selecta: De officiis clericorum,* ed. R. O. Gilbert, VIII, *Bibliotheca patrum ecclesiasticorum Latinorum selecta* (Leipzig, 1839), 49: "Nihil enim fucatum placet." Ambrose is arguing that one should move "naturally": "Is not Nature herself our teacher, who has perfectly formed every part of our body?"

48. *Elegies* i.2.14: "Volucres nulla dulcius arte canunt." Trans. H. E. Butler (Loeb Classical Library; London, 1912), pp. 6–7. *Essays,* III.xxx, trans. Florio, ed Henley, I, 221.

49. Ed. Mrs. P. S. Allen (Oxford, 1925), p. 67. See also p. 66: "Nature . . . is ever best where she is least adulterated with Art."

50. "A Treatie of Humane Learning," ed. Geoffrey Bullough, *Poems and Dramas of Fulke Greville, First Lord Brooke* (New York, 1945), I, 158 and 160.

51. Ben Jonson, "Timber," *Ben Jonson,* ed. C. H. Herford, Percy and Evelyn Simpson, VIII (Oxford, 1947), 639.

52. "Religio Medici," *Works,* ed. Geoffrey Keynes, I (London, 1928), 22–23. Nature as the Art of God was a commonplace even before Dante.

53. George [?] Puttenham, *Arte of English Poesie,* p. 304.

54. This complicated notion may only be touched on here. An excellent short account appears in Madeleine Doran, *Endeavors of Art* (Madison, 1954), pp. 53–84. Miss Doran considers "Art *vs.* Nature" and "Art as Imitation" as complementary parts of the general problem of "Verisimilitude" in Renaissance literature.

55. Quintilian, *Institutio oratoria* i.pr.26. Cf. H. E. Butler's trans. (Loeb Classical Library; London, 1921), I, 19.

56. Bartholomaeo Keckermanno, *Gymnasivm logicvm* (London, 1606), p. 9.

57. *The French Academie,* trans. T. Bowes (London, 1586), p. 750.

58. *Arte of English Poesie,* p. 304. Here Puttenham is not talking about literary imitation, which for him (as for Aristotle) is creative as well as imitative.

59. For "The Ape as Metaphor" see Ernst R. Curtius, *European Literature and the Latin Middle Ages,* trans. Willard R. Trask (New York, 1953), pp. 538–40. The simile is commonplace in the Middle Ages and Renaissance and is by no means always prejudicial. In *Theophila, or Loves Sacrifice: A Divine Poem* (London, 1652), p. 194, Edward Benlowes sees virtue in proper imitation, vice in its reverse:

As Prudence fram'd Art to be Natures Ape;
So Pride forms Nature to Arts Shape.

The famous portrait of the Earl of Rochester—the Earl is crowning his pet monkey with the poet's laurels—burlesques the tradition by inverting the commonplace: the ape as nonmetaphor.

60. Longinus, *On the Sublime* xxii.1, trans. W. Hamilton Fyfe (Loeb Classical Library; London, 1953), p. 193. The next clause restores the classical balance: "and Nature succeeds only by concealing art about her person."

61. *Institutio oratoria* i.11.3. Cf. the trans. by H. E. Butler, I, 185. For another *locus classicus* see Ovid, *Metamorphoses* x.252: *Ars adeo latet arte sua,* rendered "so does his art conceal his art" by F. J. Miller (Loeb Classical Library; London, 1916), II, 83.

62. "A Poste with a Packet of Mad Letters" (1637), ed. A. B. Grosart, *Works* (Edinburgh, 1879), II, 11.

63. *Arte of English Poesie,* p. 303.

64. Giambattista Gelli, "I Capricci del Bottaio," *La Circe e I Capricci del Bottaio,* ed. Severino Ferrari and G. G. Ferrero (Florence, 1957), p. 203: "Se la natura producesse tutte le sue cose perfette, non bisognerebbe l'arte; e se l'arte potesse farle perfette da se stessa, non bisognerebbe la natura."

65. Greville, *Poems and Dramas,* I, 159. The lines display what Puttenham calls the dry mock, for here and elsewhere Greville sees in Art the vanity of human learning. For similar sentiments, delivered without irony and undisturbed by Calvinistical pessimism, see Arthur Wilson's dedicatory poem to Edward Benlowes, *Theophila, or Loves Sacrifice* (London, 1652), sig. C2ᵛ.

Though the brute Creatures by the height of Sense
Foretell their calm and boystrous Influence,
Yet to finde out their Motions is Mans part,
Not by the help of Nature, but of Art,
Which rarifies the Soul, and makes it rife,
And sees no farther than that gives it Eyes

. . . .

It sees plain Natures Face, how rude it looks
Till it be polished by Men and Books:
And most of her dark Secrets can discover
To open View of an industrious Lover.
What ever under Heav'ns great Throne we prize
Or value, in Arts Chamber-practise lies.

66. *Essays,* I.xxx, trans. Florio, ed. Henley, I, 221.

67. Greville, *Poems and Dramas,* I, 160. The context makes it clear that the poet's dislike for Art is balanced by his Pauline distrust of all but divine Nature.

CHAPTER II: *Classical Backgrounds*

1. *Primitivism and Related Ideas in Antiquity* (Baltimore, 1935), pp. 447–56. Primitivism, someone has said, is the intriguing notion that man can add a cubit to his stature by not taking thought. The pairing of Nature and Art may or may not convey primitivistic sentiments.

2. *The Dialogues of Plato,* trans. Benjamin Jowett (New York, 1937), II, 631.

3. "Nature and Convention," Ch. V of *The Open Society and Its Enemies* (Princeton, 1950).

4. *Primitivism and Related Ideas,* pp. 103–16. I simplify in the next few paragraphs a complicated series of shifts in meaning, adapting the argument of Lovejoy and Boas to my own purposes. For the interested reader they provide a detailed, fully documented account of how these semasiological changes relate to primitivism.

5. This particular distinction appeared in the pre-Socratic "physiologers." Plato (*Laws* x.891c.) and Aristotle (*Physics* ii.193a.9 ff.) use the word Nature to refer to this earlier contrast between intrinsic qualities and those apparent to the senses; here Nature is synonymous with "essence."

6. Cf. John Burnet's argument that the Greek tendency to deny the reality of the everyday world in order to find its ultimate "nature" in

some basic substance was paralleled in ethical speculation by an attempt to discern the "nature" of morality beneath everyday "use" or convention. "Law and Nature in Greek Ethics," *Essays and Addresses* (London, 1929), pp. 23–28.

7. The shift of "physis" into the terminology of ethics was intensified by the tendency of the *Hippocratica* to identify "natural state" with "normal condition" or "health." By the end of the fifth century the dignity of the term was increased even further by its having come to designate the cosmos as a whole.

8. In literary criticism there is the related distinction, later encountered in medieval and Renaissance rhetoric, between *naturalis* or *physikos*— the simple and unadorned—and *artificiosus* or *technikos*—complex and consciously articulated.

9. See Lovejoy and Boas, *Primitivism and Related Ideas,* pp. 103–16, especially pp. 111–12. Since Lovejoy is interested in the genesis of the normative use of "nature" as it pertains to the history of primitivism, it has been necessary to summarize from my own point of view and hence to adapt his research to slightly different (but consonant) conclusions.

10. *Essays,* I.xxx, trans. John Florio (1603), ed. W. E. Henley, introd. by George Saintsbury (Tudor Translations; London, 1892–93), I, 222.

11. See *Primitivism and Related Ideas,* pp. 167–68.

12. *Sophist* 265, trans. Jowett, II, 276.

13. *Laws* x.889, trans. Jowett, II, 631.

14. *Laws* x.890, trans. Jowett, II, 632. See also Aristotle, *Physics* 199b.30, and cf. Polixenes' argument—"over that art/ Which you say adds to nature, is an art/ That nature makes"—in Shakespeare's *The Winter's Tale,* IV.iv.90–92.

15. See Lovejoy and Boas, *Primitivism and Related Ideas,* pp. 155–68, for an analysis maintaining that finally Plato regards the antithesis as spurious. For an alternative and oversimple view, as applied to the study of literature, see C. S. Lewis, *The Allegory of Love* (London, 1936), p. 328, who implies that the absolute opposition of Nature and Art he finds (inaccurately) in Spenser is derived from Plato and Senecan Stoicism.

16. M. J. Charlesworth, *Aristotle on Art and Nature* (Philosophy Series II, Bulletin 50, Auckland University College, 1957), p. 13.

17. *Politics* i.1256b.15 ff., as trans. in Lovejoy and Boas, *Primitivism and Related Ideas,* p. 187.

18. For other senses of Nature in Aristotle, see the more fully documented account in Lovejoy and Boas, Ch. VI, pp. 169–91; here I have

culled from their argument only those senses relevant to the division between Nature and Art. Further quotations from Aristotle are as translated in *Primitivism and Related Ideas* unless otherwise noted.

19. *Nichomachean Ethics* x.1179b.20 ff. Cf. *Politics* vii.1334b.24 ff., p. 189.

20. *Politics* vii.1333a.21 ff., *The Basic Works of Aristotle,* ed. Richard McKeon (New York, 1941), p. 1297.

21. *Politics* vii.1334b.15 ff., p. 190.

22. *Politics* vii.1337a.2, p. 190.

23. *Physics* ii.199a.15 ff., p. 190. That is, Art "imitates" the *process* by which Nature brings something to completion. For a brief, excellent account of what Aristotle meant by his contention—variously read in the *Poetics*—see M. J. Charlesworth, *Aristotle on Art and Nature.* For a survey see Richard McKeon, "Literary Criticism and the Concept of Imitation in Antiquity," *Critics and Criticism,* ed. R. S. Crane (abridged ed.; Chicago, 1957), pp. 117–45.

24. *Physics* ii.199b.30, p. 190.

25. *De finibus* v.21.59–60, trans. Lovejoy and Boas, *Primitivism and Related Ideas,* pp. 248–49, whose account I summarize here from the point of view of Nature and Art. See pp. 243–59 for proof of Cicero's generally vigorous anti-primitivism, for his usually unequivocal endorsement of education, discipline, and the exercise of reason.

26. *Primitivism and Related Ideas,* pp. 252–53.

27. Trans. Thomas Cockman (1699), reprinted Everyman ed., introd. John Warrington (New York, 1955), p. 49. For Haydn's argument, see *The Counter-Renaissance* (New York, 1950), pp. 477 f.

28. *Ad Lucilium epistulae morales* xc, as trans. by Thomas Lodge, *The Workes of Lvcivs Annaevs Seneca, Newly Inlarged and Corrected* (London, 1620), p. 379. Lovejoy and Boas devote a chapter, *Primitivism and Related Ideas,* pp. 260–86, to "Stoic Primitivism"; my brief account of Seneca is indebted to this chapter.

29. See Henri Frankfort, *et al., Before Philosophy* (London, 1951), pp. 11–36.

30. *Essays,* II.xii, trans. Florio, ed. Henley, II, 151.

31. As quoted in Hiram Haydn, *The Counter-Renaissance,* p. 500. This economical way of pointing up the fundamental distinction originates with Professor Jefferson Butler Fletcher.

32. Other variations are possible, but enough has already been said to indicate the range of alternative interpretations. See Haydn, *The Counter-Renaissance,* pp. 497–524, and Lovejoy and Boas, "Chronological Primitiv-

ism in Greek and Roman Mythology and Historiography," *Primitivism and Related Ideas,* pp. 23–102. For Ovid, see *Metamorphoses* i.76–215, xv.96–142.

33. *Protagoras* 321, trans. Jowett, I, 92–93. In discussing this passage, Lovejoy and Boas, *Primitivism and Related Ideas,* p. 208, maintain that Protagoras satirizes the view that man would have been better off without Art. This seems doubtful. Protagoras wants eventually to show that virtue may be taught, and at this point he seems simply to be arguing that the practical arts are not enough, that man needs as well the political arts, which Zeus, according to Protagoras, later imparts to all men.

34. As trans. by Lovejoy and Boas, *Primitivism and Related Ideas,* p. 132.

35. Satire and pastoral were closely allied in the Renaissance, partly through an etymological confusion of "satyr" with "satire" (in many minds the railing satyr occupied the same general region of the imagination as the shepherd whose simplicity penetrates courtly artifice), compounding an earlier confusion of "satyr" with the Latin *satura* (satire). The matter is extremely complicated for us and was equally so for Renaissance commentators. See Madeleine Doran, *Endeavors of Art* (Madison, 1954), pp. 201–2.

36. Bruno Snell, *The Discovery of the Mind,* trans. T. G. Rosenmeyer (Cambridge, Mass., 1953), p. 286.

37. This insight into the significance of Vergil appears first in Erwin Panofsky, "Et in Arcadia Ego," *Philosophy and History,* ed. Raymond Klibansky and H. J. Paton (Oxford, 1936), pp. 223–54, especially pp. 223–40. But Panofsky throws off the brilliant perception in the course of another (related) argument, and consequently my greatest debt for the treatment of Vergil that appears in these pages is to Bruno Snell's thorough comparison and contrast of Vergil and Theocritus in "Arcadia: The Discovery of a Spiritual Landscape," *The Discovery of the Mind,* pp. 281–301.

38. *Historiae* iv.20; *Satires* vii.160; *Vita Apollonii* viii.7. As quoted in Panofsky, "Et in Arcadia Ego," p. 225.

39. It does in fact seem that Panofsky and Snell may be incorrect in crediting Vergil with the discovery of the ideal Arcadia. The *Eclogues* were not published until 39 B.C., but as early as 49 B.C. the figurative use of "Arcadia" seems to have been widely current. In *Ad Atticum* x.5, for example, Cicero quotes the reply of the Delphic Oracle to a Spartan envoy: "You are asking for Arcadia!" (Cf. Herodotus i.66.) E. O. Winstedt, *Letters of Atticus* (Loeb Classical Library; London, 1913),

II, 292, translates idiomatically: "You are asking for the moon." The Spartan, however, needed no translation, and Cicero appears to assume that his readers are familiar with this "Vergilian" allusion to Arcadia as a kind of unattainable ideal.

40. Snell, *Discovery of the Mind,* p. 288.

41. My generalizations about Vergil cannot be applied to the *Georgics,* where the tendency to idealize Nature is complicated by the inclination to glorify the Art of the husbandman.

42. *Metamorphoses,* trans. Rolfe Humphries (Bloomington, Ind., 1955), p. 6. Cf. Hesiod, *Works and Days:* "The fruitful earth spontaneously bore them abundant fruit without stint. And they lived in ease and peace upon their lands with many good things, rich in flocks and beloved of the blessed gods." Trans. Lovejoy and Boas, *Primitivism and Related Ideas,* p. 27. The idea of a Golden Age was so widely held that it became ripe for parody, as in the comic poet Pherecrates: "Rivers full of porridge and black soup flowed gurgling through the narrows with the very gravy sops and lumps of cheese cake, so that easily and of their own accord mouthfuls would travel, as if they were grease, down the gullets." Trans. Lovejoy and Boas, p. 39.

43. Andrew Marvell, "The Garden," *The Poems and Letters of Andrew Marvell,* ed. H. M. Margoliouth (2d ed.; Oxford, 1952), I, 49. Cf. Spenser, *The Faerie Queene,* II.xii.54, *The Complete Poetical Works of Spenser,* ed. R. E. Neil Dodge (Cambridge, Mass., 1936), p. 320:

> Archt over head with an embracing vine,
> Whose bounches, hanging downe, seemd to entice
> All passers by to taste their lushious wine,
> And did them selves into their hands incline.

44. From "Appendix on the Greek Novel," Stephen Gaselee, *Daphnis and Chloe* (Loeb Classical Library; New York, 1916), pp. 410–11.

45. There are perhaps nine romances surviving from the period before the Byzantine revival in the twelfth century, depending upon the standards one uses in counting. Of these perhaps three or four exercised any influence on the Renaissance. See. S. L. Wolff, *The Greek Romances in Elizabethan Prose Fiction* (New York, 1912) for a thorough account.

46. *Three Greek Romances,* ed. Moses Hadas (Anchor Books; New York, 1953). Numbers in parentheses will refer to the pagination of this edition. Hadas' introduction supplies the few biographical details I offer about Dio.

47. Although Lovejoy and Boas do not consider *The Hunters,* they do

make use of Dio's more specifically philosophical pronouncements in the same vein. See *Primitivism and Related Ideas,* p. 117 and *passim,* especially pp. 120–21. For the distinction between "hard" and "soft" primitivism, see pp. 9–11 of the Prolegomena.

48. As quoted in E. H. Haight, *Essays on the Greek Romances* (New York, 1943), p. 120.

49. I borrow the phrase the "green world" from Northrop Frye, "The Argument of Comedy," *English Institute Essays, 1948,* ed. D. A. Robertson, Jr. (New York, 1949), pp. 58–73. Frye uses it in a wider sense than I, making it signify a world of outdoor, magical nature, opposed to the "normal world." On p. 68, for example: "Thus the action of the comedy begins in a world represented as a normal world, moves into the green world, goes into a metamorphosis there in which the comic resolution is achieved, and returns to the normal world." My own use of the phrase is self-evident, but it may be worth while to add that while I restrict its meaning to pastoral, the phrase nevertheless serves much the same function in pointing to a world of "comic resolution."

50. Crane does not consider *Daphnis and Chloe,* but I quote his formulation here to acknowledge a general debt to his "Literature, Philosophy, and the History of Ideas." The quotation is from *MP,* LII (1954), 81.

51. Not that Tasso was allowed to be proper merely about what pleased. Naturalistic ethics were sharply attacked, producing the literary imbroglio over pastoral that eventually engaged the attention of Guarini.

52. *Comus,* ll. 706–55, *The Poems of John Milton,* ed. James Holly Hanford (New York, 1936), pp. 103–4. *The Countesse of Pembrokes Arcadia,* III.10, *The Prose Works of Sir Philip Sidney,* ed. Albert Feuillerat (Cambridge, 1962), I, 403 ff.

CHAPTER III: *The Medieval Contribution*

1. See George Boas, *Essays on Primitivism and Related Ideas in the Middle Ages* (Baltimore, 1948), pp. 105–6.

2. Fulke Greville, "Treatise of Religion," st. 7, *The Remains of Sir Fulk Grevill Lord Brooke: Being Poems of Monarchy and Religion* (London, 1670), p. 178.

3. "Epithalamion," l. 179. *Poems of John Donne,* ed. Sir H. J. C. Grierson (London, 1933), p. 123.

4. Thomas à Kempis, *Of the Imitation of Christ,* trans. Thomas Rogers (London, 1584), pp. 259 and 255. Two chapters are devoted almost en-

tirely to discriminating the "diuers motions betwene Nature and Grace."

5. Bernardus, unlike Alanus, verges at times on pagan humanism in his tendency to remove God from the creation. The history of the Goddess Natura is important but complicated. See Edgar G. Knowlton, "The Goddess Natura in Early Periods," *JEGP,* XIX (1920), 224–53; "Nature in Early German," *JEGP,* XXIV (1925), 409–12; "Nature in Early Italian," *MLN,* XXXVI (1921), 329 ff.; "Nature in Middle English," *JEGP,* XX (1931), 186 ff.

6. "Ars, licet imitetur naturam, tamen ad plenum opus naturae attingere non potest." Albertus Magnus, *De mineralibus* I.i.3, *Opera omnia,* ed. August Borgnet, V (Paris, 1890), 4.

7. See Vincent de Beauvais, *Speculum naturale* (Strassburg, c. 1481), I.viii.84: "Artificialia quoque non sunt eo modo quo naturalia. nec tam certa licet propinquo sint et similia. Quoniam ars debilior est natura. Nec consequitur eam licet multum laboret."

8. *Inferno* XI, trans. J. D. Sinclair (New York, 1948), p. 149. In *Purgatorio* X, Dante comes into the presence of divine sculptures that are Nature but nevertheless remain Art; for a brilliant analysis of this paradox, see J. A. Mazzeo, "The Analogy of Creation in Dante," *Speculum,* XXXII (1957), 706–21, especially 717 f.

9. Guillaume de Lorris and Jean de Meun, *Le Roman de la rose,* ed. Ernest Langlois (Société des Anciens Textes Français, 5 vols.; Paris, 1914–24), ll. 21,346–694. As translated by Harry W. Robbins, ed. Charles W. Dunn (New York, 1962), pp. 454–61; the remaining quotations are from Ch. 78 of Dunn's edition, translating ll. 16,005–248 of the Langlois edition, IV, 128–39. The F. S. Ellis translation, even as corrected when reprinted in Charles W. Jones, *Medieval Literature in Translation* (New York, 1950), badly distorts the meaning of this section on the traditional strife between Nature and her simian Art.

10. Many of the commonplaces appearing in *The Romance of the Rose* might be traced almost indefinitely. Ernst R. Curtius, for example, in *European Literature and the Latin Middle Ages,* trans. Willard R. Trask (New York, 1953), pp. 538 ff., sees the metaphorical use of *simia* in Sidonius, John of Salisbury, Josephus-Iscanus, Alanus ab Insulis, Geoffrey of Vinsauf, Dante, and others. To take another instance: the notion of *naturam vincere,* which in de Meun has been emasculated, appears more vigorously in antiquity, reappears in *Pearl,* ed. E. V. Gordon (Oxford, 1958), ll. 749–52, again in Chaucer (see Oxford edition, IV, 290 f., and note, V, 260–61, for other citations), and again in Shakespeare and other Renaissance writers. For Shakespeare and later examples, see J. H. Hag-

strum, *The Sister Arts* (Chicago, 1958), especially pp. 66–114. But to trace a variety of such commonplaces would only repeat the obvious.

11. The third was constant practice (*exercitatio*). See *English Literary Criticism: The Medieval Phase* (New York, 1943), p. 73.

12. See G. C. Fiske, *Cicero's De Oratore and Horace's Ars Poetica* (University of Wisconsin Studies in Language and Literature, No. 27; Madison, 1929), pp. 74 ff. Also Marvin T. Herrick, *The Fusion of Horatian and Aristotelian Literary Criticism, 1531–1555* (Illinois Studies in Language and Literature, No. 32; Urbana, 1946), p. 8. The earliest formulation known to me occurs in Pindar, *Nemea* i.25, but it does not seem to have been influential.

13. See John Edwin Sandys, *History of Classical Scholarship* (Cambridge, 1903), I, 56, and J. W. H. Atkins, *English Literary Criticism: The Renascence* (London, 1947), pp. 327–28.

14. See Herrick, *The Fusion of Horatian and Aristotelian Literary Criticism*, pp. 7–27, especially p. 25.

15. These minor controversies, intimately a part of the study of medieval rhetoric, may not be considered here because of their variety and complexity. The work by J. W. H. Atkins, *English Literary Criticism: The Medieval Phase*, may be supplemented by Richard McKeon, "Rhetoric in the Middle Ages," *Speculum*, XVII (1942), 1–32; Charles Sears Baldwin, *Medieval Rhetoric and Poetic* (New York, 1928); Thomas M. Charland, *Artes praedicandi: Contribution à l'histoire de la rhétorique au moyen âge* (Paris, 1936); and *European Literature and the Latin Middle Ages*, especially Chs. 3, 4, 11, and 12, in which Curtius considers medieval rhetoric more or less directly. The history of Nature and Art in relation to rhetoric is important but complicated. Quintilian, for example, argues for the use of both Nature and Art and says that the final aim of Art is to efface itself, but the historian cannot afford to leave the matter here. Curtius points out (p. 296) that Quintilian's purpose was to systematize the criteria of Ciceronian classicism and that this purpose ran contrary to the literary trends of his time, a time of mannerist poetry and Senecan prose: Quintilian, then, is not necessarily representative, and his work is to some undetermined degree polemical. When Quintilian was arguing for a particular balance between Nature and Art, the scales had already begun to tip toward Art.

To take another example, Curtius (p. 539) holds that Sidonius had about equal weight with Horace as a teacher of rhetoric in the twelfth century. Since the two men hold opposed views of the proper relationship of Nature to Art, the historian again experiences difficulty in generalizing about the period. Finally, even such qualifications as these ignore the further difficulty of interpreting what seems to be adherence to the "same" maxims. Curtius remarks (p. 539), for example, that Sidonius interprets Horace's warning against "purple patches" as an invitation to make a lot of them. What can it mean, then, to say that such and such a rhetorician "adheres" to the Horatian position in regard to Nature and Art? Before such generalizations can have much significance, it is necessary to test practice against theory, critical example against critical precept. Pious citations of authority may signify many things. Fortunately, an understanding of how Nature and Art reached the Renaissance does not depend on a detailed survey of medieval rhetoric.

16. *The Metalogicon of John of Salisbury: A Twelfth-Century Defense of the Verbal and Logical Arts of the Trivium,* trans. Daniel D. McGarry (Berkeley and Los Angeles, 1955), pp. 24, 33, and 34. See, in general, I.vi–xi. The standard Latin edition is that of C. C. J. Webb (Oxford, 1929). Cf. Atkins, *English Literary Criticism: The Medieval Phase,* pp. 72–73, and Herrick, *Fusion of Horatian and Aristotelian Literary Criticism,* p. 25, n. 66.

17. See Curtius, *European Literature and the Latin Middle Ages,* p. 77, and *Metalogicon,* ed. Webb, p. 7.

18. *Metalogicon,* ed. McGarry, p.35. Cf. *Laws* x.890 and *The Winter's Tale* IV.iv.88–97 with *Metalogicon* 839b, ed. Webb, p. 30: "Quia artium natura mater est, merito in iniuriam parentis redundat contemptus earum."

19. For example, Robert R. Cawley's *The Voyagers and Elizabethan Drama* (MLA Monograph Series, VIII; Boston, 1938) and his *Unpathed Waters: Studies in the Influence of the Voyagers on Elizabethan Literature* (Princeton, 1940) are of limited use because they ignore the influence of ideas. Douglas Bush's section on travel literature in *English Literature in the Earlier Seventeenth Century* (New York, 1945), pp. 170–80, addresses itself to problems different from those relevant here. C. S. Lewis, on the other hand, recognizes that the encounter with the savage could set up philosophical and literary reverberations. Although he does not choose to pursue the implications of his references to the voyagers (*English Literature in the Sixteenth Century* [Oxford, 1954], pp. 15–17, 307–8, and 437–38), on p. 17 he poses in a few words the problem of how America affected "philosophical thought" with its "image of the Savage, or Natural Man." Lewis points out that it is an "ambivalent image," for the "Natural Man" might be seen as "ideally innocent" or as "brutal, sub-human." Of the writers who are in one way or another aware of what Lewis points out, R. H. Pearce, "Primitivistic Ideas in the

Faerie Queene," *JEGP,* XLIV (1945), 139–51, provides the most useful examination of travel literature in the Renaissance. See also Frank Kermode's excellent introduction to Shakespeare's *Tempest* (Arden Shakespeare, rev. ed.; Cambridge, Mass., 1954); its usefulness is not restricted to Shakespeare, and it has particular pertinence here because Kermode discusses the accounts of the voyagers in relation to Nature and Art.

20. See Arthur O. Lovejoy and George Boas, "The Noble Savage in Antiquity," *Primitivism and Related Ideas in Antiquity* (Baltimore, 1935), pp. 287–367, for the citation of numerous examples.

21. Adam of Bremen is perhaps representative. See George Boas, *Essays on Primitivism,* pp. 152–53. My account of the medieval attitude toward savage man is based on pp. 129–74. *Vide* also Richard Bernheimer, *Wild Men in the Middle Ages: A Study in Art, Sentiment, and Demonology* (Cambridge, Mass., 1952).

22. The *topos* of the *locus amoenus,* and the rhetorical-poetical tradition of the ideal landscape in general, afford independent confirmation of this generalization. See Curtius, *European Literature and the Latin Middle Ages,* pp. 183–202.

23. "A Treatise of Monarchy," st. 1, *Remains of Sir Fulk Grevill,* p. 1. Greville refers to the Golden Age, a time of harmony between ruler and subject before "Pow'r turns Nature into Art."

24. As quoted by R. H. Pearce, "Primitivistic Ideas," p. 141, from Richard Hakluyt, *Principal Navigations Voiages Traffiques & Discoveries of the English Nation, 1600* (Glasgow, 1904), VIII, 305.

25. Peter Martyr, *The Decades of the Newe Worlde or West India,* trans. Richard Eden (London, 1555), fol. 8^r. Cf. the trans. by Michael Lok, *De nouo orbe, or the Historie of the West Indies. . . . in eight decades. . . . Whereof three, haue beene formerly translated into English, by R. Eden, whereunto the other fiue, are newly added by . . . M. Lok* (London, 1612), fol. 249^r: "They had the golden age, mine, and thine, the seedes of discord, were farre remoued from them: the rest of the yeere from seede time, & haruest, they gaue themselues to tennis, dancing, hunting, and fishing: concerning iudiciall courts of Iustice, suits of law, & wrangling, and brawling among neighbours, there is no mention at all."

26. *An Elegant and Learned Discourse of the Light of Nature* (London, 1652), p. 85.

27. Hakluyt, *Principal Navigations,* VII, 224, quoted by Pearce, "Primitivistic Ideas," p. 140.

28. Hakluyt, *Principal Navigations,* IX, 386, as quoted by Pearce, "Primitivistic Ideas," p. 149. Such examples might be multiplied; as Pearce

demonstrates, they far outnumber the more famous accounts of the golden world.

29. *Essays,* I.xxx, trans. John Florio, ed. W. E. Henley, introd. by George Saintsbury (Tudor Translations; London, 1892–93), I, 221–22.

30. Trans. Richard Eden, sig. A2ᵛ.

31. *The Arte of English Poesie,* ed. G. D. Willcock and Alice Walker (Cambridge, 1936), p. 38.

32. F. J. E. Raby's *History of Christian-Latin Poetry from the Beginnings to the Close of the Middle Ages* (2d ed.; Oxford, 1953) does not consider the subject. Ernst Curtius, *European Literature and the Latin Middle Ages,* asserts (p. 459) that a "monograph on this genre is one of the desiderata of medieval literary history."

33. *Pastoral Poetry and Pastoral Drama* (London, 1906), p. 19. This is the only full-length study in English. Another and more comprehensive work by Professor W. Leonard Grant of the University of British Columbia is in preparation.

34. Ernest Dümmler, ed., *Poetarvm Latinorvm medii aevi: Poetae Latini aevi Carolini,* I (Berlin, 1881), *Monumenta Germaniae historica,* 270 ff. Hereafter cited as PLMA.

35. The use of the Vergilian eclogue form to treat specifically Christian matters is found, for example, as early as the fourth century in a Vergilian cento by Pomponius (otherwise anonymous). See Curtius, *European Literature and the Latin Middle Ages,* p. 261.

36. L. Traube, ed., PLMA, III (Berlin, 1896), 45–51, prints the poem and the prologue.

37. Cf. F. R. Hamblin, *The Development of Allegory in the Classical Pastoral* (Published dissertation; University of Chicago Library, 1928), pp. 74–75.

38. "No more, mother," then says Sister Galathea. "These things which have now been considered we shall perhaps sing better of at that later time when joyful paradise shall in the course of things grow green about us. And yet meanwhile, until that time when allelulias shall sound about, pluck lilies and flowers of the field. Scatter the way with violets, the field with flowers of virtues, the path with roses; with lilies strew the courts." Traube footnotes echoes and borrowings from Vergil in this passage and in others; the point is worth emphasizing, for many medieval poems in this way turned Vergil to new uses.

39. E. Dümmler, ed., PLMA, I, 384–91.

40. "Charles holds together the people and the nations with his kingly protection; he rules all kingdoms throughout the world, and with his

holy power dominates the entire earth. For long now have I thought of him under the name of the sun that shines with bright gleams over the whole world."

41. *Development of Allegory in the Classical Pastoral,* p. 74.

42. *European Literature and the Latin Middle Ages,* pp. 261 *et passim.*

43. "Theodulus: A Medieval Textbook," *MP,* VII (1909), 169 ff.

44. The poem formed part of *Auctores octo morales,* a schoolbook representing the final canon of medieval authors; see Curtius, *European Literature and the Latin Middle Ages,* p. 261, n. 38.

45. Chapters I and II, *Development of Allegory in the Classical Pastoral.*

46. My account of the problem follows Curtius, *European Literature and the Latin Middle Ages,* pp. 443 ff.

47. See E. F. Wilson, "Pastoral and Epithalamium in Latin Literature," *Speculum,* XXIII (1948), 43 ff.

48. *European Literature and the Latin Middle Ages,* pp. 458 ff.

49. From the metrical foreword to his Gospel epic, as quoted in Curtius, *ibid.,* p. 459.

50. The story is one that requires no detailed reexamination here. For a useful account see W. W. Greg, *Pastoral Poetry and Pastoral Drama,* pp. 17–30 *et passim.*

51. *Pilgrim's Progress,* introd. Louis Martz (New York, 1949), p. 126.

52. *The Complete Poetical Works of Spenser,* ed. R. E. Neil Dodge (Cambridge, Mass., 1936), p. 27.

53. Not all pastoral, of course, contains religious allegory, and of the pastoral that does, not all exhibits these particular symbolic equivalences. Nevertheless, I describe the general pattern of religious pastoral and there is more of it in the Renaissance than is usually conceded.

54. There is indeed a widespread tendency in literature and elsewhere to confuse Elysium, Paradise, the Blessed Isles, Eden, the Hesperides, the Golden Age, and all the similar great dreams of mankind. No doubt they are all versions of a single archetypal pattern, psychologically exemplified in the individual by the desire to return to the womb . . . but such speculations must be waived in this study. They are outside my area of competence and have dubious pertinence to the kind of literary questions I want to raise.

55. *The .xv. Bookes of P. Ouidius Naso, entytuled Metamorphosis, translated oute of Latin into English meeter* (London, 1575), sig. A7ʳ.

56. Robert Herrick, *Poetical Works,* ed. L. C. Martin (Oxford, 1956), p. 153.

CHAPTER IV: *Spenser's Legend of Courtesy*

1. See *The Faerie Queene: Books Six and Seven,* eds. J. G. McManaway, D. E. Mason, and B. Stirling, Appendix I, p. 346, Vol. VI of *The Works of Edmund Spenser,* general eds. Edwin Greenlaw, C. G. Osgood, *et al.* (Baltimore, 1938–49). Further references will be to the more accessible text of R. E. Neil Dodge, *The Complete Poetical Works of Spenser* (Cambridge, Mass., 1936).

C. S. Lewis, *The Allegory of Love* (London, 1936), is one exception to the critical attitude I have been describing; on p. 350, for instance, he attacks the widely held notion that the pastoral episode represents a digression by pointing out that Spenser did not regard courtesy as specifically a courtly virtue. That it is therefore necessarily a pastoral virtue, however, is defective logic and, I shall try to show, oversimple reading.

Another notable exception is A. C. Hamilton's stimulating *Structure of Allegory in The Faerie Queene* (Oxford, 1961). On p. 204 it appears that the "story of Pastorella is the consummation of Spenser's fiction." Mr. Hamilton's conclusion grows out of the conviction that "what the image means, it is." I agree with the conclusion but feel uneasy about the conviction, partly because of my own conviction that "imagery" has less importance in the Renaissance than "theme." On the importance of "theme" in this sense, see Robert Langbaum's use of the word "plot" in his "Character versus Action in Shakespeare," *The Poetry of Experience* (New York, 1957), pp. 160–81; and, more particularly, William Nelson's cogently informative *The Poetry of Edmund Spenser* (New York, 1963).

2. Donne commits himself immediately:

> since there must reside
> Falshood in woman, I could more abide,
> She were by art, then Nature falsify'd.

"The Primrose," ll. 18–20, p. 61, *Poems of John Donne* (London, 1933), ed. H. J. C. Grierson.

3. Documentation for the assertion that Spenser was aware that noble birth did not automatically make a man virtuous might be culled from many of Spenser's references to courtly life, but it should be enough to point out that in the same canto that contains the commonplace analogy to the trotting stallion the fair Priscilla prefers—the implication is, quite properly, prefers—the "lusty Aladine, though meaner borne," to a "great

pere," because Aladine's "valour . . . did adorne/ His meanesse much, and make her th' others riches scorne" (iii.7).

Castiglione's arguments are worth quoting at some length here because they reflect orthodox opinion (in this case, Spenser's) and make use of the familiar analogies to maintain that, though Nature remains of fundamental value, Art may also be of use: "It chaunceth alwaies . . . that the moste famous menne are gentlemen. Because nature in every thing hath depely sowed that privie sede, thich geveth a certain force and propertie of her beginning, unto whatsoever springeth of it, and maketh it lyke unto her selfe. As we see by exaumple not onely in the race of horses and other beastes, but also in trees, whose slippes and graftes alwayes for the moste parte are lyke unto the stocke of the tree they came from: and yf at any time they growe out of kind, the fault is in the husbandman. And the lyke is in men, yf they bee trayned up in good nourtour, moste commonlye they resemble them from whom thei come. . . . Truth it is . . . some there are borne indued syth suche graces, that they seeme not to have bene borne, but rather facioned with the verye hande of some God, and abounde in all goodnesse bothe of bodye and mynde. As againe we see some so unapte and dull, that a man wyl not beleve, but nature hath brought them into the worlde for a spite and mockerie. . . . But . . . there is yet a meane, and they that are not by nature so perfectly furnished, with studye and diligence maye polishe and correct a great part of the defaultes of nature." Count Canossa is the speaker, in the first book of *The Courtier,* trans. Sir Thomas Hoby (1561), ed. W. E. Henley (Tudor Translations; London, 1900), pp. 44–46, and on the next page he deals with the objection that many men of noble blood are cads.

The controversy over the relation of birth to true honor appears in Aristotle (*Ethics* 1124a) and all over the Renaissance. See, among others, G. B. Nenna, *Discourse whether a Nobel Man by Birth or a Gentleman by Desert Is Greater in Nobilitie,* trans. W. Jones (London, 1600), p. 90; Sir John Ferne, *The Blazon of Gentrie* (London, 1586), pp. 14 *et passim;* Annibale Romei, *The Courtiers Academie,* trans. John Kepers (London, 1598), p. 187; Antonio de Guevara, *Familiar Epistles,* trans. E. Hellowes (London, 1577), p. 59.

4. *Works,* ed. Dodge, p. 136.

5. From the Preface of Peter Martyr, *The Decades of the Newe Worlde or West India,* trans. Richard Eden (London, 1555), sig. A2ᵛ; the attempt is to justify Spanish seizure of cannibal land.

6. Montaigne took those accounts of the voyagers that gave him the opportunity to dwell on the natural dignity of primitive man living in

the earthly paradises across the sea. However, we have seen that the majority of writers had a more favorable view of civilized man and consequently regarded the wild men with distaste. See R. H. Pearce, "Primitivistic Ideas in the *Faerie Queene*," *JEGP*, XLIV (1945), 139–51, for the conclusion that Spenser was a chronological but not a cultural primitivist, which agrees by extension with the stand taken in this chapter.

7. *Essays*, I.xxx, trans. John Florio (1603), ed. W. E. Henley; introd. George Saintsbury (Tudor Translations; London, 1892–93), I, 221.

8. Peter Martyr, *De nouo orbe, or the Historie of the West Indies. . . . in eight decades. . . . Whereof three, haue beene formerly translated into English, by R. Eden, whereunto the other fiue, are newly added by . . . M. Lok* (London, 1612), fol. 140ᵛ.

9. This is, as we have seen, the orthodox position of Christian humanism in regard to Nature and Art. Renaissance educational theory sanctioned the idea of Art complementing Nature just as Renaissance poetic (see Rosemond Tuve, *Elizabethan and Metaphysical Imagery* [Chicago, 1947], pp. 383–89) encouraged the same relationship between the terms.

10. The knight-hermit was commonplace. See H. C. Chang, *Allegory and Courtesy in Spenser* (Edinburgh, 1955), pp. 109–13, for a note on the history of this figure.

11. "Second Eclogues," *Poems*, ed. William A. Ringler, Jr. (Oxford, 1962), p. 69.

12. Pearce, "Primitivistic Ideas," p. 143, remarks, in a passing reference to the shepherds: "*They*, it is noteworthy, have no knowledge of the blatant beast. How they have achieved such a life does not seem to concern Spenser." Of course it "concerns" Spenser, and most fundamentally at that, but there is no need to state what may be assumed—that the green world is free of the Blatant Beast because it must stand for a type of Eden in an otherwise fallen world. Cf. the June eclogue, where Colin Clout apostrophizes the pastoral life (*Shepheardes Calender*, in *Works*, ed. Dodge, p. 29):

> O happy Hobbinoll! I blesse thy state,
> That Paradise hast found, whych Adam lost.

13. Varro, *De re rustica* iii.1. "And no marvel, since it was divine nature which gave us the country, and man's skill (*ars humana*) that built the cities." Trans. W. D. Hooper, rev. H. B. Ash (Loeb Classical Library; Cambridge, Mass., 1934), p. 423.

14. Greenlaw pointed out very early, for anyone who cared to listen, that Sidney did not want to idealize Basilius' retreat to shepherd land.

"Sidney's *Arcadia* as an Example of Elizabethan Allegory," *Kittredge Anniversary Papers* (Boston, 1913), pp. 327–37, esp. p. 337.

15. Since all things are ordered according to God's Providence, disrupters of the status quo are dealt with summarily in Spenser: Mutabilitie is haled before Dame Nature herself, and the "equalitarian" Gyant of Book V is abruptly heaved off a cliff by Talus. For Calidore to fail to return would be to deny his own nature. Spenser's commitment to the principle of hierarchy makes it impossible for his lovers to return to live, like Daphnis and Chloe, in the green world.

16. It is of course possible that Sir Calidore's vision of the Graces is purely decorative; indeed, there are readers who tacitly assume this view, and if the assumption were exposed would perhaps argue that it is more "poetic" that way. Our knowledge of Renaissance poetic does not, however, bear out the view that the sixteenth-century poet cared for the purely ornamental. See, for example, "Images and a Redefined Didactic Theory," Chapter XIV of Rosemond Tuve's *Elizabethan and Metaphysical Imagery*.

17. *Allegory of Love,* p. 351. Hamilton, *Allegory in the Faerie Queene,* pleads throughout for a reading on the literal level of the "image" and offers such generalizations as these about Book VI: It is "the triumph of Spenser's fiction" (p. 191); "Book VI resolves the arguments of the previous books, as their fulfilment or consummation" (p. 192); "The . . . climactic emblem of woman is Calidore's vision of the graces" (p. 199); "The story of Pastorella is the consummation of Spenser's fiction" (p. 204); "at the centre of the whole book is the story of Mirabella" (p. 196); "Calidore's vision of the graces is the allegorical centre of the book, and the whole poem" (p. 200). This is heady stuff and may even, on occasion, appear self-contradictory. One can sympathize with Mr. Hamilton's effort to restore the literal sense of the poem—it is much like the Protestant attempt to collapse the medieval four levels back into the *sensus literalis* of the Bible—without subscribing to such statements as "what the image means, it is" (p. 204). Mr. Hamilton may seem overly general, even extravagant and self-contradictory, only because we may fail at first to understand that for him the "image" is usually an "archetype" in Northrop Frye's sense. Since Spenser's method of constructing parallel situations depends as much on *contrast* as comparison, I suspect that reading for the "image" may at times blur necessary distinctions.

18. *Imagines Deorum* was the widely circulated Latin version of Vincenzio Cartari's *Le Imagini dei Dei degli Antichi.* See DeWitt T. Starnes and Ernest William Talbert, *Classical Myth and Legend in Renaissance Dictionaries* (Chapel Hill, 1955), p. 26. Starnes and Talbert establish

Spenser's use of these and other standard works of reference in treating the Graces; see pp. 50 ff. and 88–93.

19. *The Consolation of Philosophy,* trans. W. V. Cooper (Modern Library; New York, 1943), p. 32.

20. *Allegory of Love,* pp. 327–28.

21. Lewis' position in regard to the Bower and the Garden has already been contested by N. S. Brooke, "C. S. Lewis and Spenser: Nature, Art, and the Bower of Bliss," *Cambridge Journal,* II (1949), 420–34. Brooke cites passages to show that Lewis oversimplifies in stating that Nature and Art are always in conflict for Spenser. I believe Brooke's qualifications are sound, and they reinforce by implication my position on Book VI. Cf. also Millar MacClure, "Nature and Art in *The Faerie Queene,*" *ELH,* XXVIII (1961), 1–20, and Hans P. Guth, "Allegorical Implications of Artifice in Spenser's *Faerie Queene,*" *PMLA,* LXXVI (1961), 474–79.

22. A. O. Lovejoy, "The Parallel of Deism and Classicism," *Essays in the History of Ideas* (Baltimore, 1948), pp. 85–86, distinguishes this position in the eighteenth century with the label "rationalistic anti-intellectualism." The term is apt also for those in the Middle Ages and the Renaissance who argued that too much use of the intellect was contrary to Right Reason, that speculation could be oversubtle and morally vitiating; in short, that the proper use of human reason depended in part on avoiding the vice of *curiositas.*

23. "Religio Medici," *Works,* ed. Geoffrey Keynes, I (London, 1928), 22–23.

CHAPTER V: *Shakespeare's* The Winter's Tale

1. References will be to the accessible one-volume *Complete Works of Shakespeare,* ed. George Lyman Kittredge (Boston, 1936).

2. "The Last Plays," *An Approach to Shakespeare* (2d ed., rev.; Doubleday Anchor Books; New York, 1956), p. 261.

3. This is particularly true of the more obviously experimental romances, *Pericles* and *Cymbeline.*

4. See F. C. Tinkler's ingenious article on *The Winter's Tale, Scrutiny,* V (1937), 344–64.

5. See S. L. Bethell, *The Winter's Tale: A Study* (New York, 1947).

6. Since Kermode has discussed the matter so thoroughly and admirably in his introduction to the play (Arden Shakespeare; 5th ed., rev.; Cambridge, Mass., 1954), I merely allude to his work here. The quotation appears on p. xxiv.

7. I am aware that my own language is not entirely neutral. "Harmony and alienation" may, as a pair, have for some readers theological associations, and "harmony," in particular, has musical connotations. My main effort is simply to avoid forcing the reader to choose between, say, the theological interpretation of S. L. Bethell and the anthropological interpretation of F. C. Tinkler; my own argument does not require the acceptance of either.

8. It seems appropriate to remark that Shakespeare, like Spenser, satirizes the "art o' th' court" without actually questioning the status quo: Nature that is admirable without benefit of Art almost invariably turns out to be royal or at least noble Nature.

9. *Physics* 199b.30–31, *The Basic Works of Aristotle*, ed. Richard Mc-Keon (New York, 1941), p. 251.

10. *Laws* x.890, *The Dialogues of Plato*, trans. Benjamin Jowett (New York, 1937), II, 632. See also John of Salisbury's *Metalogicon* i.8, ed. Clement C. J. Webb (Oxford, 1929), pp. 29 ff.

11. See *The Book of the Courtier*, trans. Charles S. Singleton (Anchor Books; New York, 1959), pp. 65 f.

12. There is no warrant in the play for ascribing either position to Shakespeare. But despite the uncertainties arising from the dramatic form, it seems possible to determine Shakespeare's "own" position by seeking what he assumed rather than gave to characters, and by correlating generalizations about Nature and Art with his own artistic practice and with the conduct of "normative" characters. This, however, demands a thorough study of all the plays and is clearly beyond the scope of this chapter.

13. Generally Shakespeare associates Nature with life, Art with death; see the citations from *Venus and Adonis* and the *Rape of Lucrece* at the beginning of this chapter.

14. As quoted by Jean H. Hagstrum, *The Sister Arts: The Tradition of Literary Pictorialism and English Poetry from Dryden to Gray* (Chicago, 1958), in his discussion of Nature and Art in the Renaissance, pp. 81–88. Hagstrum emphasizes the idea of contest or competition between the artist and nature, seeing *The Winter's Tale* as the "negation of one element in the pictorialist and iconic tradition."

15. C. H. Herford, Introduction to *The Winter's Tale*, *The Works of William Shakespeare* (Eversley Shakespeare; 10 vols.; New York, 1899), IV, 268; the phrase is used without the specific application it has in my argument. Cf. Samuel L. Wolff, *The Greek Romances in Elizabethan Prose Fiction* (New York, 1912), p. 432. Wolff associates this use of pas-

toral, perhaps a little vaguely, with the long tradition of "escapes" from the "life active" to the "life contemplative" of the Lower World or the Fortunate Islands. He also points out that pastoral is not so used in Sannazaro, Tasso, or Guarini, all of whom lack the "urban enveloping action," which leads him to hazard, I believe correctly, that "this employment of pastoral is distinctive of Elizabethan fiction." There is some precedent, however slight, in Longus, but it seems that the Elizabethans were the only ones to exploit fully this social use of pastoral.

CHAPTER VI: *Marvell's Garden of the Mind*

1. *The Poems and Letters of Andrew Marvell,* ed. H. M. Margoliouth (2d ed.; Oxford, 1952), I, 119. Subsequent numbers in parentheses within the text refer to the pagination of the first volume of this two-volume edition.

2. It is possible to use external or direct internal evidence to date a number of Marvell's poems, especially the satires and those few published before 1650. But by far the greater part of his lyric poetry appeared only posthumously in 1681. One may speculate, and speculate quite reasonably, that much of the pastoral verse must have been written in the early 1650s at Nunappleton, when Marvell was tutor to Mary Fairfax: an earlier Fairfax had translated Tasso; the house and grounds favored contemplation; an audience educated in the subtleties of pastoral literature remained at hand; the pastorals reveal technical accomplishments lacking in the poems before 1650 and show few overt affinities with the later satires; and the long "Upon Appleton House" betrays many similarities with the short pastoral pieces. But in the absence of further evidence these speculations remain speculations.

3. *Elizabethan Critical Essays,* ed. G. Gregory Smith (Oxford, 1904), I, 175.

4. *The Arte of English Poesie,* ed. G. D. Willcock and Alice Walker (Cambridge, 1936), p. 38. Both Sidney and Puttenham refer to the "allegorical" rather than the "decorative" tradition of pastoral. John Fletcher's definition, on the other hand, refers to the latter tradition: "Understand, therefore, a pastoral to be a representation of shepherds and shepherdesses with their actions and passions, which must be such as may agree with their natures, at least not exceeding former fictions and vulgar traditions; they are not to be adorned with any art, but such improper ones as nature is said to bestow, as singing and poetry; or such as experience may teach them, as the virtues of herbs and fountains, the ordinary course of the

sun, moon, and stars, and such like." "To the Reader," *The Faithful Shepherdess*, in *The Works of Francis Beaumont & John Fletcher*, ed. W. W. Greg (London, 1908), III, 18.

5. M. C. Bradbrook and M. G. Lloyd Thomas, *Andrew Marvell* (Cambridge, 1940), pp. 49–50, tend to identify the faun with Agnus Dei and see the "love of the girl for her fawn" as a "reflection of the love of the Church for Christ." Everett H. Emerson, "Andrew Marvell's 'The Nymph Complaining for the Death of her Faun,'" *Etudes Anglaises*, VIII (1955), 107–10, argues that while the poem is not an "allegory," it nevertheless embodies Marvell's emotional response to the Church of England in the 1640s. This poem, like the "Horatian Ode," has become the occasion for numerous articles; it is an academic *cause célèbre*, plunder in the running battle between Historical Scholar and New Critic. My own feeling is that the poem is best read as a pastoral epicedium on the loss of love, but I do not hazard a full-scale interpretation here because it would not be entirely pertinent to the rest of my argument and because my purpose is not polemical.

6. Only some 64 (Stanzas XLIX–LVI) of the 776 lines of "Upon Appleton House" are devoted to the Mowers as the poet, oscillating between physical and spiritual topography, moves in verse from house to garden to meadow to wood. Courtly compliment to Lord Fairfax is a major theme of this extraordinary work, but Marvell also explores the relation of man to nature and a variety of other important themes. The informing principle of the entire poem lies in an ideal of conduct embodying "measure" and "proportion" in the "vast and all-comprehending Dominions of Nature and Art."

7. *The .xv. Bookes of P. Ovidius Naso, entytuled Metamorphosis, translated oute of Latin into English meeter* (London, 1575), sig. A7ʳ. Cf. *The Shepheardes Calender*, "June," ll. 9–10, *The Complete Poetical Works of Spenser*, ed. R. E. Neil Dodge (Cambridge, Mass., 1936), p. 29.

8. Frank Kermode, whose sensitive, learned criticism is useful in any reading of Marvell, locates the poem within the established terms of the Nature-Art controversy and cites a number of relevant documents outside Marvell; see "Two Notes on Marvell," *Notes and Queries*, CXXVII (1952), 136–38, and "The Argument of Marvell's *Garden*," *Essays in Criticism*, II (1952), 225–41. A more general view of Marvell in relation to Nature may be found in J. H. Summers, "Marvell's Nature," *ELH*, Vol. XX (1953); Summers chooses to emphasize only one aspect of the Mower (p. 126): "He symbolizes man's alienation from nature."

9. Like John Rea, who maintains that a "green Medow is a more de-

lightful object" than the "Gardens of the new model" because "there Nature alone, without the aid of Art, spreads her verdant Carpets, spontaneously imbroydered with many pretty plants and pleasing Flowers, far more inviting than such an immured Nothing." *Flora: seu, De florum cultura. Or, a Complete Florilege* (London, 1665), p. 1.

10. The literary and philosophical contrast between two kinds of gardens is an important theme in medieval and Renaissance literature. Readers of the *Romance of the Rose* will be familiar with the theme, but of course the famous example occurs in Spenser, where the Garden of Adonis in which Art complements Nature is contrasted with the Bower of Bliss in which Art usurps the proper functions of Nature.

11. "Andrew Marvell," *Selected Essays* (New York, 1932), p. 251.

12. The allusion to Matthew 7:20 ("Wherefore by their fruits ye shall know them") implies the entire poem: flowers must become fruits through the Grace of God.

Works Cited

Abrams, M. H. *The Mirror and the Lamp: Romantic Theory and the Critical Tradition.* New York, 1958.

Agrippa, Henry Cornelius. *Three Books of Occult Philosophy.* Translated by J. F. London, 1651.

Albertus Magnus. *De mineralibus.* Vol. V of *Opera omnia.* Edited by August Borgnet. Paris, 1890.

Ambrose, Saint. *S. Ambrosii episcopi mediol. selecta: De officiis clericorum.* Edited by R. O. Gilbert. Vol. VIII of *Bibliotheca patrum ecclesiasticorum Latinorum selecta.* Leipzig, 1839.

Apuleius. *The Golden Ass.* Translated (1566) by W. Adlington, revised by Stephen Gaselee. Loeb Classical Library. London, 1947.

Aristotle. *The Basic Works of Aristotle.* Edited by Richard McKeon. New York, 1941.

Atkins, J. W. H. *English Literary Criticism: The Medieval Phase.* New York, 1943.

—— *English Literary Criticism: The Renascence.* London, 1947.

Bacon, Francis. *The Works of Francis Bacon.* Edited by James Spedding, Robert Leslie Ellis, and Douglas Denon Heath. 14 vols. London, 1887–1902.

Baldwin, Charles Sears. *Medieval Rhetoric and Poetic.* New York, 1928.

Benlowes, Edward. *Theophila, or Loves Sacrifice: A Divine Poem.* London, 1652.

Bernheimer, Richard. *Wild Men in the Middle Ages: A Study in Art, Sentiment, and Demonology.* Cambridge, Mass., 1952.

Bethell, S. L. *The Winter's Tale: A Study.* New York, 1947.

Boas, George. *Essays on Primitivism and Related Ideas in the Middle Ages.* Baltimore, 1948.

—— See also Lovejoy, Arthur O.

Boethius. *The Consolation of Philosophy.* Translated by W. V. Cooper. Modern Library. New York, 1943.

Bradbrook, M. C., and M. G. Lloyd Thomas. *Andrew Marvell.* Cambridge, 1940.

Breton, Nicholas. *Works.* Edited by A. B. Grosart. 2 vols. Edinburgh, 1879.

Brooke, N. S. "C. S. Lewis and Spenser: Nature, Art, and the Bower of Bliss," *Cambridge Journal*, II (1949), 420–34.

Browne, Sir Thomas. *Works*. Edited by Geoffrey Keynes. 6 vols. London, 1928–31.

Bulwer, John. *Anthropometamorphosis: Man Transform'd . . . . the Native and Nationall Monstrosities That Have Appeared to Disfigure the Humane Fabrick*. London, 1653.

Bunyan, John. *The Pilgrim's Progress*. Introduction by Louis Martz. New York, 1949.

Burnet, John. "Law and Nature in Greek Ethics," in *Essays and Addresses*. London, 1929.

Burton, Robert. *The Anatomy of Melancholy*. Edited by Floyd Dell and Paul Jordan-Smith. New York, 1955.

Bush, Douglas. *English Literature in the Earlier Seventeenth Century*. New York, 1945.

Castiglione, Baldassare. *The Book of the Courtier*. Translated by Charles S. Singleton. Anchor Books. New York, 1959.

—— *The Courtier*. Translated by Sir Thomas Hoby and edited by W. E. Henley. Tudor Translations. London, 1900.

Cawley, Robert R. *Unpathed Waters: Studies in the Influence of the Voyagers on Elizabethan Literature*. Princeton, 1940.

—— *The Voyagers and Elizabethan Drama*. MLA Monograph Series, VIII. Boston, 1938.

Chambers, E. K. "The English Pastoral," in *Sir Thomas Wyatt: And Some Collected Studies*. London, 1933.

Chambers, E. K., ed. *English Pastorals*. London, n.d.

Chang, H. C. *Allegory and Courtesy in Spenser*. Edinburgh, 1955.

Charland, Thomas M. *Artes praedicandi: Contribution à l'histoire de la rhétorique au moyen âge*. Paris, 1936.

Charlesworth, M. J. *Aristotle on Art and Nature*. Philosophy Series II, Bulletin 50. Auckland University College, 1957.

Charron, Pierre. *Of Wisdome*. Translated by Samson Lennard. London, 1640.

Chaucer, Geoffrey. *Complete Works*. Edited by W. W. Skeat. 6 vols. Oxford, 1894.

Cicero, Marcus Tullius. *De legibus*. Translated by C. W. Keyes. Loeb Classical Library. London, 1928.

—— *Letters to Atticus*. Translated by E. O. Winstedt. Loeb Classical Library. London, 1913.

—— *Offices.* Translated by Thomas Cockman; introduction by John Warrington. New York, 1955.

Cooper, Thomas. *Thesavrvs lingvae Romanae & Brittanicae.* London, 1584.

Cowley, Abraham. *Essays, Plays and Sundry Verses.* Edited by A. R. Waller. Cambridge, 1906.

—— *Poems.* Edited by A. R. Waller. Cambridge, 1905.

Craig, Hardin. *The Enchanted Glass.* New York, 1936.

Crane, Ronald S. "Literature, Philosophy, and the History of Ideas," *MP,* LII (1954), 73 ff.

Culverwel, Nathanael. *An Elegant and Learned Discourse of the Light of Nature.* London, 1652.

Curtius, Ernst R. *European Literature and the Latin Middle Ages.* Translated by Willard R. Trask. New York, 1953.

Dante. *Inferno.* Translated by J. D. Sinclair. New York, 1948.

Denham, Sir John. *Poems and Translations; with the Sophy, a Tragedy.* London, 1709.

Dio Chrysostom. "Hunters of Euboea," in *Three Greek Romances.* Edited by Moses Hadas. New York, 1953.

Donne, John. *Poems of John Donne.* Edited by Sir Herbert J. C. Grierson. London, 1933.

Doran, Madeleine. *Endeavors of Art: A Study of Form in Elizabethan Drama.* Madison, 1954.

Drayton, Michael. *Works.* Edited by J. William Hebel, K. Tillotson, and B. H. Newdigate. 5 vols. Oxford, 1931–41.

Dümmler, Ernest, ed. *Poetarvm Latinorvm medii aevi: Poetae Latini aevi Carolini.* Vol. I. *Monumenta Germaniae historica.* Berlin, 1881.

Eliot, T. S. *Selected Essays: 1917–1932.* New York, 1932.

Eliot, Sir Thomas, trans. *The Education or Bringinge Vp of Children.* London, n.d.

Emerson, Everett H. "Andrew Marvell's 'The Nymph Complaining for the Death of her Faun,'" *Etudes Anglaises,* VIII (1955), 107–10.

Empson, William. *Some Versions of Pastoral.* London, 1935.

Erasmus, Desiderius. *Praise of Folly.* Translated by John Wilson and edited by P. S. Allen. Oxford, 1925.

Ferne, Sir John. *The Blazon of Gentrie.* London, 1586.

Fiske, G. C. *Cicero's De Oratore and Horace's Ars Poetica.* University of Wisconsin Studies in Language and Literature, No. 27. Madison, 1929.

Fletcher, John. *See* W. W. Greg.

Fludd, Robert. *De macrocosmi historia.* Vol. I of *Utriusque cosmi maioris scilicet et minoris metaphysica, physica atque technica historia.* Oppenheim, 1617.

Frankfort, Henri, *et al. Before Philosophy.* London, 1951.

Frye, Northrop. "The Argument of Comedy," in *English Institute Essays, 1948.* Edited by D. A. Robertson, Jr. New York, 1949. Pp. 58–73.

Gang, Theodor. "Nature and Grace in the *Faerie Queene:* The Problem Revisited," *ELH,* XXVI (1959), 1–22.

Gaselee, Stephen. "Appendix on the Greek Novel," in *Daphnis and Chloe.* Loeb Classical Library. New York, 1916.

Gelli, Giambattista. *La Circe e I Capricci del Bottaio.* Edited by Severino Ferrari and G. G. Ferrero. Florence, 1957.

Gerhardt, Mia Irene. *La Pastorale: Essai d'analyse littérature.* Assen, 1950.

Golding, Arthur. *The .xv. Bookes of P. Ovidius Naso, entytuled Metamorphosis, translated oute of Latin into English meeter.* London, 1575.

Goulart, Simon. *Commentaires et annotations sur la sepmaine de la creation dv monde de Gvillavme de Saluste Seigneur du Bartas.* Paris, 1583.

Gracián y Morales, Balthasar. *The Courtiers Manual Oracle, or, The Art of Prudence.* Printed 1647, Englished 1685. No translator given. London, 1685.

Greenlaw, Edwin. "Sidney's *Arcadia* as an Example of Elizabethan Allegory," in *Kittredge Anniversary Papers.* Boston, 1913.

Greg, W. W. *Pastoral Poetry and Pastoral Drama.* London, 1906.

Greg, W. W., ed. "The Faithful Shepherdess." Vol. III of *The Works of Francis Beaumont & John Fletcher.* London, 1908.

Greville, Fulke, Lord Brooke. *Poems and Dramas of Fulke Greville, First Lord Brooke.* Edited by Geoffrey Bullough. 2 vols. New York, 1945.

—— *The Remains of Sir Fulk Grevill Lord Brooke: Being Poems of Monarchy and Religion.* London, 1670.

Guazzo, Stefano. *The Civile Conversation of M. Steeven Guazzo.* First 3 books translated by George Pettie (1581), 4th book translated by Bartholomew Young (1586). Edited by Charles Whibley. 2 vols. Tudor Translations, Second Series. New York, 1925.

Guevara, Antonio de. *Familiar Epistles.* Translated by E. Hellowes. London, 1577.

Guillaume de Lorris and Jean de Meun. *Le Roman de la rose.* Edited by Ernest Langlois. Société des Anciens Textes Français. 5 vols. Paris, 1914–24.

—— *The Romance of the Rose.* Translated by Harry W. Robbins and edited by Charles W. Dunn. New York, 1962.

Guth, Hans P. "Allegorical Implications of Artifice in Spenser's *Faerie Queene*," *PMLA*, LXXVI (1961), 474–79.

Hadas, Moses, ed. *Three Greek Romances*. New York, 1953.

Hagstrum, Jean H. *The Sister Arts: The Tradition of Literary Pictorialism and English Poetry from Dryden to Gray*. Chicago, 1958.

Haight, E. H. *Essays on the Greek Romances*. New York, 1943.

Hamblin, F. R. *The Development of Allegory in the Classical Pastoral*. Published dissertation, University of Chicago Library. Chicago, 1928.

Hamilton, A. C. *Structure of Allegory in The Faerie Queene*. Oxford, 1961.

Hamilton, G. L. "Theodulus: A Medieval Textbook," *MP*, VII (1909), 169–85.

Haydn, Hiram. *The Counter-Renaissance*. New York, 1950.

Heliodorus. *An Aethiopian History*. Translated by Thomas Underdowne (1587). Edited by W. E. Henley; introduction by Charles Whibley. Tudor Translations. London, 1895.

Herford, C. H., ed. *Works of William Shakespeare*. Eversley Shakespeare. 10 vols. New York, 1899.

Herrick, Marvin T. *The Fusion of Horatian and Aristotelian Literary Criticism, 1531–1555*. Illinois Studies in Language and Literature, No. 32. Urbana, 1946.

Herrick, Robert. *The Poetical Works of Robert Herrick*. Edited by L. C. Martin. Oxford, 1956.

John of Salisbury. *Metalogicon*. Edited by Clement C. J. Webb. Oxford, 1929.

—— *The Metalogicon of John of Salisbury: A Twelfth-Century Defense of the Verbal and Logical Arts of the Trivium*. Translated with introduction and notes by Daniel D. McGarry. Berkeley and Los Angeles, 1955.

Johnson, Samuel. *Works*. Literary Club Edition from Type. 16 vols. New York, 1903.

Jones, Charles W. *Medieval Literature in Translation*. New York, 1950.

Jonson, Ben. *Ben Jonson*. Edited by C. H. Herford, Percy Simpson, and Evelyn Simpson. 11 vols. Oxford, 1925–52.

Keckermanno, Bartholomaeo. *Gymnasivm logicvm*. London, 1606.

Kermode, Frank. "The Argument of Marvell's *Garden*," *Essays in Criticism*, II (1952), 225–41.

—— "Two Notes on Marvell," *Notes and Queries*, CXXVII (1952), 136–38.

214 *Works Cited*

Kermode, Frank, ed. *English Pastoral Poetry: From the Beginnings to Marvell.* Life, Literature, and Thought Library. London, 1952.

—— *The Tempest.* William Shakespeare. Arden Shakespeare. Rev. ed. Cambridge, Mass., 1954.

Knowlton, Edgar G. "The Goddess Natura in Early Periods," *JEGP,* XIX (1920), 224–53.

—— "Nature in Early German," *JEGP,* XXIV (1925), 409–12.

—— "Nature in Early Italian," *MLN,* XXXVI (1921), 329 ff.

—— "Nature in Middle English," *JEGP,* XX (1931), 186 ff.

Kyd, Thomas. *The Works of Thomas Kyd.* Edited by F. S. Boas. 2d ed. Oxford, 1955.

Langbaum, Robert. *The Poetry of Experience.* New York, 1957.

La Primaudaye, Pierre de. *The French Academie.* Translated by T. Bowes. London, 1586.

Lawson, William. *New Orchard and Garden.* Reprinted from 3d ed. (1626) by Eleanour S. Rohde. London, 1937.

Lewis, C. S. *The Allegory of Love: A Study in Medieval Tradition.* London, 1936.

—— *English Literature in the Sixteenth Century.* Oxford, 1954.

Lodge, Thomas, trans. *The Workes of Lvcivs Annaevs Seneca, Newly Inlarged and Corrected.* London, 1620.

Longinus. *On the Sublime.* Translated by W. Hamilton Fyfe. Loeb Classical Library. London, 1953.

Longus. "Daphnis and Chloe," in *Three Greek Romances.* Edited by Moses Hadas. New York, 1953.

Lovejoy, Arthur O. *Essays in the History of Ideas.* Baltimore, 1948.

—— *The Great Chain of Being.* Cambridge, Mass., 1936.

Lovejoy, Arthur O., and George Boas. *Primitivism and Related Ideas in Antiquity: Contributions to the History of Primitivism.* Vol. I. Baltimore, 1935.

Lyly, John. *Euphues: The Anatomy of Wit.* Edited by Edward Arber. English Reprints. London, 1869.

MacClure, Millar. "Nature and Art in *The Faerie Queene," ELH,* XXVIII (1961), 1–20.

MacDonald, Hugh, ed. *England's Helicon.* Edition of 1600 with additions from 1614. Cambridge, Mass., 1950.

McKeon, Richard, ed. *The Basic Works of Aristotle.* New York, 1951.

—— "Literary Criticism and the Concept of Imitation in Antiquity," in *Critics and Criticism.* Edited by R. S. Crane. Abridged ed. Chicago, 1957. Pp. 117–45.

—— "Rhetoric in the Middle Ages," *Speculum,* XVII (1942), 1–32.

Martyr, Peter (Pietro Martire d'Anghiera). *The Decades of the Newe Worlde or West India.* Translated by Richard Eden. London, 1555.

—— *De nouo orbe, or the Historie of the West Indies. . . . in eight decades. . . . Whereof three, haue beene formerly translated into English, by R. Eden, whereunto the other fiue, are newly added by . . . M. Lok.* London, 1612.

Marvell, Andrew. *The Poems and Letters of Andrew Marvell.* Edited by H. M. Margoliouth. 2 vols. 2d ed. Oxford, 1952.

Mazzeo, J. A. "The Analogy of Creation in Dante," *Speculum,* XXXII (1957), 706–21.

Milton, John. *The Poems of John Milton.* Edited by James Holly Hanford. New York, 1936.

Montaigne, Michel de. *Essays.* Translated by John Florio (1603) and edited by W. E. Henley with introduction by George Saintsbury. Tudor Translations. 3 vols. London, 1892–93.

Nelson, William. *The Poetry of Edmund Spenser.* New York, 1963.

Nenna, G.-B. *Discourse whether a Nobel Man by Birth or a Gentleman by Desert Is Greater in Nobilitie.* Translated by W. Jones. London, 1600.

Nicolson, Marjorie H. *The Breaking of the Circle.* Evanston, Ill., 1950.

Ovid. *The .xv. Bookes of P. Ovidius Naso, entytuled Metamorphosis, translated oute of Latin into English meeter.* Translated by Arthur Golding. London, 1575.

—— *Metamorphoses.* Translated by Rolfe Humphries. Bloomington, 1957.

—— *Metamorphosis.* Translated by F. J. Miller. 2 vols. Loeb Classical Library. London, 1916.

Panofsky, Erwin. "Et in Arcadia Ego," in *Philosophy and History.* Edited by Raymond Klibansky and H. J. Paton. Oxford, 1936. Pp. 223–54.

Pearce, R. H. "Primitivistic Ideas in the *Faerie Queene," JEGP,* XLIV (1945), 139–51.

Pearl. Edited by E. V. Gordon. Oxford, 1958.

Pettie, George, trans. *The Civile Conversation of M. Steeven Guazzo.* First 3 books translated by George Pettie, 4th book translated by Bartholomew Young. Edited by Charles Whibley. 2 vols. Tudor Translations, Second Series. New York, 1925.

Plat, Sir Hugh. *Delightes for Ladies, to Adorne Their Persons, Tables, Closets, and Distillatories.* Reprinted from edition of 1627 by Violet and H. W. Trovillion. Herrin, Ill., 1942.

Plato. *The Dialogues of Plato.* Translated by Benjamin Jowett. Reprinted from 3d ed. 2 vols. New York, 1937.

Popper, Karl. *The Open Society and Its Enemies.* Princeton, 1950.

Porta, John Baptista. *Natural Magick.* London, 1658.

Propertius. *Elegies.* Translated by H. E. Butler. Loeb Classical Library. London, 1912.

Puttenham, George [?]. *The Arte of English Poesie.* Edited by G. D. Willcock and Alice Walker. Cambridge, 1936.

Quintilian. *Institutio oratoria.* Translated by H. E. Butler. Loeb Classical Library. 4 vols. New York, 1921–22.

Raby, F. J. E. *History of Christian-Latin Poetry from the Beginnings to the Close of the Middle Ages.* 2d ed. Oxford, 1953.

Raleigh, Sir Walter. *History of the World,* in *Works.* Edited by William Oldys and Thomas Birch. London, 1829.

Rand, William, trans. *The Mirrour of True Nobility & Gentility: Being the Life of the Renowned Nicolaus Claudius Fabricius, Lord of Peiresk.* London, 1657.

Ravenscroft, Thomas. *A Briefe Discourse . . . , 1614,* "Of Ale and To-bacco," in *English Madrigal Verse.* Edited by E. H. Fellowes. 2d ed. Oxford, 1929.

Rea, John. *Flora: seu, De florum cultura. Or, a Complete Florilege.* London, 1665.

Romei, Annibale. *The Courtiers Academie.* Translated by John Kepers. London, 1598.

Sandys, John Edwin. *History of Classical Scholarship.* 3 vols. Cambridge, 1908–21.

Seneca, Lucius Annaeus. *Ad Lucilium epistulae morales.* Translated by Richard M. Gummere. Loeb Classical Library. 3 vols. London, 1917–25.

—— *The Workes of Lvcivs Annaevs Seneca, Newly Inlarged and Cor-rected.* Translated by Thomas Lodge. London, 1620.

Shakespeare, William. *Complete Works.* Edited by George Lyman Kit-tredge. Boston, 1936.

Shirley, James. *The Poems of James Shirley.* Edited by Ray Livingstone Armstrong. New York, 1941.

Sidney, Sir Philip. *The Poems of Sir Philip Sidney.* Edited by William A. Ringler, Jr. Oxford, 1962.

—— *The Prose Works.* Edited by Albert Feuillerat. 4 vols. Cambridge, 1962.

Smith, G. Gregory, ed. *Elizabethan Critical Essays.* Oxford, 1904.

Snell, Bruno. *The Discovery of the Mind.* Translated by T. G. Rosenmeyer. Cambridge, Mass., 1953.

Spencer, Theodore. *Shakespeare and the Nature of Man.* New York, 1955.

Spenser, Edmund. *The Complete Poetical Works of Spenser.* Edited by R. E. Neil Dodge. Cambridge, Mass., 1936.

—— *The Faerie Queene: Books Six and Seven.* Edited by J. G. McManaway, D. E. Mason, and Brents Stirling. Vol. VI of *The Works of Edmund Spenser,* general editors Edwin Greenlaw, C. G. Osgood, *et al.* Baltimore, 1938–49.

Spitzer, Leo. "Classical and Christian Ideas of World Harmony," *Traditio,* II (1944), 409–65; III (1945), 307–64.

Sprat, Thomas. *History of the Royal-Society of London.* London, 1702.

Starnes, DeWitt T., and Ernest William Talbert. *Classical Myth and Legend in Renaissance Dictionaries.* Chapel Hill, 1955.

Summers, J. H. "Marvell's Nature," *ELH,* XX (1953), 126 ff.

Swift, Jonathan. *Gulliver's Travels.* Edited by Arthur E. Case. New York, 1938.

Taverner, Richard. *Proverbes or Adagies with Newe Addicions Gathered out of the Chiliades of Erasmus.* London, 1539.

Thomas à Kempis. *Of the Imitation of Christ.* Translated by Thomas Rogers. London, 1584.

Tillyard, Eustace Mandeville Wetenhall. *The Elizabethan World Picture.* New York, 1944.

—— *Shakespeare's Last Plays.* London, 1938.

Tinkler, F. C. "*The Winter's Tale,*" *Scrutiny,* V (1937), 344–64.

Traube, Ludwig, ed. *Poetarvm Latinorvm medii aevi: Poetae Latini aevi Carolini.* Vol. III. *Monumenta Germaniae historica.* Berlin, 1896.

Traversi, Derek A. *An Approach to Shakespeare.* 2d ed., rev. Doubleday Anchor. New York, 1956.

Trilling, Lionel. *The Liberal Imagination.* New York, 1953.

Turbervile, George. *Epitaphes, Epigrams, Songs and Sonets.* London, 1567.

Tuve, Rosemond. *Elizabethan and Metaphysical Imagery.* Chicago, 1947.

Varro. *De re rustica.* Translated by W. D. Hooper, revised by H. B. Ash. Loeb Classical Library. Cambridge, Mass., 1934.

Vincent de Beauvais. *Speculum Naturale.* Strassburg, *ca.* 1481.

Weld, Charles R. *A History of the Royal Society with Memoires of the Presidents.* 2 vols. London, 1848.

Wilmot, John, 2d Earl of Rochester. *Poems on Several Occasions.* Antwerp, 1680. Facsimile edition; edited by James Thorpe. Princeton Studies in English, No. 30. Princeton, 1950.

Wilson, E. Faye. "Pastoral and Epithalamium in Latin Literature," *Speculum,* XXIII (1948), 35–57.

Wilson, Harold S. "Nature and Art' in *Winter's Tale,* IV.iv.86 ff.," *Shakespeare Association Bulletin,* XVIII (1943), 114–19.

Wilson, John, trans. *Praise of Folly.* Edited by P. S. Allen. Oxford, 1925.

Wilson, Thomas. *Arte of Rhetorique.* Edited by G. H. Mair. Oxford, 1909.

Wither, George, trans. *The Nature of Man: A Learned and Usefull Tract Written in Greek by Nemesius.* London, 1636.

Wolff, Samuel L. *The Greek Romances in Elizabethan Prose Fiction.* New York, 1912.

Woodhouse, A. S. P. "The Argument of Milton's *Comus,*" *University of Toronto Quarterly,* XI (1941), 46–71.

—— "Nature and Grace in the *Faerie Queene,*" *ELH,* XVI (1949), 194–228.

—— "Spenser, Nature and Grace: Mr. Gang's Mode of Argument Reviewed," *ELH,* XXVII (1960), 1–15.

Index